INCEST

A Psychological Study
of Causes and Effects
with Treatment
Recommendations

Karin C. Meiselman

INCEST

▣ ▣ ▣ ▣ ▣ ▣ ▣ ▣ ▣ ▣ ▣ ▣ ▣ ▣ ▣ ▣

A Psychological Study of Causes and Effects with Treatment Recommendations

P.

p.196

Jossey-Bass Publishers
San Francisco · Washington · London · 1979

INCEST
A Psychological Study of Causes and Effects with Treatment Recommendations
    Karin C. Meiselman

Library of Congress Catalogue Card Number LC 78-62557

International Standard Book Number ISBN 0-87589-380-5

Manufactured in the United States of America

JACKET DESIGN BY WILLI BAUM

FIRST EDITION
        First printing: September 1978
        Second printing: January 1979

Code 7820

The Jossey-Bass
Social and Behavioral Science Series

Preface

When I began to review the psychological literature on incest in connection with preparing a college-level course in human sexuality, I was struck by the repeated statements of numerous authors that there is a dearth of literature on overt incest. It seems to be a time-honored tradition among researchers in this field to bemoan the absence of substantive information before presenting a few additional cases of incest to their professional colleagues. As I continued to read these studies, I realized that the often-cited scarcity is gradually diminishing as studies of overt incest become more acceptable, and hence more publishable, in the wake of the wave of sexual openness that swept over us in the 1960s. (Fifty years ago, articles on incest appeared only in the *American Journal of Urology and Sexology*!) As a psychologist, however, I realized that the question of the effects of incest trauma on psychological

functioning was still largely unanswered. At the same time, I recalled that I had often heard therapists comment on the surprising frequency of incest cases that they encountered in practice,
and I began to contemplate an effort to fill in this remaining
gap in our knowledge about overt incest.

My research began with the naive idea that I would gather
a sufficient sample of incest and control cases in, say, six or
eight months, analyze the data, and write one or two journal
articles before going on to my next project. This is the kind of
time-limited, precise research activity for which young academic
psychologists are generally reinforced. Over four years later, I
can be amused at the difficulties I encountered, but there were
times when I thought that I should abandon the entire effort
and take up rat psychology.

My first difficulty soon became apparent when I approached therapists, who had previously exclaimed about the
frequency of incest histories in their caseloads, and requested
that they provide descriptions of their current cases of incest. I
then discovered that most of them had not seen a case of incest
for the past two or three years and that their statements about
the frequency of incest really meant that they had never expected to encounter the few cases that they had indeed seen. I
had to play a waiting game in collecting the cases that passed
through the clinic; sometimes two months would go by without
any incest discoveries, and then one visit to the clinic might
yield as many as three or four new cases. As my case collection
grew in fits and starts, I became inured to this unpredictable
means of gathering data, and I became increasingly absorbed in
the accumulating qualitative information on the incest experience and its aftermath. I dropped my idea of a quick, crisp
study and settled in for a long, but interesting, siege.

Although my data collection did not proceed as smoothly
as anticipated, this was no fault of the clinic therapists. In order
to provide the most complete anonymity to the patients described in this book, I cannot name the individual therapists
who were most helpful to me in providing descriptions of incest
cases, but I wish to acknowledge their support of the project
and their willingness to wedge interviews with me into their

crowded schedules. At the time, their only reward was my personal thankfulness. I hope that the publication of this book will enable them to feel that they made a personal contribution to the body of knowledge about incest and that future patients may benefit from their efforts to understand the causes and effects of overt incest.

After about three years of research, I had sufficient clinical information and new hypotheses about the effects of incest to write three or four journal articles. I had always assumed that such articles would be the best way to address other professionals, but it became increasingly apparent to me that mental health professionals would benefit from some prior knowledge of how incestuous situations develop and what their sequels tend to be. Although my library research had shown me that there is not really a dearth of incest literature and although I thought that my own study would help to fill in one of the remaining gaps, it seemed unrealistic, to say the least, to expect a professional who encounters a case of incest to consult numerous and often obscure journals and out-of-print books to get a sense of what is known about incest. Thus I decided that a book about the psychology of incest would be a more useful addition to the literature than additional articles.

In this book, I have integrated the previous literature on the psychology of incest with my own findings. The first chapter summarizes anthropological and sociological views on the origin and maintenance of the incest taboo; Chapter Two provides a discussion of the advantages and inherent problems of various strategies for doing research on overt incest behavior; and Chapter Three delineates the data collection methods that were employed in my own study and gives a preliminary description of the psychotherapy sample of incest cases and a control group of nonincestuous clinic patients. The emphasis throughout the remainder of the book is on the psychological causes and effects of overt incest. Chapters Four, Five, and Six are devoted to extensive description of father-daughter incest—its causes, the course of the incest "affair," and its immediate and long-term aftereffects. Other forms of heterosexual incest, notably sibling incest and mother-son incest, are discussed in

Chapters Seven and Eight; Chapter Nine summarizes what little is known about homosexual incest; Chapter Ten provides a discussion of several patterns of multiple incest; and Chapter Eleven makes suggestions for improved detection and treatment of incest cases.

I hope that this assemblage of findings will stimulate both clinicians and academics to do further research in the many areas where our knowledge of this subject is still quite tentative. The major purpose of the book, however, is to provide mental health professionals who may be encountering occasional incest cases with the accumulated observations and hypotheses of numerous clinicians and researchers, including myself, over the past fifty years. Readers should emerge with an intellectual perspective on the psychology of incest that will be useful in evaluation and treatment of incest cases.

Pasadena, California   Karin C. Meiselman
July 1978

Contents

⊞ ⊞ ⊞ ⊞ ⊞ ⊞ ⊞ ⊞ ⊞ ⊞ ⊞ ⊞ ⊞ ⊞ ⊞ ⊞ ⊞ ⊞ ⊞

The Author

Karin Carlson Meiselman is a clinical psychologist in private practice in Pasadena, California and assistant professor of psychology at the Claremont Colleges. She received the B.A. degree in sociology at Case-Western Reserve University (1963) and the Ph.D. degree in clinical psychology at the University of California at Los Angeles (1971).

In the course of her training at UCLA, she did psychotherapy, testing, and clinical research at the UCLA Psychology Clinic and at the Wadsworth and Sepulveda Veterans Administration Hospitals in Los Angeles. She was licensed as a clinical psychologist by the State of California in 1973 and is a member of the Division of Clinical Psychology of the American Psychological Association. Her major research interest as a graduate student was the study of cognitive processes in schizophrenia, and she has published the results of two research projects in this area, in the *Journal of Consulting and Clinical Psychology* and the *Journal of Abnormal Psychology.* She accepted her present position at the Claremont Colleges in 1972 and has been teaching courses related to her clinical interests for the past six years. One of these courses, Problems in Human Sexuality, stimulated her interest in incest as a research area, and she began the study on which this book is based in 1973.

Originally from upstate New York, the author and her husband of fifteen years, Herbert Meiselman, have lived in the vicinity of Pasadena, California, for twelve years. Their first child, a daughter, was born between Chapters Three and Four of this book.

To my family,
especially Herb and Sharon Rachel

INCEST

A Psychological Study
of Causes and Effects
with Treatment
Recommendations

Origins of the Incest Taboo

The incest taboo is widely believed to be universal. While prohibitions against sexual relations or marriage between uncles and nieces, aunts and nephews, cousins, and relatives by marriage vary considerably among cultures, there are almost always severe penalties for sexual relations within the nuclear family, with the obvious exception of husbands and wives. Various intriguing exceptions to this universality have been described in the anthropological literature, and the interested reader is advised to consult more extensive summaries of incest customs in ancient and primitive societies (Weinberg, 1955, pp. 3-40; Maisch, 1972, pp. 11-64). Since it is beyond the intended scope of a book devoted to the psychology of incest to go into the anthropological literature in detail, we shall examine only a few of the most commonly cited exceptions to the incest taboo before proceeding to a consideration of its origins.

Probably the most widely cited example of a culturally accepted abrogation of the taboo on nuclear family incest is the case of the ruling families of ancient Egypt. According to Middleton (1962), brother-sister marriages definitely occurred in the royal family during the Pharaonic and Ptolemaic periods— Cleopatra was the best-known sibling spouse of the latter period. Very rarely, the historical record describes royal father-daughter marriages, but there is no evidence that nuclear family marriages of any sort were allowed to ordinary citizens until after the Roman conquest of Egypt. During the Roman period, there is sufficient written evidence in the form of wedding invitations, marriage contracts, and other kinds of genealogical records to attest to the social acceptability of brother-sister marriages. Middleton speculated that the royal custom had filtered down to other social classes over the centuries and that brother-sister marriage was often seen as a means of maintaining family property intact and avoiding the eventual splintering of an estate among the surviving siblings. Brother-sister marriage was, of course, again prohibited with the advent of Christianity.

There also seems to be agreement that some primitive societies, while strictly prohibiting nuclear family marriages, allow some kinds of incestuous sexual relations in the context of magical rituals. An interesting example of this kind of suspension of the incest ban is described by Jounod (cited in Masters, 1963), who observed that villagers in an area of Africa that specializes in hippopotamus hunting believe that a hunter can ensure his success in the field by having sexual relations with his own daughter immediately prior to embarking on an expedition. The rationale given for this belief is that consummation of an incestuous act requires that the father kill something within himself, which makes him a murderer who is capable of courageously attacking hippopotamuses. Lest the reader think that such magical beliefs are confined to the backwaters of primitive cultures, it should be noted that Weinberg (1955) has found that there is a belief in some subcultures in the United States that incest with a young, prepubertal daughter can cure a man of venereal disease because he can "catch" the purity of his daughter in the same manner that he caught the disease originally.

Again, these descriptions of socially sanctioned incest are

a few of the instances most agreed on among many that have been mentioned in the incest literature. It is probably a good idea to read many of the other descriptions of exceptions to the taboo on nuclear family incest with a measured degree of skepticism. Throughout the years, examples of accepted incest in primitive and ancient cultures have been described as fact and then later retracted after failing to withstand scientific scrutiny. One should also be aware of the nearly universal human tendency to ascribe what are considered depraved beliefs and practices to ancient or foreign cultures. Some of the earlier incest researchers erred in this manner. Marcuse (1923), for instance, thought that incest must have been much more common in the ancient world than it is today because myths depicting the relationships of the gods frequently have incest themes. Similarly, Rohleder (1917) believed that incest was more frequent in certain foreign countries, where the natives were often quite flagrantly accepting of the practice; to bolster this claim, he gave an account of having been approached by an Italian prostitute who offered to sell him herself and her two children in any combination he might desire. In a similar vein, the historical record contains many accusations of incest against such groups as the Gnostics, the Cathars, and participants in the Witches' Sabbath (Masters, 1963). All such descriptions should be taken with several grains of salt because they are usually most sensibly construed as an attempt by the "historian" to stir up popular outrage against a supposedly heretical group and to justify an official persecution of its members. Trumped-up charges of incest were also sometimes brought against individuals, such as Ann Boleyn, in order to enlist public support for their execution.

But let us now return to the major point of this section. The taboo on nuclear family incest *is* more or less universal. The exceptions that are so frequently listed often serve to distract the reader from apprehending the truly remarkable degree of regularity with which nuclear family incest is prohibited. Of the thousands of cultural groupings that we have knowledge of, both past and present, only a few have been shown to permit nuclear family incest of any kind, and these groups have stopped far short of allowing intrafamilial promiscuity. Incestuous marriages have almost always been restricted to brother-sister marriages within a privileged group, and incest during magical rites has been condoned in a few societies that hold to strict incest rules most of the time. Murdock (1949) surveyed 250 primitive societies that had been thoroughly studied by anthropologists and reported that *all* of them banned nuclear family incest. While a few societies allowed half brothers and sisters to marry, all of them extended the taboo to some or all relatives outside of the nuclear family. All but eight of the societies banned marriage with some or all first cousins; a substantial majority forbade marriage to some or all aunts, uncles, nephews, or nieces; and a minority extended the taboo to cover everyone who was known to be even remotely related to an individual.

Murdock (1949, p. 288) also remarked that "incest taboos and exogamous restrictions, as compared with other sexual prohibitions, are characterized by a peculiar intensity and emotional quality." He went on to describe the "grisly horror" that incest inspired in most peoples, as evidenced by the frequency with which the death penalty was prescribed for offenders. In some societies, there is no legally institutionalized sanction for incest at all, and on careful investigation he found that in these societies the taboo is so strongly internalized and the potential horror at its violation so great that the people consider the consummation of an incestuous act to be simply unthinkable. If asked, people in such societies will say that if an incestuous act ever were to occur the gods or other supernatural powers would punish the guilty parties, and no human intervention would be necessary.

The nearly universal nature of the incest taboo and the intense emotions engendered by its violation have elicited the interest of many social scientists, especially anthropologists, and numerous theories have been constructed to explain the origin of the taboo and its persistence over time. In the remainder of this chapter, I shall review some of the more influential ideas advanced by incest theorists in the twentieth century, explain the relatively recent rekindling of interest in the "old-fashioned" biological explanation of the taboo, and, finally, summarize what I believe to be a sensible view of the multidetermined nature of this fascinating social phenomenon.

The Early Biological Theory

In the late nineteenth century, biological explanations began to be advanced to support the age-old incest prohibition that had been largely explained on ethical and religious grounds prior to that time. In his well-known historical account of ancient society, L. H. Morgan (1877) exemplified the early biological view of incest in his belief that consanguineous marriages were once the common lot of humanity but were abandoned in favor of exogamy because of the damaging effects of such marriages on the offspring. Morgan and other early exponents of this view framed their theories without the benefit of any knowledge of the infant science of genetics; thus their arguments used such phrases as "mental and moral degeneration," which have a peculiar, superstitious ring in the ears of modern readers. The evidence advanced for such views was largely impressionistic. Westermarck (1922), for example, cites the beliefs of some unnamed animal breeders and reports on the condition of inbred populations in remote areas of the world, such as the island of Foula in the Shetlands, as evidence that close inbreeding results in physical weakness, mental retardation, and deaf-mutism.

After the turn of the century, these early biological theories began to fall by the wayside. Their abandonment was partially attributable to a general rebellion in the social sciences against biological explanations in many areas of human behavior. In criminology, for instance, Lombroso ([1876] 1911) had "explained" antisocial behavior by more or less saying that criminals are "born that way." In psychology, McDougall (1908) and others had postulated literally hundreds of instincts to "explain" a great variety of human behaviors. But these largely unprovable hypotheses became less and less satisfactory, especially since they did not seem to stimulate further research and since they often were used to stifle attempts to improve the human condition. A fresh wind was blowing, and explanations of human behavior in terms of learning processes, social interaction, and economics were becoming popular.

Of course, there were also some excellent arguments against the early biological theories and the kinds of evidence that had been advanced in their favor. Some of the counterarguments that appeared frequently in the literature were as follows:

1. The inferiority of inbred populations, if and where it exists, could be due to the inferiority of the founders of these populations—that is, perhaps the founding fathers of such places as Foula were very much like their modern descendants, and thus the inbreeding per se has had no particular effect.

2. Geneticists had already pointed out that the chances that individuals might inherit a pair of mutant recessive genes are greatly enhanced if their parents are related to each other and that such a combination of recessives can result in congenital malformations. However, it was also thought that recessive genes were just as frequently beneficial to offspring. Inbreeding could therefore be positive in its effects as well as negative, depending on the nature of the recessive genes carried by parents.

3. Even if inbreeding has some deleterious effects, it seems difficult to believe that primitive peoples would have noticed these outcomes, attributed them to the relationship of the parents, and formulated a universal taboo on the basis of their awareness of the effects of inbreeding. Even today, there are tribes that seem to have no knowledge of the connection between sexual intercourse and pregnancy, yet these same peoples dread incest and have evolved elaborate rules governing exogamy.

4. Infrahuman animals have no scruples about breeding with fathers, mothers, and siblings, as witnessed by the indiscriminate sexual behavior of animals observed in zoos and domestic settings. If inbreeding has serious adverse effects, one would expect such animals to suffer from their lack of selectivity.

5. Some breeders contended that superior strains of animals and plants could be produced if inbreeding were controlled

skillfully. Especially if members of a superior "family" were in-bred, one ought to be able to produce a super strain.

These and other arguments allowed incest theorists to gloss over or entirely dismiss any biological basis for the incest taboo for the next fifty years and to advance a series of fascinating hypotheses about the social and psychological aspects of the incest taboo.

Anthropological, Sociological, and Psychological Theories

Westermarck (1922), although he was inclined to think that the taboo had a biological origin, was among the first to postulate a noninstinctive psychological mechanism by which the taboo is maintained in the lives of individuals. Quite simply, his theory stated that a natural aversion to mutual sexual expression develops among persons who live together from early childhood. Since nuclear (and sometimes extended) families nearly always live together, this tendency to develop sexual aversion for one another becomes codified as the incest taboo and may later be extended to some persons outside of the living group who are also categorized as relatives.

Much later, Fox (1962) suggested a means by which an aversion to sex could arise among siblings raised together. Fox hypothesized that if prepubertal brothers and sisters are allowed to freely interact, a certain amount of sexually stimulating physical contact would take place and that the aroused sexual drives could not be satiated by orgasm in sexually immature individuals. The aroused and frustrated sexual feelings would then prove aversive to the siblings, who would learn to avoid physical contact with each other well before they attained sexual maturity, and this avoidance behavior would be strong enough to continue through adolescence into adulthood. Fox cites some interesting evidence that societies that allow very free contact between young brothers and sisters do not have extremely strong prohibitions against sibling incest because there seems to be little temptation to perform such acts, but he stops short of making the most interesting recommendation that seems to follow from his theory—that young brothers and sisters be urged to sleep together in order to prevent incest!

The Westermarck-Fox "natural aversion" hypothesis has met with a barrage of well-deserved criticism (Bagley, 1969). If incest aversion really arises so naturally, why has such an intensely enforced taboo evolved to prevent incest behavior in most past and present cultures? Is not the mere arousal of the sexual drive sometimes rewarding whether or not it culminates in orgasm? How would one explain the many examples that anthropologists have given of customary (and successful!) marriages between unrelated persons who have been raised together? And what about Kinsey's (1948, 1953) data showing that many children are capable of achieving orgasm well before puberty? In short, there seems to be ample evidence from numerous sources to allow us to reject this theory as a primary explanation for incest avoidance. Yet an aura of general plausibility still surrounds it. Weinberg (1955), for instance, found that brothers and sisters who had been separated for long periods of time during their youth seemed less restrained by the incest taboo, and there is also some intriguing evidence, cited by Fox (1962), that children raised together in Israeli kibbutzim reject each other as potential sex partners even though they are not related.

Freud ([1913] 1946) rejected arguments for a biological basis for the incest taboo and also rejected the Westermarck theory. From his extensive experience with patients undergoing psychoanalysis, he concluded that the desire for incestuous experience, far from being extinguished in the intimacy of the nuclear family, becomes intense in early childhood and persists throughout life as a repressed desire. A proper explanation of Freud's personality theory is beyond the scope of this discussion, but it suffices to emphasize that he viewed the inevitable clash between the incest taboo—as enforced by the parents—and the child's incestuous desires to be a universal human experience that is central to personality development, normal and abnormal. He believed that the persistence of repressed incest wishes could explain the peculiar emotional intensity that is associated with maintenance of the incest taboo—that is, indi-

viduals are defending themselves against their own repressed impulses by severely condemning such impulses or behavior in
others.

However, Freud remained puzzled as to the origin of the
incest prohibition, and in *Totem and Taboo* ([1913] 1946) he
proposed a quasi-anthropological solution. Citing Darwin's belief that early humans lived in a horde controlled by a violent,
tyrannical father who kept all the females for himself and drove
away his sons to prevent their competition, Freud suggested
that the mistreated sons eventually joined forces, overwhelmed
the father, and ate him in a cannibalistic victory celebration.
However, their jubilation was short-lived. Remorse set in, for
they had also admired their father, and with remorse came the
realization that their original plan of gaining sexual access to
their father's women would create a savage competition among
themselves that would destroy the power that they had found
in unity. They therefore joined together in renouncing sexual
claims on the women by creating the incest taboo and concomitant rules of exogamy.

Perhaps best regarded as an allegory about the state of
primitive families, the "primal horde" story has never gained
wide acceptance. Freud himself was dissatisfied with it, and anthropologists viewed it as "nothing short of fantastic" (Murdock, 1949, p. 292). Yet Freud's original insights into the role
of incestuous feelings in the individual psyche constitute his
most important contribution to this field and are alive and well
today (see, for example, Lindzey, 1967).

Another family-oriented theory was advanced by the
prominent anthropologist Malinowski (1927). In his view, intrafamilial sex (except between marriage partners) was taboo because it would have been extremely disruptive to family relationships: "Incest would mean the upsetting of age distinctions,
the mixing up of generations, the disorganization of sentiments,
and a violent exchange of roles at a time when the family is the
most important educational medium. No society could exist
under such conditions" (p. 251). If the sexual attachment
between two individuals is characterized by possessiveness and
jealousy of possible interlopers, promiscuous sex within the

family would certainly create the chaotic conditions foreseen by the brothers in the primal horde! Moreover, Malinowski believed that parent-child relationships, especially those involving the mother, are vital to the adequate development of the young and that such relationships of necessity involve an attitude of dependence, submission, and respect from the young child. Mating with a parent would involve courtship behaviors that would be completely inconsistent with a properly "childlike" attitude.

Some authors (Aberle and others, 1963) have pointed out that an alternative solution—controlled, institutionalized sexual access within the family, as in polygynous and polyandrous families—was available to early humans but was not adopted by any society of which we have knowledge. But Malinowski's ideas in general are still accepted as descriptive of the present function of the incest taboo, if not necessarily of its origin, and have been elaborated and extended by more recent authors (Parsons, 1954; Schwartzman, 1974).

In 1948, L. A. White suggested that the most adequate explanation of the incest prohibition was of an economic nature. Strongly rejecting instinctual and biological theories, he accepted the psychological premise that individuals have a tendency to desire sexual union with persons with whom they are in close proximity, therefore making incest a very likely occurrence in the absence of a taboo. In human groups, the acquisition of symbolic language enabled early humans to develop and extend cooperative behaviors that had been impossible for even the most intelligent apes and that had definite survival value in the vigorous struggle for existence. The incest taboo, by guaranteeing the occurrence of interfamilial and intergroup marriages, enabled our species to forge larger networks of cooperation, which made life more secure and increased the exchange of ideas and commodities that is so necessary for cultural evolution. Groups that failed to establish exogamy rules would have been at a competitive disadvantage and thus would have died out unless they eventually learned to marry out.

White's line of argument is very convincing as a description of the function and by-products of the incest taboo on a sociocultural level. There is, however, lingering doubt among social scientists that his theory can entirely account for the origin of the taboo or for its peculiar absoluteness and emotional intensity.

Murdock (1949), for one, thought that an adequate explanation of the incest taboo required a multidisciplinary approach utilizing ideas drawn from psychoanalysis, sociology, behavioristic psychology, and cultural anthropology. Freud's theory of a universally repressed desire for incestuous relationships could account for the intensity of incest horror through the ego defense mechanism of reaction formation—the strong condemnation in others of ideas or behaviors that one is struggling to keep repressed in oneself. On a sociological level, the incest taboo would serve the function of preventing sexual competition and jealousy within the family—an extremely important function, since societies depend on families that are adequate for their primary role of socialization of children. Also, along lines suggested by White (1948), the incest taboo would increase "internal diffusion," the process by which customs and inventions are spread throughout the culture, and promote cooperative, peaceful ties between family groups. In turn, behavioristic psychology can help to explain the extension of the incest taboo beyond the nuclear family through its concept of "stimulus generalization"—that is, relatives who are seen as being very similar to nuclear family members would tend to become taboo as sexual partners whether or not they were related by blood. Cultural anthropology, with its knowledge of the structure of kinship systems, by providing information on just which relatives will be seen as very similar to nuclear family members, can explain how stimulus generalization is channeled in various cultures. Murdock (1949) believed that in this way one could account for the confusing variability in application of the incest taboo to extended family members.

Although it is difficult to do justice to Murdock's concepts in such a short summary, the reader should take away a general impression of his multidisciplinary approach and his rejection of any one theory as an explanation for the complex nature of the incest taboo. His approach, if not each and every idea presented in his 1949 formulation, is a sensible, intelligent one that continues to be favored by incest theorists (see, for example, Bagley, 1969).

In the 1950s, two social scientists, Parsons (1954) and Slater (1959), made significant contributions to incest theory by elaborating on points that had been neglected by prior theories. Parsons emphasized the importance of the incest taboo in personality development and in promoting the learning of "transfamilial roles" that are vital to society as a whole. His view of personality development is essentially Freudian in its emphasis on the role of incestuous desire in motivating psychological growth. A very young child, he says, is capable of a kind of diffuse erotic excitement, and the mother is the main source of stimulation that produces such excitement in early life. The child's yearning for this kind of stimulation provides the incentive to progress to higher, more difficult stages of development; such progress depends, however, on the mother's ability to frustrate the child at appropriate times and use the sexually tinged attachment to her to push and pull the child through developmental stages. "Thus the child's erotic attachment to the mother is the 'rope' by which she pulls him up from a lower to a higher level in the hard climb of 'growing up' " (Parsons, 1954, p. 111).

During the latency period, children turn their efforts to mastery of the extrafamilial roles, the learning of which is imperative to the adequate functioning of the larger society. At this time also, average children join a same-sex peer group and repress sexual feelings both for their mothers and, by stimulus generalization, for all other members of the nuclear family. According to this view, overt incest, especially with the mother, would disrupt both personality development for the individual and the optimum functioning of society. Parsons was aware, however, that his description pertained mainly to how incest desires and their prohibition currently function within families and did not necessarily shed any light on how the incest prohibitions originally came into being.

In contrast, Slater (1959) introduced a theory that she felt explained the origin of the incest taboo. Essentially, Slater contended that incest prohibitions and exogamy rules are rather late developments and that in actuality nuclear family matings were largely nonexistent in primitive times because of the conditions of life to which early humans were subject. If one assumes that life expectancy was short, that sexual maturity occurred rather late in the life span, and that offspring were usually born one at a time and nursed for a long period (thus extending the average time period between births), then one can conclude that the parents in such primitive families would typically have been dead by the time their children reached sexual maturity. Parent-child incest would thus be virtually impossible. Siblings would tend to form sexual attachments to extrafamilial individuals as soon as they reached sexual maturity, thus making it very unlikely that two sexually mature siblings would remain with the nuclear family long enough to permit sibling incest. Slater drew up tables illustrating the effects of various assumptions about life span and sexual maturity and also produced evidence from contemporary primitive societies to show that these assumptions are reasonable. Nuclear family incest, therefore, was very rare in the first place. Institutions and taboos later developed that codified the existing situation and continued in force long after the original conditions of family life had changed, perhaps because the taboo had proven to be adaptive in other ways.

Although interesting and thought provoking, Slater's theory makes a rather uncomfortable number of assumptions. Even if one accepts all of the "vital statistics" suggested for primitive families, there is another, unstated assumption that seems questionable; namely, that there can be little or no sexual experience prior to puberty. The Kinsey studies (1948, 1953) disprove any such assumption quite resoundingly, and in fact there are many cases of overt nuclear family incest on record that involve prepubertal children. If sexual activity among children and between children and adults occurred in early times, why was it prohibited by incest taboos that were devised to describe the status quo? And why, in particular, is incest with young children so intensely condemned?

At the beginning of the 1960s, then, a wide variety of incest theories had been advanced, each of which could claim to have at least some validity in explaining some aspect of the incest taboo and its effect on human behavior. All of these theories, however, seemed less than satisfactory as explanations of the *origin* of the incest taboo as opposed to its present function. Some vital ingredient seemed to be missing.

Resurgence of the Biological Theory

The methodological weaknesses that characterized earlier observational studies of the biological consequences of inbreeding have already been described. Research in genetics continued, of course, during the ensuing fifty years, and methods of carrying out controlled experiments with animals and selecting more appropriate comparison groups for human samples were substantially improved. Results of these improved experiments were summarized and brought forcefully to the attention of psychologists by Gilbert Lindzey's presidential address to the American Psychological Association in 1967. Although he attributed some validity to the older theories, he decried many of their advocates as having been believers in "simple and sovereign solutions" and denied that any of these theories was sufficient to explain the origin of the incest taboo, although they may be helpful in understanding how the taboo is maintained.

Lindzey resurrected the biological theory that had been rejected for so long as the best candidate for a truly convincing explanation of the origin of the taboo. He maintained, quite simply, that the consequence of inbreeding, both in animals and in humans, is a decrease in fitness that seriously affects the long-term survival prospects of the individual and the group. He further maintained that the effects of inbreeding would be especially prominent and deleterious in humans because their slowness in reaching sexual maturity and their limited number of offspring make human children far less expendable than the young produced by more prolific species. Thus any human group that were to practice inbreeding, either by prescribing it or by failing to proscribe it, would be at a selective disadvantage and would be very likely to lose out in competition with groups that practice exogamy. Over a long period of time, therefore, we would expect the inexorable process of natural selection to eliminate most or all inbreeding groups.

The alert reader may recall at this point that one of the early arguments against a biological explanation for the origin of the incest taboo was that, even if inbreeding were truly deleterious, primitive humans could not have had sufficient insight into the connection between inbreeding and diminished fitness to explain the creation of the incest taboo. However, this argument becomes absurd when one thinks of the elaborate kinds of adaptive behavior that have evolved in many animal species. Nest building in birds is obviously an adaptive behavior with the "purpose" of protecting the young and enhancing their survival potential. But to what extent is a bird aware of the connection between its successful assemblage of materials into a hollowed-out structure and the benefits of insulation of the young who will eventually be hatched there? Of course, such an awareness of cause and effect becomes increasingly plausible to us as we ascend the scale of animal intelligence, but the salient point here is that the process of natural selection of adaptive physical and behavioral traits is not at all dependent on awareness and is very seldom mediated by insight on the part of individuals or groups. Incest avoidance behaviors could have been selected for in the complete absence of awareness of the effects of inbreeding.

Recent evidence indicates, however, that the effects of nuclear family inbreeding in the human species are often rare, dramatic conditions that are recognizable fairly soon after birth —albinism, dwarfism, and severe congenital sensory losses are examples. It is not wildly implausible to suppose that primitive peoples sought explanations for these "curse of the gods" phenomena and that at least sometimes they seized on the parents' relationship as a possible cause. Lindzey (1967) cites an unpublished study by Segner and Collins (1967) as evidence that some degree of insight may have been present. Segner and Collins found that approximately one third of known myths containing incest themes described deformed offspring or infertility as being a consequence of the incestuous relationship. Such myths were formerly discounted as primitive superstitions with no basis in fact, but now it seems quite likely that they sometimes related to actual observations of the dramatic results of close inbreeding. When such insights existed, they probably helped to sustain enforcement of the incest taboo, but, again, no awareness at all would have been necessary for the *creation* of the taboo—only the operation of natural selection, favoring the preservation of incest avoidance behaviors.

But what are the kinds of evidence that enable us to make such definite statements about the deleterious effects of inbreeding? A brief survey of the newer animal and human research will be carried out, drawing heavily from Lindzey's review (1967).

It has been shown that hybrids are superior to inbred individuals with regard to such physical characteristics as body size, fertility, longevity, and resistance to disease, and these differences have been demonstrated in a wide range of species, such as chickens, rats, mice, honeybees, and fruit flies. Even more interesting to psychologists, however, have been demonstrations that inbred individuals tend to be inferior in various behavioral traits that would have important survival value for a species. Appetitive learning, aversive learning, and exploratory behavior tend to be impaired in the inbred individual. Resistance to stress may also be affected, as suggested by a study showing that a group of inbred mice stressed by loud noises in infancy were inferior to nonstressed inbred mice in their adult maze learning behavior, while no such effect could be demonstrated for hybrid mice. It seemed as if the hybrids possessed some ability to recover from infantile trauma that was lacking in inbred individuals, and it is easy to see how such resilience would have survival value in a hostile environment.

The effects of close inbreeding over many generations can be fatal to a group in at least two ways. Frequently, it has been shown to lead to increasing infertility in the offspring so that the strain literally inbreeds itself out of existence in a relatively short number of generations. But even if a strain could continue to reproduce itself, it would face the additional hazard of increasing homozygosis (the extent to which an individual possesses identical pairs of genes), which would mean that the offspring would be less and less variable. These "homogenized" offspring might survive and reproduce satisfactorily so long as the environment remained constant, but any important change in the environment would initiate a possibly fatal crisis for the group, because it would have lost the variability that ordinarily enables it to produce at least some individuals who can survive under the new conditions.

Although one formerly heard claims that carefully con-trolled inbreeding could produce a superior strain of animals, there is very little evidence that this is possible. True, one can select a few characteristics, such as milk production in cows or olfactory acuity in bloodhounds, and produce a strain that is superior with regard to the chosen qualities by inbreeding indi-viduals who possess the desired characteristics; however, the re-sultant strain regularly shows an overall loss of fitness and adaptability that would most probably ensure its elimination in a natural habitat.

While we are considering animal studies, let us reexamine the contention that the incest barrier is uniquely human—that is, that other animals have no compunction whatsoever about breeding with family members. Our observations of the sexual behavior of animals in zoos or domestic settings are no doubt accurate, but they are also likely to be quite atypical. In the field or forest, various conditions exist that render nuclear family matings either very improbable or virtually impossible. In species that are quick to reach sexual maturity, have large numbers of offspring, and care for them for a very limited time, there is no family in the sense of a permanent or semipermanent attachment bond between a male and a female for the purpose of producing and nurturing the young. After weaning, the young wander off and will mate promiscuously if and when they reach sexual maturity. Although possible, it is highly un-likely that they will produce offspring through nuclear family matings, even though they seem to have no innate aversion to them. In any event, an occasional incest-produced litter would be of little concern, since a large number of relatively expend-able offspring allows any truly unfit individuals to fall by the wayside without significantly affecting the species as a whole.

In larger, more intelligent animals, fewer young are born, and they require care over longer periods of time, thus making attachment bonds between parents highly adaptive. The possibilities for incest are also multiplied by these familylike arrangements, and the impact of increasing the probability of bearing unfit young would be greater, since the offspring are much less expendable. We would therefore expect incest avoidance behaviors to evolve under these conditions, and a variety of them have been described. A rather spectacular example is given by ethologist Eckhard Hess in his observations of families of the Canadian goose (described by Aberle and others, 1963). In this species, males and females mate for life and produce goslings each year; the goslings remain with their parents for approximately three years and form families of their own on reaching sexual maturity. Despite ample opportunity to mate with their siblings or parents, they invariably seek out eligible geese from other families as mates. Experimental work on this species indicates that this incest avoidance is produced by what is called *asexual imprinting*—that is, the other individuals a gosling sees during a critical period in the first weeks or months of life are permanently "imprinted" in its brain as being inappropriate sex objects. Thus the only way that such a fastidious bird could be induced to mate with a member of its nuclear family would be to isolate it from its family from the moment of hatching and to reintroduce it much later. This has been done experimentally, but the probability that such situations would occur in nature is of course quite negligible.

Asexual imprinting is not known to occur in mammals, but mammals that form attachment bonds and nuclear families, thus making inbreeding statistically more likely in the absence of an incest barrier, appear to have evolved behavioral tendencies that decrease the probability of close inbreeding (Aberle and others, 1963). The most frequent mechanism is a strong tendency for parents to expel their young from the family group as soon as sexual maturity is attained. The expulsion typically arises from a competitive struggle between same-sex parents and juveniles, father versus son and mother versus daughter. Since the parent is nearly always of superior size and strength, the competition usually results in the juvenile's being forced to seek a sexual partner elsewhere. Sibling incest is also rendered unlikely, since the presence of two sexually mature juveniles of the opposite sex within the family living unit would seldom occur, especially if the species is given to having single births.

In humans, the incest barrier persists, but the nature of incest avoidance behavior has changed to conform with the needs and abilities of an intelligent and culturally well-developed animal. Creation of the incest taboo was made possible by, and probably coincided with, the development of human language. The symbolization in language of a prohibition against intrafamilial sex enabled human families to stay together after the young became sexually mature while also avoiding the dangers of inbreeding. The abandonment of pubertal expulsion from the nuclear family would have constituted a significant adaptive advantage for early humans in that juvenile family members would then have sufficient time to master the collective knowledge and skills of their culture (Aberle and others, 1963). As a result, the possibilities for cultural transmission of knowledge would have been expanded, and advantages would have also been realized from the continued cooperation and mutual protection that family members afforded each other.

Once established, the incest taboo and resultant exogamous marriage customs have the advantage of forging links of cooperation and shared knowledge between family units that would have survival value for the larger group. Thus the verbally mediated incest taboo of early human groups would soon prove to have economic and cultural advantages, as described by White (1948), and there would be a tendency to extend the taboo to more distant relatives. Although the biological dangers of breeding with relatives outside the nuclear family are slight (see Schull and Neel, 1965) or nonexistent in the case of relatives by marriage, the advantages of intermarriage between larger and larger groups would have made the extended incest taboo highly adaptive in a cultural sense. Indeed, today the extension of the incest taboo is almost as universal as its existence (Murdock, 1949), and some of the most extreme forms of extension and exogamy are found in very primitive cultures, such as the Australian aborigines, where cooperation between local bands is vital to survival.

Thus far, we have discussed the evidence from animal studies for the harmful effects of inbreeding, the mechanisms that other species have evolved to avoid it, and the probable course of the development of incest avoidance in early human groups. The harmful effects of nuclear family inbreeding in humans have been assumed to exist, but the most convincing evidence is yet to be presented. The kinds of controlled experiments that allow the demonstration of such subtle effects as reduced variability are not possible with human groups, of course. But the most dramatic effects of inbreeding (mentioned earlier in discussing whether primitive peoples would have noticed them) are congenital conditions caused by the pairing of two mutant recessive genes that determine the expression of maladaptive characteristics. The marriage of unrelated individuals ensures an extremely low probability that both parents will possess an identical mutant recessive that could be manifested in their offspring. Family members, however, are much more similar to each other in genetic structure than unrelated persons, and thus there is a much higher probability that the offspring of an incestuous relationship will receive a pair of mutant recessive genes. Although it was formerly thought that such recessives would be equally likely to produce favorable and unfavorable characteristics, it is now evident that a happy combination of mutant recessives is a very rare event (Lindzey, 1967). Proof of this last statement rests partly on modern studies of "children of incest," who are compared with appropriate control groups. Three of these studies will now be summarized.

Schull and Neel (1965), taking advantage of the fact that first-cousin marriages are legal in Japan, obtained a sample of children of marriages in Hiroshima and Nagasaki between first cousins, first cousins once removed, and second cousins and compared them on a large number of physical and psychological variables to a matched control group of children of nonconsanguineous marriages. The children of unrelated parents were somewhat larger, less susceptible to infection, and more intelligent, as measured by the Wechsler Intelligence Scale for Children. There was also a slight but highly significant difference in the presence of major congenital defects: 11.7 percent in the inbred group versus 8.5 percent in the control group. As would be expected, the percentage of children with such defects increased with the closeness of relationship of their parents, the children of first cousins having more defects than the children of second cousins. Although it should be emphasized that the differences found in this careful study were modest, they are consistent with the small amount of genetic material shared by first and second cousins. One would expect much more striking differences to be found in the children of nuclear family members, since they are much more closely related.

In 1967, Adams and Neel reported a study of eighteen children resulting from nuclear family incest, twelve from brother-sister and six from father-daughter matings. The incestuous mothers were located, before their children were born, through the cooperation of social agencies that aid unwed mothers in the state of Michigan. A control group of nonincestuous unwed mothers being seen by the same agencies was matched as closely as possible to the incestuous mothers on the variables of age, race, weight, stature, intelligence, and socioeconomic status. The children were examined at birth and at the age of six months. Only seven of the eighteen children of incest were considered to be normal and ready for adoption at six months. Five were stillborn or had died in early infancy; two were severely retarded and subject to seizures; three were being kept under observation because of evidence of borderline intelligence; and one had a bilateral cleft lip. In contrast, fifteen of the eighteen control children were considered normal and ready for adoption. None had died; none was severely retarded; none had given evidence of borderline intelligence, although three were being retained for further testing; one had a major congenital defect. Of course, the small number of cases examined in this study should cause us to view its findings as a preliminary, although highly suggestive, report.

Seemanova (1971) has presented a much larger series of

children of incest reported by various public agencies in Czecho-
slovakia over an eight-year period. Examinations were performed on a total of 161 children of confirmed incestuous
origin, 88 from father-daughter, 72 from brother-sister, and 1
from a mother-son union. Control cases consisted of 95 half siblings of the children of incest—that is, children later born to
incestuous mothers as a result of relationships with unrelated
males. Although the control group was necessarily somewhat
younger, it was quite comparable to the incest group in background variables other than relatedness of the father. Unlike the
group studied by Adams and Neel (1967), very few infant
deaths were reported in either group, probably due to the fact
that Seemanova's cases were reported by agencies that encountered the children some time after birth. In other respects, the
results were quite similar. Moderate to severe mental retardation
was found in 25 percent of the incest group and 0 percent of
the control group; 20 percent of the incest and 5 percent of the
control group had one congenital malformation or some other
serious abnormality, such as deaf-mutism or epilepsy; and 6 percent of the incest group and 0 percent of the control group had
multiple malformations. All in all, 89 percent of the control
group children were found to be normal, while only 43 percent
of the incest group could be thus described.

To be sure, no one study is perfect and absolutely conclusive; there is always some possibility for bias to enter into the
selection of groups or the judgment of which defects are "major" ones, for instance. But, taken as a whole and combined
with the evidence produced by animal studies, the new emphasis on a biological, evolutionary view of the origin of incest prohibitions appears to be amply justified.

Limitations of the Biological Theory

The biological explanation of the origin of the incest taboo has been reasserted quite successfully, and most or all of
the objections raised by earlier theorists have been answered by
more recent research. It now seems that the harmful effects of
inbreeding are sufficient to have mediated the natural selection

of incest avoidance behaviors in both animals and humans, and it has become customary to refer to such behaviors in animals as the *incest barrier,* reserving the term *taboo* for humanity, since it describes a kind of verbal, symbolic behavior that is prominent only in our species (Frances and Frances, 1976). In no way, however, should the reemergence of the biological explanation be taken to imply that humans have an innate, instinctive aversion to incest; there is no evidence that strongly suggests that the incest taboo is not learned by each individual through his or her early interactions with family members and other societal agents. The biological explanation states only that those groups or societies that successfully inculcate incest restraints in their young, by whatever method, will thereby avoid the negative effects of inbreeding and will have a selective advantage over groups that lack incest restraints.

The biological explanation, despite its present prominence, cannot pretend to be the only explanation of the incest avoidance behaviors commonly observed in humans. The fact that the incest taboo is extended beyond the nuclear family in very different ways in different societies still strongly suggests that it serves other social and psychological purposes. Since the biological effects of inbreeding decrease drastically outside the nuclear family, one would not expect the taboo to be extended beyond first cousins, yet Murdock's sample of societies contains many that include all known relatives no matter how distant plus various nonrelatives, such as those who worship the same totem animal. Many cultures also allow marriages with first cousins on either the maternal or paternal side of the family but taboo marriages with very remote relatives on the other side. Such variations do not lend themselves to biological explanations, and one thus returns to Murdock's suggestion that, once established within the nuclear family, the taboo would tend to generalize to other relatives in a pattern dependent on the kinship system of each society. Such extensions would be preserved and possibly expanded even further if the exogamy systems thus established proved to have social benefits of their own. Murdock's concept of "social diffusion" and White's theory of the survival value of cooperative links between social groups would seem quite plausible as explanations of the social benefits of exogamy above and beyond the biological benefits of discouraging close inbreeding.

Another well-established characteristic of the incest taboo is that the intensity of the prohibition varies markedly within the nuclear family. Almost universally, brother-sister incest is less severely taboo than father-daughter incest, while mother-son incest inspires the greatest horror. This differential cannot, of course, be explained by the harmful effects of inbreeding because all three of these unions would be equally likely to produce defective offspring on a purely genetic basis. In fact, the mother-son relationship would be the least likely to produce any offspring, since the mother would often be past the age of optimum fertility when her son reached puberty, yet this union is by far the most strongly condemned.

I suggest that, while the taboo on nuclear family incest probably had its origin in the advantages of avoidance of inbreeding, from the earliest times the incest taboo has been influenced by many other social conditions, taboos, and psychological factors that have nearly always been present in the nuclear family situation. Four such influences will be suggested here, but the list is not intended to be exhaustive, and readers can no doubt think of additional factors.

First, in humans and most other higher animals there is commonly a series of dominance relationships within any family or social grouping. Older, bigger individuals tend to be dominant over younger ones, and males are usually dominant over females within the same age grouping, due to the males' greater size and aggressiveness. Initiation of sexual relationships is importantly connected with the dominance hierarchy: Males are usually the initiators, and they tend to succeed with females who are less dominant than themselves. On the basis of these facts, one would expect that father-daughter and older brother-younger sister sexual relationships would be both more common and less socially reprehensible (since they do not violate social expectations about dominance) than mother-son or older sister-younger brother incest.

Societies commonly taboo sexual relationships involving

adults and prepubertal individuals, particularly if the latter are very young. In our own culture, one has only to think of our stereotype of the "child molestor" to realize the strength of this prohibition in cases where the adult and child are not at all related. Within the nuclear family, then, one would certainly expect father-daughter and mother-son relationships to seem more loathesome than sibling incest, because they would be more likely to involve an adult and a child.

A related point is that, even when neither of the sexual partners is prepubertal, societies display an almost unanimous preference for sexual unions and marriages to occur between individuals of the same generation, possibly because same-age marriages enhance the likelihood that both partners will survive long enough to nurture and instruct their offspring. This preference suggests greater censure for parent-child incest, even when the "child" is actually an adult.

A fourth and final factor to be discussed here is the special nature of dependency relationships involving nurturance of one individual by another. It has long been maintained (see Malinowski, 1927) that the intense dependency relationship between a young child and its parents, especially the mother, is incompatible with overt sexuality and its concomitant courtship behaviors. Although there may well be distinctly erotic components in the parent-child relationship, theorists (for example, see Parsons, 1954; Schwartzman, 1974) are generally agreed that direct erotic expression would be extremely confusing for the child and might be expected to interfere with his or her emotional development. If the destructiveness of overt incest is greatest for the most intense dependency relationship, then we would expect mother-son incest to be the most intensely taboo and sibling incest to be the least.

These factors could be expected to interact with each other to produce the definite variation in the incest taboo's intensity within the nuclear family despite the biological equivalence of the three mating combinations. All four of the factors would go strongly against mother-son incest; none of the factors would affect the sibling incest situation, unless one partner were much older than the other; and the father-daughter incest combination comes out in an intermediate position, since such unions would not violate dominance relationships and would also tend to involve less intense dependency-nurturance relationships than would mother-son incest. Again, it is not represented that the factors presented are a complete set, nor is a really new theory of the incest taboo being advanced. My intention is to reemphasize the essential wisdom of the multidisciplinary approach proposed by Murdock, although its components have been somewhat modified over the past thirty years to reflect our knowledge of the biological necessity involved in the incest taboo.

Research on
Overt Incest

The incest taboo has been discussed at some length in Chapter One in order to provide the reader with background material and a historical context for a consideration of the central question addressed in this book—the psychological causes and effects of overt incest. As intensely as the taboo has been enforced in most places and at most times, it is also nearly a universal experience that members of any society have heard of at least one case of real incest (usually a few generations back or several miles from the individual reporting). The first scientifically oriented attempts to study cases of overt incest were made in the late nineteenth century; case histories were published in Latin by Richard von Krafft-Ebing ([1886] 1965) and other physicians of the time. Research on incest continued to appear in German language journals and books in the early twentieth century, and some articles (for instance, Rohleder, 1917; Marcuse, 1923) were translated into English and published in the *American Journal of Urology and Sexology*. American research began with a trickle (Bender and

Blau, 1937; Sloane and Karpinski, 1942) in the 1930s and 1940s, but accounts of incest did not appear in the professional literature with regularity until the 1950s. Since 1950, at least twenty-five articles and books reporting cases of overt incest have been published in this country, and important contributions have been reported in foreign journals with increasing frequency, particularly in the British Commonwealth nations and in France, Israel, and Japan.

This chapter summarizes some of the more important problems and issues that have confronted incest researchers over the years and gives the reader a global impression of the characteristics of the research carried out to date. A tabulation of these characteristics appears in this chapter. Summaries of the actual findings of these studies and the hypotheses generated by them will appear in appropriate places throughout the book.

The Incidence of Overt Incest

The question of the incidence of overt incest is interesting in its own right; however, it will be discussed here because it constitutes a major problem for the incest researcher. The introductions of many studies give an incidence figure of one in a million "detected cases" per year, after which the author hastens to add that the true incidence of incest must surely be much higher than that. The one-in-a-million figure refers to the incidence of incest in criminal statistics, which have generally reported between one and two cases per million inhabitants per year in this country and have reported rather similar figures from other countries, according to Weinberg (1955). When deviations from this figure do occur, it is exceedingly difficult to make statements about differences among countries or even among different time periods within one country, because there are so many divergent ways of keeping criminal statistics. Sometimes, for instance, the incidence figure refers to the number of individuals who have been investigated by law enforcement agencies, and in other cases it refers to the number of persons who are actually tried and convicted of incest. Such statistics have been eagerly examined in attempts to discern trends in the incidence of detected incest in relation to such variables as rural-urban residence patterns, population density, and the state of the economy, but no consistent differences have emerged. The one finding that has been replicated in several countries at different times is that the rate of detected incest tends to fall during wartime, when fathers and older sons are generally separated from their families, and tends to rise again in the postwar period.

As stated earlier, authors seem to agree that the true rate of overt incest must far exceed the rate of detected incest. A few even state that incestuous experiences are "common," but it is difficult to know what is meant by this when no figures are attached. There is certainly good reason to believe that many or most cases of incest are never reported to any social authority, least of all the police, but are kept as skeletons in the family closet or revealed to a very limited number of extrafamilial persons. The penalties for reporting incest are certainly very severe, since one or more family members may be subject to a long prison sentence. And, whether or not a sentence is imposed, a public accusation will usually result in the family's being stigmatized in the community, deprived of financial support in the event that the breadwinner leaves, and subjected to all the other unpleasant results of the anger that the accusation will create within the family. No wonder that incestuous families have a reputation for being "collusive"! It is common for a public accusation to be made only in the context of a major family argument and then to be retracted when the dust settles down. It should be emphasized, however, that a reluctance to report incest should not be construed to mean that the family is happy with the incestuous situation—just that the family is avoiding an alternative that it perceives to be even more aversive.

Impressions of the true incidence of overt incest vary greatly with the kind of subject sample that the researcher is in a position to observe. Generally, if the researcher is dealing with a delinquent population the impression will be that incest is very common indeed. Samples of "sexually delinquent" or "promiscuous" young women tend to yield especially high numbers of incestuous backgrounds. Halleck (1962) has reported that approximately 15 percent of a group of delinquent teen-age girls who were confined to a state training school had had sexual relations with their fathers or stepfathers. Lukiano-wicz (1972) found that approximately 10 percent of young women being seen by a social service agency reported incest, while only 4 percent of female psychiatric patients told their therapists of incestuous experiences. Similarly, in a study of women who had had three or more illegitimate pregnancies, Malmquist, Kiresuk, and Spano (1966) reported that 25 percent of their sample confessed to incestuous experiences prior to their careers as unwed mothers. There are also indications that a sample of sexually disturbed males will yield a high rate of in-cest histories. For instance, the Kinsey Institute study of sex offenders (Gebhard and others, 1965) reported that 9 percent of a sample of imprisoned rapists admitted to researchers that they had had sexual relations with sisters, aunts, or mothers.

A researcher who studies a more representative sample will get a very different impression. Greenland (1958) reviewed 2,439 letters to an "advice column" dealing with sex- and court-ship-related problems and found only seven letters that reported actual incidents of incest. And in the Kinsey Institute study of sex offenders (Gebhard and others, 1965) a control group of 477 noncriminal, mostly working-class males revealed only a .2 percent incidence of incest with sisters, aunts, or mothers.

Probably the best information now available to us on the real incidence of incest in the United States is contained in the Kinsey studies of sexual behavior in the human male (Kinsey, Pomeroy, and Martin, 1948) and the human female (Kinsey and others, 1953). These studies assembled large samples of care-fully taken sexual histories that are reasonably representative of the general population, although only Caucasians were sampled. In the male sample, the finding of incest was so rare that the usually cautious Kinsey made a statement to the effect that in-cest "occurs more frequently in the thinking of clinicians and social workers than it does in actual performance" (1948, p. 558). In the study of females Kinsey and others (1953) found a somewhat higher incidence, with about 4 percent of the sample reporting that they had been approached in a sexual manner by an uncle, father, brother, or grand-father prior to adolescence. Thus about one in twenty-three adult females reported some kind of incestuous experience to researchers.*

From this evidence, it is not possible to give any definite incidence figure for incest, but I think that some tentative conclusions can be stated. It appears that incest occurs much more frequently than the one or two per million per year figure for detected cases and that it is realistic to think of incest as an event that occurs in one or two lifetimes out of a hundred. Although its incidence is much higher than many people would guess, it still qualifies as a relatively rare event, much more rare than most other forms of stigmatized sexual behavior. It may be accurate to refer to incest as "common" only in certain kinds of clinically defined groups. Thus clinicians are likely to describe incest as rather common, while researchers such as Kinsey, who are in contact with a more representative group of subjects, are likely to think of most incest being "in the thinking of clinicians"!

Methods of Obtaining Case Samples

The incidence of overt incest, plus the emotional intensity of the incest taboo, plus the very real and severe social and legal sanctions against incestuous behavior add up to a well-nigh insurmountable barrier for any researcher who dreams of doing the "ideal" study of incest behavior. The ideal study would require a large sample of incest participants who could be said to be truly representative of all incest participants. How could this be done? Could a random sample of numbers in the phone book be called or could people emerging from supermarkets in a representative community be confronted? Such methods would be feasible in a study of political preferences, but it is ludicrous to

*These figures were calculated from percentages given in the Kinsey report on females (Kinsey and others, 1953, p. 118), on the assumption that there was little or no overlap between groups involved with uncles, fathers, and brothers.

think of their application to incest behavior, because the disclosure of incestuous experience under such circumstances is socially inappropriate in the extreme. After approaching literally thousands of persons in such a manner, the researcher would obtain a small sample of individuals who boldly disclose their incestuous acts, and one would certainly wonder about the degree to which such persons would represent the real population of incest participants!

The serious study of incest behavior necessarily involves the use of skewed, nonrepresentative samples, since the most feasible approach to obtaining a sample is to work under the auspices of a legal, social, or clinical agency that frequently encounters cases of incest in the population it serves. After incest cases are studied in a variety of settings, it is hoped that a composite picture of the "true" nature and scope of incest in our society will eventually emerge. In the meantime, individual researchers need to be very conscious of their own sample's skew—that is, the manner in which their particular research setting influences their findings about incest.

Courts and prisons are fairly obvious settings in which to do incest research. Even though the incidence of reported incest cases is low, a researcher working through the court system in a metropolitan area can hope to obtain an adequate sample within a reasonable time period. If permission to interview imprisoned incest offenders can be obtained in several different localities, then a fairly large number of cases can be obtained within a short period of time. Using this method, the Kinsey Institute group (Gebhard and others, 1965) has done the largest, most thorough study of males imprisoned for incest offenses. Over a period of about fifteen years, the group interviewed 165 incest offenders who were imprisoned in Indiana and California for relations with daughters, sisters, or nieces.

The court or prison setting is probably our best opportunity to study males who have actively initiated incest, inasmuch as these individuals seldom are seen in other settings and tend to be quite uncooperative. Incest offenders who are already imprisoned may be very cooperative in order to expiate their guilt feelings; however, Gebhard and others (1965) reported that a minority of them continued to deny the offense despite what seemed to be overwhelming evidence that it had actually occurred. Efforts to interview the rest of the family may be successful, but the researcher has to deal with a very high level of defensiveness under these circumstances. Since the interviewees are likely to be either potential or past witnesses against a member of their own family, there will usually be high levels of ambivalence and guilt and thus efforts to defend their own positions at the possible expense of accurate reporting.

A court- or prison-collected sample will, of course, tend to be skewed toward a lower socioeconomic level in that lower-class males are more likely to actually go to jail for any offense, given their lack of sophistication and resources. Although imprisoned incest offenders are not a particularly criminal group, they may be somewhat more criminal than incest offenders who do not go to jail. A person with a clean record who has some degree of support and sympathy in his community is far less likely to be tried for incest than is a black sheep type who has already acquired a reputation as a public nuisance or menace.

Incest cases that never come to court may be located through various other social agencies—juvenile detention facilities, homes for unwed mothers, family service agencies, to name a few. Sometimes incest is a direct cause of contact with the agency; in many cases, however, it comes to light almost accidentally in the course of investigating some other kind of family difficulty. Once a caseworker enjoys the confidence of family members, reports of incest may be elicited that would never be made to law enforcement authorities. Although some of these cases may also eventually turn up in court, most of them are handled in a less drastic manner.

Collecting cases through social agencies also tends to limit sampling to the lower socioeconomic groups, since middle- and upper-class families are more likely to seek aid from private practitioners of various sorts. Researchers must also be acutely aware that the specific nature of the agency through which cases are collected will have an important effect on the results of the study. For example, if it were hypothesized that incestuous experience leads to sexual promiscuity and if evidence were then gathered from cases of incest reported in a home for delinquent girls, it would almost certainly be found that girls with incestuous case histories tend to be promiscuous, simply because sexual promiscuity may actually be the norm in that setting. Thus the population served by an agency is always an important piece of information to be reported along with the information gathered through the agency.

A third promising source of incest cases would be a psychotherapeutic setting, such as a psychiatric hospital, crisis intervention center, or child guidance clinic. Psychotherapists, especially those with a younger female clientele, frequently remark that they are surprised by the number of patients who admit to past incestuous experience in the course of their psychotherapy. Seen through the patient's eyes, the therapeutic situation is a unique opportunity to disclose forbidden thoughts and misdeeds with very little danger of repercussions. Such an opportunity can be especially important to a person who has been involved in incest because of the difficulty and risk encountered in disclosure to friends and relatives. Since the revelation of incest is so likely to be treated with horror and disbelief and since a breach of confidence could lead to legal proceedings that the incest participant may be quite unprepared for, use of a trusted therapist as the patient's "confessor" becomes especially attractive. When incest is disclosed, the patient will often say something like "I'm not sure that this has anything to do with my present difficulties, but I've always wanted to tell somebody that. . . ."

The collection of incest cases in a psychotherapeutic setting has some decided advantages. First, the therapist often possesses a rich store of information about the patient, obtained over many therapeutic interviews and enhanced by the opportunity to observe the patient's behavior over a period of months or even years. The "portrait" of an incest participant in psychotherapy thus has the potential of being much more complete and lifelike than the more limited view afforded when a participant is interviewed in prison or a case is reported by a social agency. A second advantage is the opportunity to see and evaluate incest participants at widely varying intervals after the

incest. Some reports of current, ongoing incest situations may
be elicited, especially in cases where adolescents are involved as
patients either in family therapy or individually. But many
other reports are given five, ten, twenty, or more years after the
incestuous relationship has ended, and such accounts are needed
in order to piece together some kind of tentative picture of the
long-term aftereffects of incestuous experience. A third advantage is the possible avoidance of a sample skewed toward subjects from a lower socioeconomic level. Since involvement in
psychotherapy is much more socially acceptable than encounters with law enforcement or other social agencies, samples of
psychotherapy patients are more likely to include middle- and
even upper-class individuals. The sample may be skewed toward
the upper or lower end of the socioeconomic scale, depending
on the kind of psychotherapy clientele that is being served, but
at least there is the possibility of obtaining a sample that is reasonably representative with regard to social class.

A number of reports of small numbers of incest cases or
of just one especially interesting case have appeared in the incest literature, and, while these case histories are interesting and
suggestive in their own right, they do not begin to constitute
adequate samples of incestuous behavior. A very small number
of cases (less than ten) can hardly be termed a *sample* at all, and
when all the cases are described by the same therapist there will
be a definite bias in the direction of his or her theoretical beliefs
about incest. It is then virtually impossible for the reader to
decide whether the case material supports the therapist's theory
or whether the theory itself has determined the therapist's interpretation of the case material. A large sample that is also somewhat freer of the theoretical biases of therapists could be gathered by collecting observations of incest cases seen by a group
of therapists practicing in a given setting. Since it would be unlikely that a group of therapists would be completely homo-
geneous in their beliefs about incest, no one theory would
strongly bias the results of such a study. This approach, however, has seldom been attempted.

Of course, any sample of psychotherapy patients will include only those incest participants who are motivated to seek

psychotherapy either by themselves or through referral by some authority figure who perceives them as disturbed. The sample is therefore skewed to some extent in the direction of psychological disturbance, because there is no possibility of sampling the hypothetical population of incest participants who are either undisturbed or who have no desire or opportunity for therapy. The degree of psychological disturbance that is found will, of course, depend on the nature of the psychotherapeutic setting. Psychiatric hospitals, or their affiliated out-patient clinics, obviously produce samples skewed toward psychosis, psychoanalytic settings yield neurosis or character disorders, sex therapists find sexual dysfunction, and family therapists usually discover "communication difficulties." Research in a setting that tends to attract patients with a wide range of difficulties and various degrees of disturbance is most desirable, because it is then possible to discover whether incest participants tend to be over- or underrepresented in certain diagnostic categories, such as psychosis or sexual dysfunction. In any case, the characteristics of the clinical population in which incest cases are collected should always be specified by the researcher so that the findings about incest participants can be correctly interpreted.

A few studies have used other methods of case collection. Greenland's (1958) study of several thousand letters received by an "advice column" has already been mentioned. Another example is Landis (1956), who asked students in an introductory psychology course to fill out anonymous questionnaires on early sexual experiences with adults. Out of 1,800 replies, a few described sexual approaches by adults who were well known to them as children, although Landis does not make clear whether the adults were actually related to the children. Again, studies that use these miscellaneous methods of case collection seem to require that one examine a very large number of subjects in order to obtain a very small number of incest case histories, and even this sample will be skewed in a subtle way toward whatever factors may be operating to allow a person to report an extremely personal event to a stranger.

Once an appropriate setting for incest research has been selected, there are several important questions that should ideally be answered before data collection begins: How will it

be decided if a report of incest is "real"? What kinds of activities constitute a sexual relationship? Is homosexual incest to be
included? How many relatives, by blood or marriage, should be
included in the definition of incest? And, finally, what kinds of
information will be collected for each appropriate case that has
been found?

Assessing the Reality of Incest Reports

There seems to be a widespread notion that reports of incest in a patient's early history are very likely to be fantasies
that serve some psychodynamic purpose in the patient's personality structure. Similarly, accusations of incest by adolescent
girls may not be taken at face value because, like reports of
rape, they may be seen as an attempt to get revenge or to excuse an illegitimate pregnancy. Freud's well-known conclusion
that reports of sexual trauma in his early case studies were fantasized is often given as a reason for discounting reports of
incest. However, at least some recent clinical researchers (for instance, Berry, 1975; Peters, 1976) have been impressed by the
frequency with which childhood sexual trauma, including
incest, actually occurs and have suggested that the extreme skepticism engendered by Freud's statement about fantasies should
be seriously reconsidered.

Peters (1976) gives an interesting historical account of
Freud's ideas about the role of childhood sexual trauma in the
etiology of neurosis and suggests that social pressure was a
major factor in Freud's "rejection" of his earlier theory. When
Freud and Breuer began to treat cases of hysteria in the 1890s,
they were surprised to hear reports of childhood sexual trauma
from their patients; a role for such trauma in the genesis of
neurosis ran counter to their previous training and expectations,
but the frequent reports of sexual abuse in childhood could not
be denied. In "The Etiology of Hysteria," Freud ([1896] 1962a,
p. 203) concluded, "I therefore put forward the thesis that at
the bottom of every case of hysteria there are *one or more occurrences of premature sexual experiences*, occurrences which
belong to the earliest years of childhood."

Freud admitted much later that he had cautiously suppressed the fact that two of his early series of hysteria cases, on which his theory of hysteria was based, were actually cases of father-daughter incest. Nevertheless, the theory provoked a storm of criticism from his most respected colleagues, including Charcot, his own mentor in the study of neurosis. Breuer retreated into pulmonary physiology, leaving Freud to withstand the resistance of both his patients and the scientific community until he gradually shifted his emphasis from childhood sexual trauma to oedipal fantasies. In 1924, he added a footnote to his earlier paper on hysteria. The most widely quoted section of this note read, "At that time I was not yet able to distinguish between my patients' fantasies about their childhood years and their real recollections. As a result, I attributed to the etiological factor of seduction a significance and universality which it does not possess." That Freud had not entirely rejected his earlier theory was indicated in a less well-known section of the footnote: "Nevertheless, we need not reject everything written in the text above [about the specific etiology of hysteria]. Seduction retains a certain etiological importance, and even today I think some of these psychological comments are to the point" ([1896], 1962a, p. 168).

According to Peters (1976), Freud's partial rejection of his earlier theory was focused on because it relieved the anxiety of *therapists*! As the idea of real sexual abuse of children is an aversive, threatening thought for adults to seriously entertain, therapists were well motivated to repress it and substitute the notion of oedipal fantasies. Since fantasies came to be considered as important as real events in childhood, therapists were also relieved of any responsibility for discerning whether or not their patients' reports were real. Thus, in Peters' opinion, psychoanalysis has for the past fifty years "oversubscribed to the theory of childhood fantasy and overlooked incidents of the actual sexual victimization in childhood" (1976, p. 401).

Of course, the issue of the "reality" of incest reports is raised here because of its importance to research on overt incest. The conclusion that seems to emerge from our consideration of the history of the psychoanalytic viewpoint is that reports of sexual trauma should not be disbelieved in an automatic, doctrinaire, "fantasy until proven reality" manner. We should instead adopt a wait-and-see attitude, looking for evidence in an impartial way and realizing that the occurrence of very real sexual trauma in the lives of children is not the extremely rare event that we might wish it to be. (Peters, 1976, has reported that 150 to 175 of the 1,000 cases of rape reported each year to an inner-city rape victim center involved victims under the age of thirteen and that in a substantial number of these cases the offender was a relative.)

Obviously, reports of incest can also be false. They may represent psychotic delusions, neurotic embroiderings of innocent events, or even deliberately trumped-up charges aimed at "getting" someone, and it is a researcher's task to set up some criteria for deciding whether a report is untrue or at least questionable. Unfortunately, even when researchers state that some of their incest reports proved to be false, they rarely describe the process of arriving at this conclusion.

If both parties involved in the reported incest admit that it has occurred, then we can be nearly 100 percent certain that it has, since it is very difficult to imagine motives for "malingering incest." If, however, a daughter or sister alleges incest and the father or brother vehemently denies it, the report may be false. The word *may* is used very deliberately here because the social and psychological costs of admitting to incest are so high for a father or brother that the motivation to falsely deny the report is much more than adequate. Even after being convicted and imprisoned, many incest offenders continue to deny the offense despite rather overwhelming evidence that the alleged incest did occur (Gebhard and others, 1965). Weinberg (1955, p. 184) describes a case where it was well substantiated that a father had sexual relations with three of his daughters over a period of several years, having impregnated one of them twice. After being imprisoned, he continued to insist that mysterious "enemies" were responsible for his plight and showed every evidence of being delusional.

If incest is denied by one party or if the report relates to events long past, it would certainly be helpful to obtain corroboration from other family members. But here too there are some serious potential problems, since other members of the family are hardly dispassionate observers—on the contrary, they tend to have strong motives of their own for keeping the family together or expelling one or more members. Weinberg (1955), who was frequently able to interview the family, has given the best description in the incest literature of the effects of incest disclosure on family dynamics. He concluded that, in cases where a father is making financial or emotional contributions that are valued by the family, members will tend to support him and to reject the daughter. However, if the father has been abusive and nonsupportive of the family, members may well join ranks and make every effort to substantiate the daughter's claims. Since family members would seldom have actually witnessed the incestuous acts, their support or rejection of the incest report rests on their interpretation of a very complex series of events and is heavily influenced by their personal biases.

Since independent corroboration of an incest report is often not obtainable or is inconclusive, it is often necessary to make some judgment about the mental state of the person reporting incest as a guide to whether or not the report should be accepted at face value. One criterion for rejecting a report has been the presence of psychosis (Medlicott, 1967), and with good reason. Clinicians often observe a preoccupation with incest in psychotic patients, who may confuse their fantasies with reality or project their own incestuous impulses on others in a desperate attempt to shore up their failing ego defenses. Since psychosis is, by definition, a condition in which a person's perception of reality is less accurate than usual, it does make sense to be skeptical about incest reports given by psychotics. Such reports should not, however, be automatically rejected simply because the person reporting is psychotic. In fact, incest is not infrequently associated with gross psychopathology (see Wahl, 1960; Kubo, 1959). The guilt and anxiety produced by a real incestuous experience can be one of the precipitating factors in a psychotic breakdown in which thoughts about incest can be expressed in morbid ruminations and hallucinations, or, conversely, psychosis can be a causative factor in incest because the psychotic person tends to be more erratic in impulse control and may attempt to act out desires that are usually firmly repressed in the nonpsychotic state. Thus it would seem that the prudent course for a researcher to follow in evaluating reports given by psychotics is to suspend judgment and seek further evidence.

If incest reports are being collected in a psychotherapeutic setting where patients are seen more than briefly, the problem is somewhat alleviated, since a therapist generally has the luxury of reserving judgment on the reality of patient reports. Over a period of weeks or months, it usually is possible to observe how the patient's account changes (if it does), to see how the reported event fits in with the patient's defense structure and whether it might be providing secondary gain, and to ascertain the extent to which the patient misinterprets or fantasizes events that the therapist can really know about. Unless a researcher insists on a very strict criterion of corroboration, these kinds of slowly-arrived-at clinical judgments are probably the best that can be obtained in questionable cases of incest.

Problems with the Research Definition of Incest

Another decision that confronts an incest researcher pertains to the kind or amount of sexual activity between related persons that will be defined as *incest*. The strictest criterion for incest is genital intercourse, and some studies (for example, Weinberg, 1955) have adhered to it, thus avoiding any ambiguity in the definition of sexual activity. But such a definition excludes a good deal of sexual activity with younger children, because genital intercourse is considerably more difficult to effect with a very young female (Gebhard and others, 1965, p. 227) and also obviously excludes the possibility of homosexual incest. Therefore, researchers have usually included such obviously sexual acts as oral-genital contact, fondling of genitals, and mutual masturbation in their incest definitions. A somewhat more questionable area would be the report of perceived attempts at sexual activity that were stopped short of sexual contact, display of genitals in a sexual context without contact, and very overtly expressed sexual interest on a verbal level. A fairly good case can be made for including such events in a definition of incest, since they are specified by certain kinds of overt behaviors. Mere "seductiveness" on the part of a relative, although it can no doubt be an important psychological reality, is too far afield to qualify as an overt incestuous relationship and has almost never been included in a research definition.

Incest has often been defined as *heterosexual* relations between family members, thus excluding half of the possible sexual combinations within a family. Homosexual incest is supposed to be rare, and authors commonly lament the lack of published case histories in this area. Cory (1963) makes an interesting conjecture to the effect that psychoanalytically oriented researchers may have shied away from this subject because homosexual incest presents them with a conceptual difficulty: If homosexuality is explained by psychoanalysts as being a "flight from incest," then how can they explain homosexual incest? Whether or not homosexual incest is a dilemma for Freudian theorists, the possibility of its occurrence should be recognized prior to designing a research project, and it should be included, if possible, in the researcher's definition of incest so that we can attain a more adequate understanding of the scope of such incest and of how its causes and effects compare with those found in heterosexual incest.

Another "inclusion" problem is the degree of relationship between sexual partners that will be defined as incestuous. The father-daughter, mother-son, and brother-sister combinations are always included; relationships between grandparents and grandchildren, aunts and nephews, uncles and nieces, and half brothers and sisters are almost always considered to be incest; and, although a relationship with a first cousin may be incest in the eyes of the law, cousin incest is very seldom included in a research definition, because the feelings associated with incest are very diluted with regard to cousins, and real social and legal censure is minimal.

A serious definitional problem concerns the "incestuousness" of relations with relatives by adoption or by marriage. Some major studies (Weinberg, 1955) have excluded such relationships entirely, but there is a good case for inclusion, especially if the study's focus is on the child or younger sibling. If a stepparent or adoptive parent or sibling is present from early childhood, then the feeling of "real" relationship is very strong. In fact, a child may not even be aware of the lack of blood relationship at the time the sexual relations occur, and even if awareness was present the person reporting the incident may feel strongly that "He was the only father I ever knew!" Thus to a child the relationship may seem vividly incestuous, even though the law defines it as being "only" child molestation. Of course, the older the child is when the adoption or marriage occurs, the less incestuous will a parent-child or sibling sexual relationship seem, and one can imagine situations in which it would be patently ridiculous to label a sexual relationship *incestuous*. If an older man marries a young woman who subsequently has an affair with a stepson who is actually older than she is, is this a case of mother-son incest? Of course not. Such a relationship would have practically none of the horror attached to it that is characteristic of mother-son incest and could be expected to have very different consequences. The researcher is thus confronted with the necessity of making an intelligent decision as to when to include relations between unrelated relatives in the incest category. A research report should carefully specify how many cases involved blood relatives as opposed to relatives by marriage or adoption.

Data Collection and Evaluation

Once a sample of incest participants is located, the researcher makes one more decision—how to gather and interpret information about the incest participants and their backgrounds. By far the most widely used method has been to report one or more case histories containing qualitative information obtained by a nonstructured interview method, either in the context of psychotherapy or otherwise. While these kinds of qualitative data are of significant importance in conveying the "feel" of an incest situation—the home atmosphere, the emotional reaction of participants, and so forth—they are subject to distortion by the theories (or prejudices) of the researcher. This bias can be alleviated to some extent by using a structured interview approach in which a series of standard questions are posed for each case of incest that is investigated.

In incest research, the structured interview method has seldom been used (see Table 1), the most notable exception having been the Kinsey Institute group (Gebhard and others, 1965). To be sure, it is not always possible to obtain the same kinds of information on each case in a sample, but an attempt to obtain the answers to a list of standard questions can yield data that are more amenable to being reported in percentage tables, the presentation method long favored by the Kinsey Institute group. Making statements in terms of percentages is a much more accurate form of communication than using such vaguely quantitative terms as *rarely, often, most,* or *many.* In addition, knowledge of the demographic characteristics (such as age, education, and ethnic group) of the sample in terms of percentages enables readers to make more informed assessments of the results and to compare the sample with those results obtained in other studies that have described samples quantitatively.

Very few studies have made use of psychological tests in the collection of data. Intelligence test scores have been reported most frequently; projective tests of personality, such as the Rorschach, have occasionally been used; and objective personality tests, such as the Minnesota Multiphasic Personality Inventory (MMPI), have been least frequently reported, probably because they are relatively recent developments on the clinical research scene. While all of the better-known standardized tests contribute some additional knowledge beyond that gained by interviews alone, the increased reporting of objective test results would be especially desirable, because these results are less likely to be affected by the subjective biases of the researcher and because of the interesting possibility that results obtained from different samples by different researchers could be combined, which is especially intriguing in a field of research where small samples are almost the rule.

Finally, the researcher must decide how to evaluate and interpret the data obtained from a sample of incest cases. It is

Table 1. Studies of Overt Incest

Author(s) and Date	Country	N	Research Setting	Incest Criteria[a]	Method[b]
Rasmussen (1934)	Norway	14	Court	Sexual contact with relative by blood or marriage	Interviews and third-person reports
Bender and Blau (1937)	United States	4	Psychiatric hospital (court referred)	Sexual approach by blood relative	Interviews, Stanford-Binet
Riemer (1940)	Sweden	58	Court referred for psychiatric evaluation	Intercourse (?) with blood relative	Interviews
Tompkins (1940)	United States	1	Psychiatric hospital (?)	Sexual contact with blood relative	Interviews (psychotherapy)
Sloane and Karpinski (1942)	United States	5	Referred by family service agency (?)	Intercourse (?) with blood relative	Interviews
Rascovsky and Rascovsky (1950)	Argentina	1	Psychiatric practice	Sexual intercourse with blood relative	Interviews (psychoanalysis)
Kaufman, Peck, and Tagiuri (1954)	United States	11	Referred by court or social agencies	Intercourse (?) with relative by blood or marriage	Interviews (psychotherapy), Stanford-Binet or Wechsler, Rorschach, TAT, Draw-a-Man
Weinberg (1955)	United States	203	Reported by "authorities"	Intercourse with blood relative	Structured interview
Weiss and others (1955)	United States	26	Court referred for psychiatric evaluation	Sexual contact with relative by blood or marriage	Interviews, Rorschach, TAT, Draw-a-Person
Barry and Johnson (1958)	United States	?[c]	Private practice (?)	Sexual contact (?) with blood relative	Interviews (psychotherapy)
Greenland (1958)	Great Britain	7	Letters to advice column	Sexual intercourse with relative by blood or marriage	Letters to advice column

(continued on next page)

Table 1 (Continued)

Author(s) and Date	Country	N	Research Setting	Incest Criteria[a]	Method[b]
Martin (1958)	United States	30	Prison	Sexual intercourse with blood relative	Blacky Test, TAT, Michigan Picture Test; control groups of 21 sex offenders and 20 other prisoners
Howard (1959)	United States	2	Referred by court and social agency	"Advances" by blood relative	Interviews (psychotherapy)
Kubo (1959)	Japan	36	Reported by "various institutions, consultation centers, or welfare agencies"	Attempts at incest by relative by blood or marriage	Interviews
Schachter and Cotte (1960)	France	18	Referred by court or social service agencies	Intercourse (?) with blood relative	Interviews, intelligence testing, Rorschach
Wahl (1960)	United States	2	Psychiatric hospital	Intercourse with blood relative	Interviews (psychotherapy)
Hersko and others (1961)	United States	3	Home for delinquent girls	Intercourse (?) with blood relative	Interviews (psychotherapy)
Rhinehart (1961)	United States	4	Psychiatric hospital and private practice	Sexual contact with blood relative	Interviews (psychotherapy)
Cormier, Kennedy, and Sangowicz (1962)	Canada	27	21 in prison; 6 court, social agency, or psychiatrist referred	"Abnormal" sexual interest in blood relative	Interviews
Merland, Fiorentini, and Orsini (1962)	France	34	Court referred	Sexual approach by blood relative	Interview
Szabo (1962)	France	96	Court	Intercourse with blood relative (?)	Study of court records
Weiner (1962)	United States	5	Self-referred and court referred for psycho-	Sexual contact with blood relative	Interviews (psychotherapy), Rorschach, WAIS,

Study	Country	N	Setting	Definition	Method/Comments
Heims and Kaufman (1963)	United States	20	Psychiatric clinic and private practice	"Strong incestuous wishes" for relative by blood or marriage	Interviews (psychotherapy)
Gebhard and others (1965)	United States	165	Prisons	Sexual approach by relative by blood or marriage	Structured interview, two control groups and comparison with other groups of imprisoned sex offenders
Bigras and others (1966)	Canada	9	Psychiatric hospital	Sexual approaches by blood relatives over a period of at least one year	Interviews (psychotherapy), three "comparison cases"
Cavallin (1966)	United States	12	Prison or parole board referred	Intercourse (?) with relative by blood or marriage	Interviews, MMPI
Lustig and others (1966)	United States	6	Court referred (?) in a military setting	Intercourse (?) with blood relative	Interviews (psychotherapy)
Gligor (1966)	United States	57	Court records	Intercourse (?) with blood relative	Court records; control groups
Yorukoglu and Kemph (1966)	United States	2	Court referred for psychiatric treatment	Intercourse with blood relative	Interviews (psychotherapy)
Machotka, Pittman, and Flomenhaft (1967)	United States	4	Psychiatric hospital	Sexual approach to blood relative	Interviews (psychotherapy)
Medlicott (1967)	New Zealand	35	Psychiatric practice (?)	Sexual approach (?) to a blood relative	Interviews (psychotherapy)
Raphling, Carpenter, and Davis (1967)	United States	1	Physician referred for psychiatric evaluation	Intercourse with blood relative	Interviews, unspecified objective and projective psychological tests
Eist and Mandel (1968)	United States	1	Out-patient psychiatric clinic	Intercourse (?) with blood relative	Interviews (family therapy)
Langsley, Schwartz, and Fairbairn (1968)	United States	1	Psychiatric hospital	Sexual contact with blood relative	Interviews (psychotherapy)

(continued on next page)

Table 1 (Continued)

Author(s) and Date	Country	N	Research Setting	Incest Criteria[a]	Method[b]
Magal and Winnick (1968)	Israel	5	Psychiatric hospital	Intercourse with blood relative	Interviews (psychotherapy)
Raybin (1969)	United States	1	Psychiatric hospital	Sexual contact with blood relative	Interviews (psychotherapy)
Woodbury and Schwartz (1971)	United States	1	Private practice	Sexual contact with blood relative	Interviews (psychotherapy)
Lukianowicz (1972)	Northern Ireland	55	Psychiatric hospital, out-patient clinics, child guidance clinic, home for wayward girls	Intercourse (?) with blood relative	Interviews (psychotherapy)
Maisch (1972)	West Germany	78	Court system	Sexual approach by relative by blood or marriage	Court records and questionnaires filled out during legal proceedings, intelligence testing
Santiago (1973)	United States	1	Psychiatric practice	Intercourse with blood relative	Interviews (psychotherapy)
Berry (1975)	United States	5	Self-referred for psychotherapy	Sexual contact with blood relative	Interviews (psychotherapy)
Molnar and Cameron (1975)	Canada	18	Psychiatric practice	Intercourse with blood relative	Interviews (psychotherapy)
Shelton (1975)	United States	4	Court referred	Intercourse with blood relative	Interviews
Awad (1976)	Canada	1	Court referral for psychiatric evaluation	Sexual contact with blood relative	Interviews, MMPI, Sentence Completion, TAT, Rorschach

Peters (1976)	United States	100	4 from private psychiatric practice, 96 from urban rape crisis center	Sexual contact with relative by blood or marriage ("surrogate fathers" and members of "extended family" included)	Interviews (psychotherapy and evaluation)
Browning and Boatman (1977)	United States	14	Psychiatric clinic	Sexual contact with relative by blood or marriage	Interviews (psychotherapy)
Herman and Hirschman (1977)	United States	15	Private practice	Sexual contact with blood relative	Interviews (psychotherapy)

Note: Table 1 lists, in chronological order, published studies of incest behavior; theoretical or review articles are not included. An attempt has been made to include all studies with samples larger than five that have been reported in this country plus as many single case histories and small samples as possible. Foreign studies that have made important contributions to the incest literature have also been included.

[a] The criteria stated in this column refer to the minimal degree of sexual interaction and family relationship that was required for inclusion in the incest sample in each study. The frequent question marks indicate that the criteria were not at all clear but were inferred by myself on the basis of information presented in the research article.

[b] Abbreviations used: TAT (Thematic Apperception Test), WAIS (Wechsler Adult Intelligence Scale), MMPI (Minnesota Multiphasic Personality Inventory).

[c] The authors state that their conclusions are based on "many" cases, but they only cite three of them.

always acceptable, of course, to describe the characteristics found in the incest group, but in the absence of an appropriate control group it is not possible to conclude that these characteristics are especially prevalent in the incest group. For instance, Kaufman, Peck, and Tagiuri (1954) have described a three-generation sequence of family interactions that are said to culminate in a pattern of family dynamics leading to incest of the father-daughter variety: A cold, depriving maternal grandmother raises a love-starved but sexually frigid daughter who is very dependent on her husband but incapable of fulfilling her role as wife and who thus encourages her own daughter to assume a wifely role within the family. An appealing, plausible theory, the description given by Kaufman and his colleagues has been cited again and again in the incest literature since the 1950s, yet when one asks what evidence was originally presented in its favor it is found that Kaufman, Peck, and Tagiuri were describing the family histories of eleven adolescent girls referred to a clinic by courts or protective agencies. No matter how accurate their description of these incest families, the lack of a control group makes it impossible to state that the family history and dynamics found in father-daughter incest is *specific* to incest cases. It may well be the case that this composite picture of the incestuous family is equally descriptive of the families of the majority of disturbed adolescent girls—without an appropriate control group, this possibility cannot be ruled out.

It is therefore very desirable for researchers to compare their incest samples with groups that are similar in all important respects except for the occurrence of incest—a sample of incest cases should be compared with a group of prisoners, persons referred by courts for psychiatric evaluation, psychotherapy patients, or other group, depending on the setting in which the incest cases have been collected. However obvious this research design may seem to the reader, only Martin (1958), Gebhard and others (1965), and Gligor (1966) have employed it. In the entire history of incest research, I have been unable to find another instance of the use of an appropriate control group!

The Psychotherapy Sample

■■■■■■■■■■■■■■■■

Although incest can still be described as a relatively rare life event, it does occur frequently enough to warrant our concern about its impact on the lives of incest participants, especially children. The peculiar emotional intensity associated with the incest taboo and the severe social and legal censure that may be incurred by its violation should make overt incest a rather traumatic event when it does occur. From a psychoanalytical point of view, the repression of incestuous desires in early childhood, their sublimation in socially approved activities, and their eventual redirection to appropriate sexual partners in adulthood constitute an essential sequence of events in personality development. The acting out of incestuous wishes, especially with the opposite-sex parent, should therefore be a severely disruptive experience with potential impact on adult personality structure.

From a nonpsychoanalytical viewpoint, incest would still have the potential of being a major life stress in that it would be likely to disrupt family relationships, causing conflicts both within the family and between the family and the larger society. Gebhard and others (1965, pp. 207-208), for instance, speculated as follows about the consequences of breaking the taboo on father-daughter incest: "Such incest would create an intrafamily competition and favoritism that would threaten the continued existence of the family unit; any resultant procreation would intolerably complicate the inherited obligations and rights that form the basis of human organization; and, moreover, it would interfere with the daughter's forming a liaison with a male outside the family." The stress created by overt incest would not necessarily be different in its effects on the child from stresses generated by other negative life events, such as divorce, serious accidents or illness, loss of financial support, and so forth. It is not far-fetched, however, to consider that the long-term effects of incest stress might be manifested more specifically in the sphere of sexual functioning than are stresses less specifically sexual in nature.

Previous Studies of the Consequences of Incest

Studies of incest behavior and clinical experience with incest participants have generated numerous hypotheses about the consequences of incest (to be reviewed in Chapter Six), but very few researchers have directly addressed the question of long-term aftereffects in the lives of child incest participants. Small samples and the absence of a control group have characterized these studies. Sloane and Karpinski (1942) reported a follow-up of five incest cases that had been seen by social service agencies; Bender and Grugett (1952) obtained follow-up information on four cases of incest that had been described in the Bender and Blau report in 1937. Among studies that have not specifically focused on long-term aftereffects, as of 1973 only six American research reports on samples of ten or more incest cases had appeared in the professional literature.*

*Heims and Kaufman (1963) have not been included, because their sample of twenty consisted of both overt incest cases and patients with

1. Weinberg (1955) has reported the largest study—203 cases. Since the interviews were done shortly after the cases were reported to the research group by courts or social agencies, the major focus of the study was on the immediate antecedents and consequences of incest in the family milieu. There are a few comments (pp. 147-152) on long-term aftereffects, based on an undisclosed number of participants who were interviewed a few years after the incest incident. There was no control group.

2. Kaufman, Peck, and Tagiuri (1954) studied eleven cases of father-daughter incest, which had been referred for psychiatric evaluation by courts or social agencies, but these cases were studied in depth, with a series of interviews of family members plus psychological testing. Emphasis was on the description of antecedents of incest within the nuclear family. There was no control group.

3. Martin (1958) administered the Blacky Pictures Test and the TAT to thirty imprisoned incestuous fathers and control groups of twenty-one men convicted of statutory rape and twenty men serving sentences for breaking and entering. He was primarily interested in ascertaining the presence of certain psychoanalytic personality constructs (such as oral eroticism and castration anxiety) in the incest group.

4. Gebhard and others (1965) reported on 165 cases of incest (mostly father-daughter) in which the male participant had been convicted and imprisoned. Their major focus was on the sexual histories of the fathers, but they also provide an interesting description of the family circumstances preceding overt incest. There is, however, little or no information about effects on other family members, either immediate or long term. Only Caucasian incest offenders were included in the sample. There were two control groups, one consisting of men imprisoned for offenses of a nonsexual nature and the other of noncriminal men who were comparable in age and socioeconomic background. The incest offenders were also compared with other groups of imprisoned sex offenders: rapists,

---

incest fantasies, and they did not state how many cases fell into each category.

exhibitionists, "peepers," pedophiles, and homosexual offenders.

5. Cavallin (1966) studied twelve incestuous fathers referred for psychiatric evaluation by prisons or parole boards. Emphasis was on the background and personality structure of these men, and psychological testing was used in addition to interviews. There was no control group.

6. Gligor (1966) reported a study of court records pertaining to fifty-seven cases of father-daughter incest. Description of family characteristics and behavioral histories of the mostly adolescent daughters were emphasized. A control group consisted of fifty-three girls who had been adjudged delinquent because of their sexual behavior but had no history of incest.

There is some information on long-term aftereffects to be gleaned from foreign studies that have included subsets of incest cases that were studied years after the occurrence of incest. Lukianowicz' (1972) study of fifty-five incest case histories in Northern Ireland is most helpful in this regard; Medlicott's (1967) sample of thirty-five in New Zealand and Kubo's (1959) thirty-six in Japan should also be noted. However, none of these studies included a control group, and it is also difficult to assess the contribution of cultural factors to their findings.

After reviewing the major studies of incest behavior, it becomes evident that most of our knowledge to date relates to the personality and background of fathers involved in father-daughter incest, the family situations in which incest occurs, and the immediate aftereffects of an incest situation that has been disclosed to legal authorities or other social agencies. The area in which we have the least information is the long-term aftereffects of overt incest in the lives of child and adolescent participants. Whether or not disturbance is evident immediately after the incestuous incident, if it is really a traumatic event it has the potential of disrupting subsequent personality development and contributing to adjustment problems that occur much later. For instance, Peters (1976) describes an eighty-year-old patient who developed a conversion hysteria that seemed to be related to a repressed incident of rape at the age of four. Although Peters' case is a fairly extreme example, there is a widely held belief among psychotherapists that events that are remote in time can be associated with unresolved conflicts that continue to be effective motivating forces long after the original event. This lingering effect is thought to be especially likely when the original traumatic event has never been adequately "worked through"—that is, when there have been no catharsis of the emotions associated with the traumatic event and no resolution of the conflicts aroused by it.

It can be argued that this failure to work through a traumatic event would be especially likely to occur in cases of incest. Since incest is an unpleasant topic of conversation for most adults (and especially for adults within the incestuous family), children would often be denied the opportunity to ventilate their emotions and to correct misunderstandings about the nature and meaning of the event. And, since incest is specifically sexual, it might also be expected that the unresolved conflicts related to it would tend to be manifested in situations that are specifically sexual. Therefore, the full effects of overt incest might not be observable until such time as the individual is attempting to make an adult sexual adjustment.

The purpose of the study described in the remainder of this chapter was to provide more systematically collected information on the long-term effects of overt incest and thus to begin filling in the blanks in our knowledge about incest as a life event with at least a modest body of concrete knowledge. In addition, since psychotherapists regularly encounter patients with incestuous backgrounds, the formulation of some tentative recommendations in regard to therapy with patients who are or have been involved with incest was also a goal of the study. Most therapists encounter incest cases at such a low rate that it is difficult for them to build up a personal fund of clinical knowledge about the incest experience; therefore, it was thought that a summary of other therapists' perceptions of incest cases would be a useful addition to the literature.

Research Setting and Methods

The research setting was a Los Angeles psychiatric clinic that contracts to provide services to employee groups that have elected to include prepaid psychiatric care in their health care coverage. Among the many employee groups served by the clinic at the time of the study were government employees, college and university professors, members of several large labor unions, the staff of a major hospital complex, policemen and firemen, and the employees of several suburban school districts —a healthy representation of the major ethnic groups and socioeconomic classes in the Los Angeles area. Every occupational stratum, from unskilled laborers through university professors and physicians, was served by the clinic, with the exception of the very lowest and the highest. The unemployed or marginal worker is unlikely to have any health care coverage at all; the wealthy tend to seek out private practitioners.

Most employee groups had coverage that included several free out-patient visits and up to six weeks of in-patient psychiatric care per year. Only about 12 percent of patients who entered treatment were ever hospitalized, and the average patient was seen for about five visits. Some patients were seen on a long-term treatment basis, since they had the option of paying a nominal fee for visits after their allotted free visits had been used. Clinic records indicated that about 6,000 patients were seen for a total of over 30,000 visits in calendar year 1975.

After requesting treatment or being referred by a physician, the patient was seen for an intake appointment by a staff member, who wrote an evaluation report and usually continued to see the patient if psychotherapy was recommended. The professional staff of the clinic consisted of eight psychiatrists, eight psychologists, thirteen psychiatric social workers, and eight students (psychology interns, social work students, and family practice residents); the students carried small caseloads under the supervision of regular staff members. Although the traditional areas of expertise of the three professional disciplines were recognized, almost all staff members spent most of their time doing intake interviews and individual and group psychotherapy.

At the time of the intake interview, various kinds of demographic information were recorded in the patient's chart. Since it was not possible to obtain exact statistics for the entire patient population during the time period of the study, a random sample of 100 patient charts was drawn from files containing charts for all patients seen for the past five years. The demographic characteristics of the patient population, as estimated from this random sample, are presented in Table 2 in the columns with the "Control" heading. The data in Table 2 generally confirm the impression that the patient population served by the clinic was characterized by a broad spectrum of ages, ethnic groups, religions, and socioeconomic levels. Although intake reports usually contained tentative diagnoses, these were considered to be rather unreliable, and thus no attempt was made to

Table 2. Demographic Characteristics of 58 Incest Participants
and 100 Random Controls, in Percentages

Age at Intake

	Incest	Control
60+	0	4
50-59	0	8
40-49	10	15
30-39	33	15
20-29	33	35
10-19	24	22
0-9	0	1
Mean Age	27.6	31.1

Marital Status of Patients over 18

	Incest	Control
Married	59	56
Single	18	23
Divorced	11	14
Separated	11	5
Widowed	0	2

Religion

	Incest	Control
Protestant	31	42
Catholic	31	27
Jewish	3	14
None	34	17

Education of Patients over 18

Years of Education	Incest	Control
16+	7	7
15-16	16	21
13-14	25	27
11-12	41	42
9-10	11	1
< 9	0	1
Mean Years of Education	13	13.6

(continued on next page)

Table 2 (Continued)

Children of Married Patients over 18				Occupation Group of Head of Patient's Household		
	Incest	Control			Incest	Control
8	0	2		Professional	17	20
7	6	0		Skilled labor	36	23
6	0	3		Unskilled labor	7	8
5	6	0		Clerical	5	17
4	6	2		Managerial	9	6
3	22	10		Civil service	14	13
2	25	41		Police, fire	3	3
1	11	16		Student	0	5
0	25	26		Unemployed	9	5
Mean Children	2.2	1.7				

Ethnic Group				Yearly Family Income		
	Incest	Control			Incest	Control
Black	14	27		15+	29	19
Latin	19	9		10-15	43	39
White	66	63		7, 5-10	16	34
Asian	2	1		5-7, 5	6	6
				2, 5-5	4	2
				0-2, 5	2	0

estimate the distribution of clinical diagnoses in the patient population. The small percentage of patients hospitalized, the typically short course of therapy, and the general impressions of the clinical staff suggested that the patient population was characterized by a mild to moderate level of psychological disturbance. While an occasional patient proved to be acutely psychotic, a therapist generally expected to encounter patients in crisis situations revolving around marital discord, problems in handling children, and/or job-related difficulties.

Collection of incest cases began in the fall of 1973 and continued on a more or less regular basis for three years. After permission had been obtained from the clinic administration, an initial announcement of the nature and purpose of the study was made at staff meetings and a request for cases, along with a rough description of the research definition of incest, was distributed to all therapists. Reminders of the ongoing study were also distributed at yearly intervals. After the study was announced, the researcher spent one day every two weeks at the clinic, seeing as many therapists as possible and reminding them on an informal basis of the study and the kinds of cases being collected. This low-key but persistent search for incest cases probably resulted in obtaining reports on a significant number of the incest cases that were seen at the clinic over the three-year period covered by the study, but, of course, there is no way of absolutely determining the proportion of cases that were missed. Although the majority of therapists were cooperating in the study, there must surely have been cases that were forgotten, and these would probably have been patients who were seen very briefly so that they made a very weak impression on a therapist with a large caseload. In all, the reports were received from a total of twenty-five therapists, including three psychiatrists, seven psychologists, eleven psychiatric social workers, and four psychology or social work students.

When a current case of incest was reported to the researcher,* it was first of all determined whether the case fit the following research criteria for incest.

1. Sexual activity was defined as a very definite sexual approach, involving successful or unsuccessful attempts at exposure, genital fondling, oral-genital contact, and/or vaginal or anal intercourse, as perceived by the patient. Reports of "seductive behavior" that consisted only of suggestive dressing or posturing, verbal suggestions, or unusual possessiveness did not satisfy this criterion for sexual activity, which required that some sort of specific action be taken in the direction of effecting sexual contact. Incest fantasies, however intense, did not qualify as a

---

*Only cases in therapy at the time of the study were included. Most of the therapists remembered one or two highly unusual cases they had seen or heard of before the study, but their inclusion would have run counter to the researcher's goal of obtaining a sample of "typical" incest cases.

case for inclusion in this study unless they were acted out in some definite way.

2. Sexual activity with relatives by blood, by marriage, or by adoption was considered to be incest. Sexual companions of parents or other friends of the family were not included unless a long-standing "common-law" marriage had been in existence at the time of the sexual activity. In all cases of relationship by marriage, sexual activity was defined as *incestuous* only if the participants had actually lived together in related roles such that a feeling of "real" relatedness could have been achieved. In most cases, the marriage that brought about the relationship had occurred prior to the patient's adolescence. Probably the most marginal case that was included was that of a twenty-five-year-old stepdaughter who had lived with her stepfather for about three years prior to his sexual advances; since the stepdaughter was mentally retarded, it was most likely that a "real" parent-child dependency relationship had existed in their case.

3. Relatives were defined as all members of the nuclear family—fathers, mothers, brothers, and sisters—and also aunts, uncles, and grandparents. Cousins and all more distant relatives were excluded from the definition, since it is generally believed that the feeling of relationship becomes quite diluted at this point. The most distant relative included in the study was a great-uncle who had served in the role of his great-niece's father for seven years in her early childhood, during which time period the sexual activity had occurred.

4. All homosexual relationships that met the preceding three criteria were included in the research definition of incest.

5. No case of reported incest was included in the study if the therapist reporting it concluded that it was largely or wholly the fantasy of the patient. In the majority of cases, the therapist had no doubt that the events occurred substantially as reported by the patient, although judgment was often reserved as to the patient's interpretation of these events. In a few cases, designated by question marks in Table 3, the therapist thought that incest had probably occurred but seemed to have lingering doubts about the accuracy of the report because it was denied

Table 3. Descriptions of Incest Incidents

Number	Name	Present Age	Age Range at Incident	Relative(s)	Nature and Outcome
1	Ada	11	3-10	Great-uncle	Genital fondling on many occasions when living with him and her aunt. Bribes and threats used. She told aunt and great-aunt, but they laughed it off and did nothing.
2	Barbara	43	3	Uncle	Uncle attempted penetration, thereby injuring her, and she required medical treatment. Told mother and aunt, who ignored it.
3	Carol	27	8-11	Mother	Mother, described as religious and seclusive, carried out frequent pelvic exams to see if father was molesting her (he was not).
?4	Daphne	24	13	Brother, older, adoptive	Raped by older adoptive brother on one occasion. Did not tell her family about it.
5	Edith	25	8-16	Father	Raised by grandparents, but stayed intermittently with father, who came to her bed and fondled genitals and had interfemoral intercourse. Threats prevented her from telling until many years later, when father denied it.
?6	Fay	14	14	Stepfather	On probation for stealing and runaway behavior. Told probation officer of incident where stepfather attempted to initiate sexual activities, and family was referred for therapy.
7	Gabrielle	34	12	Stepfather	He approached her when home alone during day and tried to fondle her sexually—she put up fierce struggle and he desisted. She told grandmother, but no action was ever taken against the stepfather.

(continued on next page)

Table 3 (Continued)

Number	Name	Present Age	Age Range at Incident	Relative(s)	Nature and Outcome
8	Harriet	16	12-16	Stepfather	Having intercourse with sociopathic, alcoholic stepfather for over three years. Has not told anyone, by own choice, as seems to enjoy it.
9	Ida	25	5-12, 15	Father, ?stepfather	Father often came to room at night and kissed and fondled genitals—she pretended to be asleep and thought about other things. Moved in with mother and stepfather at twelve and at fifteen similar attempt by stepfather. Told mother, but never reported.
10	Jacqueline	40	12, 14	Stepuncle, stepgrandfather	Stepuncle (identical twin of stepfather) had intercourse with her at age twelve. At fourteen, reported raped several times by stepgrandfather, with whom she was living. His wife reported and had him sent to jail.
11	Karen	42	6-14	Brother (younger)	Had consensual relations with brother from very early age. Developed into intercourse; gave up these sexual relations out of fear of pregnancy. Never told parents.
12	Laura	36	?-14	Brothers (older)	As child, she was sexually molested by her older brothers when her parents were absent. When she was fourteen, one brother raped her. She evidently told no one.
13	Madeline	25	< 11	Father	Genital fondling by father on unknown number of occasions. Parents divorced when she was eleven; not known if told mother of sexual activity.
14	Nadine	34	10	Stepfather	Genital fondling by stepfather on a few occasions. Told mother, who scolded her and ordered her not to tell anyone else.
15	Olivia	25	10-14	Stepfather	Genital fondling by stepfather over period of years. Eventually told mother, who had been divorced from him and had heard that he is now molesting his new stepdaughters.

?16	Pamela	14	14	Stepfather	Genital fondling by stepfather while sleeping with both parents in king-size bed. Told mother, who then broke up marriage.
?17	Rachel	16	13-16	Father	Genital fondling by father, evidently in guise of "sex education." Told numerous people about it. Eventually placed in a home for girls, then denied incest in court.
18	Sabrina	31	15-17	Father	Intercourse with father over period of two years, beginning with rape. Told mother, who did not believe her. Left home to be married at seventeen.
19	Tania	36	13-16	Father (adoptive)	Intercourse with father began under threat at thirteen and continued until she ran away at sixteen and was placed in a convent. Afraid to tell mother.
20	Una	30	10	Father	Raped on single occasion by father, who was in state of deep depression. Told mother, who was understanding and broke off marriage shortly thereafter.
21	Valerie	17	8-17	Father	Intercourse with father over long period of time, although mother knew of situation almost from beginning. Daughter intermittently hospitalized for psychosis and told therapists, but situation continued. Had abortion at age fourteen.
22	Wendy	28	23	Stepfather	Mentally retarded woman was fondled sexually by stepfather on several occasions. Told her mother, who teased her about it. Hospitalized for recurrence of epileptic seizures and placed in protected work environment on release.
23	Yvonne	20	13-15	Stepfather	Obvious sexual interest and genital fondling while daughter pretended to be asleep. Did not tell mother, because she felt she would be blamed for marital breakup. Left home at seventeen.

(continued on next page)

Table 3 (Continued)

Number	Name	Present Age	Age Range at Incident	Relative(s)	Nature and Outcome
24	Adelaide	24	8-?	Father, grandfather, two uncles	Molested by father when he was drunk at various times since age eight. Also by grandfather, two uncles, and some neighbors. Unclear whether intercourse was involved. Apparently did not tell mother.
25	Beatrice	23	8	Foster father	Genital fondling and attempted fellatio by foster father of two months. She told foster mother and was not believed. Told social worker, who placed her in another home after one year.
26	Caroline	35	4	Grandfather	Family visited grandparents once a week; grandfather would fondle her genitals while they played together in his room. He gave her presents and persuaded her not to tell anyone.
27	Dawn	15	12-14	Father	Genital fondling and attempted intercourse under guise of "sex education" over a two-year period. Told mother, who did little to help. Attempted to run away with boyfriend at fifteen. Older sister had same experience.
28	Edna	18	14	Father	Genital fondling and attempted intercourse. She told mother, and parents were soon divorced.
29	Felicia	24	6-8	Stepgrandfather	Lived with grandparents for several years as small child. Grandfather fondled her sexually over a three-year period. Unclear whether she ever told grandmother.
30	Genevieve	15	8-15	Father	Intercourse with father for several years; threatened by him. Mother had abandoned family. Told social worker but did not report to police. Ran away at fifteen.
31	Helen	29	6-9	Grandfather	Lived with grandparents during most of childhood. Genital petting by grandfather over long time period. Not clear how it ended.

No.	Name	Age	Age(s)	Perpetrator	
32	Ingrid	29	12	Stepbrother (older)	Genital fondling; evidently told no one, as she was not especially disturbed about it.
33	Jane	26	10	Father	He got into her bed on one occasion and fondled her genitals. She pretended that it had not happened, and the incident was not repeated.
34	Kathleen	16	12-16	Father	Forced to have intercourse at age twelve. Continued intercourse and oral sex under threats from father. Tried to tell mother, who did not believe her until she saw pornographic pictures father had taken. A social worker reported case to juvenile authorities, and she was placed in foster home.
35	Leila	32	8-10	Brother (older)	Intercourse with brother, who also had relations with older sister. Brother and older sister sent to home for delinquents because of sexual behavior, but she stayed with her adoptive mother, who never learned that she had also been involved.
36	Marcia	31	5-7	Father	Genital fondling, interfemoral intercourse with father every day after school. Older sister caught them and ordered father to stop. Parents divorced when she was seven.
37	Nancy	38	12-14(?)	Brothers (two older)	Induced to manipulate their genitals by brothers, who often masturbated in front of her. Did not report it, as she was afraid of brothers and parents.
38	Pauline	15	15	Stepfather	Genital exposure, attempt to initiate sexual activities. She resisted and told mother, who refused to believe it. Asked to be placed in a foster home.
			10	?Father	May also have had sexual activity with her father prior to parents' divorce several years ago.
39	Regina	25	4, 8, 10, 14	Father	Episodic genital stimulation during periods of parental separation. Tried to tell mother many times but was always dismissed by her.

(continued on next page)

Table 3 (Continued)

Number	Name	Present Age	Age Range at Incident	Relative(s)	Nature and Outcome
40	Sally	43	8-12	Stepfather	Genital fondling and possibly some penetration whenever alone with him when twelve. She refused to be alone with him when twelve. Mother evidently knew but did nothing to stop it.
41	Therese	31	8	Brothers (older, younger)	Would tie her to bed and stimulate her with electric vibrator. Told her mother, and activity stopped.
42	Ursula	15	11-12	Father, stepbrother (older)	When eleven, raped by stepbrother, twenty-three, and a cousin. Father, when drinking, would get into bed with her and fondle her breasts. She arranged to live with a foster family for three years after these incidents, then returned to father and stepmother.
?43	Vanessa	29	10	Stepfather	Woke up and found stepfather in bed with her in nude. Was aware that he had intercourse with all of his other daughters and stepdaughters but cannot remember if he went further with her. Cannot remember if it happened again.
44	Adele	35	8	Father	Raped by drunken father. Told her mother, who beat her. No further sexual activity with father.
45	Betty	14	10	Father	Father attempted sexual fondling while he was drunk. Suspected that he also had sexual relationship with older sister. Unknown whether she told mother, but advances stopped.
46	Cassandra	26	10-12	Father	Sexual fondling by father over a period of time in her childhood. Her two sisters were also involved with him. She reported it to authorities at age twelve; he was jailed for child molestation, and she was made a ward of the court for three years.

No.	Name	Age		Relationship	Comments
47	Deanna	20	6	Uncle	Genital petting by uncle.
			13	Stepfather	Stepfather got into her bed and fondled her genitals; she pretended to be asleep and stopped it by giving obvious signs that she was waking up. She told no one, and there were no further advances.
48	Adrian	37	?	Father	Reported having had "sexual relations" with his father as a child, but other details not known since he was seen for just one session.
?49	Barry	30	10	Stepbrother (older)	Forced to have anal intercourse with stepbrother on one occasion when parents had left them alone. Felt physically threatened; told no one, and it did not recur.
50	Carl	45	33-37	Daughter	Intercourse with older daughter from age twelve until she left home. Then approached younger daughter, who refused and told his wife. Wife left him and married her own stepfather.
51	Dale	44	4-23	Mother	Masturbated by mother for three years as child and much mutual exposure and sex play in teens; intercourse with her between ages nineteen and twenty-three, ending only after his marriage.
52	Earl	38	10-29	Sister (younger)	Mutual masturbation with sister; intercourse occasionally after age fifteen, ending after her marriage.
			3-7?	Mother	Often watched his mother, a prostitute, having intercourse with clients. When very young, she slept with him, and mutual genital fondling often occurred. Unclear how relationship ended.
53	Floyd	32	32	Stepdaughter	Intercourse and oral sex with ten-year-old stepdaughter over a period of several months. She told mother, who immediately filed for divorce and suggested psychotherapy for him. Did not report to police.

(continued on next page)

Table 3 (Continued)

Number	Name	Present Age	Age Range at Incident	Relative(s)	Nature and Outcome
54	Gary	15	10-13, 14	Half sister (younger), half brother (younger), stepfather	Sex play with attempted intercourse with younger half sister; occurred very frequently over a three-year period and stopped when sister threatened to tell his friends. A few episodes of oral sex with younger half brother. Mutual masturbation with stepfather on several recent occasions, but Gary now refuses.
55	Harry	34	32-34	Daughter	Intercourse with adolescent daughter over two-year period; when she began to resist, he threatened and forced her. She left home to live with relatives and reported him to police. He was arrested but not imprisoned.
56	Jack	28	12-19	Sister (younger)	Intercourse with sister over long period, despite parents' occasional efforts to separate them. Stopped only when her muscular fiancé told him to.
57	Lee	35	33	Two daughters	Wife reported him to police for molestation of ten- and twelve-year-old daughters. They were placed in a foster home for two years, and family was reunited after undergoing family therapy and getting court permission.
58	Malcolm	30	35-38	Stepdaughter	(Same as Number 8, as stepfather was also in therapy.)

Note: Question marks indicate that therapist had doubts about report.

by other family members or because there was some obvious "payoff" for the patient in making the incest report. An example of the latter would be a case in which a mother and daughter were very close to each other, and both had developed an extreme dislike for the mother's second husband; when the daughter told her mother of sexual advances by her stepfather, the marriage was immediately ended, and both mother and daughter seemed very relieved and happy about the outcome.

When an incest case was located, the therapist reporting it was interviewed in what is best described as a "semistructured" format. In the initial phase of the interview, therapists were simply asked to describe the significant, outstanding aspects of the case in their own manner while the researcher took careful notes and interrupted only for purposes of clarification or to follow up on any therapist statements that seemed to indicate doubt about the reality of the incest report. After this mostly spontaneous description, the researcher went down a checklist of standard questions and attempted to obtain information about any areas that had been overlooked previously.

The researcher also read all information that was available in the patient's chart, including intake reports, notes on progress in psychotherapy, results of psychological testing (usually MMPI reports), communications from other agencies, and sometimes letters or diaries that the patient had personally written, often as a part of the therapeutic effort. (Information about the incest incident itself was often not included in these written records, because many therapists regarded it as too sensitive to record in writing.) All notes that were taken during the semistructured interview and the review of the patient's chart omitted the patient's name and any other possibly identifying information. Each case was assigned a code number and the information pertaining to it was kept in the exclusive possession of the researcher. No one else was allowed to read the notes, even though names had been omitted, and none of the information elicited in the interview was added to the written records in the patient's chart.

After the initial data collection on a case, the researcher often received spontaneous "updates" from the therapist if the

patient continued to be seen for psychotherapy or if the patient
returned to the clinic for additional treatment. In all the
cases studied, the patient's chart was located at the end of the
three-year study period and reviewed again to extract any additional information (usually therapy progress notes and closing
summaries) that had been added to it.

Of course, there were limits to the kinds of information
that could be gathered by the methods described; it was certainly not possible to obtain answers to all the questions
posed by the researcher in each and every case. In some cases,
the patient had been seen for only one or two interviews; in
others, the patient had described the incest incident on only
one occasion, and the therapist considered it unwise to disrupt
the course of ongoing therapy by further probing that might
cause the patient to focus on incest. Some blanks and question
marks in the tabulation of characteristics of incest cases are inevitable, but it was usually possible to obtain answers for the
majority of questions that were posed.

Description of Sample Characteristics

Over the three-year period of this study (1973-1976), 58
cases of incest were collected. Table 2 presents the demographic
characteristics of these cases; the control group for the 58 incest
cases, also shown in Table 2, consisted of the 100 randomly
drawn patient charts already mentioned. Table 3 summarizes
some basic descriptive information about each case—code number and pseudonym, age, age range at the time of the incest incident, relative(s) participating in incest, and the nature and outcome of the incestuous incident(s). Much more descriptive
information about these cases will be given in later chapters.

Of the fifty-eight cases, eleven were reports received very
soon after the incestuous incident (interval = 0), and forty-seven
cases were reports given one or more years after incest had occurred. Reports in the latter group were given an average of fifteen years after the incident, with a range of intervals from one
to forty years. This probably constitutes the largest sample of
"years after" incest reports in the literature. Three studies—
Lukianowicz (1972), Medlicott (1967), and Kubo (1959)—had

served preponderance of females is the relative reluctance of males to self-disclose in regard to emotionally charged events, even when they feel that they were the victims. For instance, one male patient had several sessions with his therapist without disclosing incest and finally, during a therapy session in which he was half-drunk and wearing dark sunglasses, told of his abuse by his older half brother. And another male, who had had several years of therapy before coming to the clinic, was unwilling to disclose any details of his sexual relationship with his mother during his first several months of therapy. When his therapist first asked him whether the relationship had included sexual intercourse, he trembled so visibly that the therapist feared he might be on the verge of a seizure. There may well be an unknown number of male patients who drop out of therapy without disclosing that they have been incest participants.

Homosexual incest was deliberately included in the research definition of incest in order to get some idea of its frequency in relation to heterosexual incest. Among the forty-seven female cases, only one involved a homosexual relationship, Number 3, in which mother-daughter incest occurred; three of the eleven male cases involved homosexual contact, Number 48 with the father, Number 49 with a half brother, and Number 54 with a half brother and stepfather. The total incidence of four cases in a sample of fifty-eight is quite comparable to that found by the only other large study that has included homosexual relationships in its sample—Medlicott (1967) reported five out of thirty-five cases to have been homosexual incest, four involving males and one involving females. Although these numbers are much too small to allow us to draw conclusions, it seems sensible at this point to hypothesize that homosexual incest constitutes a small, but not negligible, percentage (say, 5 to 15 percent) of the population of incest cases in a psychotherapeutic setting. Also, it seems that homosexual incest tends to be more commonly reported by male patients than by females, and this hypothesis fits in well with the finding of the Kinsey studies of male and female sexual behavior (Kinsey, Pomeroy, and Martin, 1948; Kinsey and others, 1953) that a higher percentage of males than females have some overt (non-

The Psychotherapy Sample

samples that were partly composed of such cases, but the
thors did not give an exact breakdown of their cases with reg
to this variable. Also, Weinberg's large sample (203 cases) m
have included a few of these reports because his book contain
short section on long-term aftereffects, but, again, we are n
told how many reports these observations are based on.

Of the sample of fifty-eight incest cases, forty-seven we
reported by female participants and eleven by males. On th
basis of chance alone, one would expect to obtain a more eve
ratio of females to males when cases are collected from the pa
tient population of the clinic, which is approximately 55 pe
cent female and 45 percent male. Therefore, we can conclud
that there was a definite tendency for more incest reports to b
given by females than by males in this research setting. Othe
studies (Medlicott, 1967; Lukianowicz, 1972) that have been carried out in a psychotherapeutic setting have also reported many
more female accounts of incest than male, but their female to
male ratios could not be statistically evaluated, because they did
not report the ratio in the patient population.

Since most cases of incest are heterosexual in nature,
there should be about one male incest participant for every female participant in the general population. Why, then, do we
find so many more females than males reporting incestuous experiences in the course of psychotherapy? One possible explanation is that the male incest participant is less likely to seek
psychotherapy than the female. Since the majority of incestu
ous incidents are initiated by males, they are no doubt mor
threatened by any possibility of exposure than are females an
may well be motivated to "forget" the incident and thus avoi
the kinds of self-examination traditionally required by psych
therapy. Females, however, usually feel that they were the "vi
tims" of incest and see the psychotherapy hour as an appr
priate and safe time to ventilate their feelings about the inc
incident. There is some impressionistic evidence to support t
notion in the psychotherapy sample in that the incestuous
thers and stepfathers who entered treatment did so at the urg
of their families or social agencies and tended to drop out
therapy as soon as the external pressure lessened.

Another factor that could have contributed to the

incestuous) homosexual experience during their lifetimes. We would therefore expect a tendency for males to become sexually involved with male relatives more frequently than females with female relatives.

The small number of homosexual incest cases found in this study—two father-son, two brother-brother, and one mother-daughter—will be reported in more specific detail in later chapters because they are additions to the very limited literature on this sort of behavior. A search of the literature revealed the following case reports of homosexual incest within the nuclear family: eleven cases of father-son incest, four by Medlicott (1967) and one each by Bender and Blau (1937), Berry (1975), Langsley, Schwartz and Fairbairn (1968), Raybin (1969), Rhinehart (1961), Shelton (1975), and Awad (1976); three cases of brother-brother incest, one each by Cory (1963), Raybin (1969), and Rhinehart (1961); and one case of mother-daughter incest by Medlicott (1967). While mother-son incest is widely regarded to be the rarest kind of sexual relationship within the nuclear family, if one includes homosexual combinations, the rarest of all must be sister-sister incest. Although it surely must occur from time to time, it is not represented in the psychotherapy sample nor are there any descriptions of it in the incest literature.

Since the research definition of incest used in the present study included relatives by marriage and adoption, it is interesting to examine the numbers of cases involving real relatives versus "step" relatives. Considering only the large father-daughter group, we find eighteen cases involving blood relatives, thirteen involving step relatives, and two cases in which a daughter was sexually involved with both her real father and a stepfather. There is very little in the literature with which to compare this result, as the largest studies that have included step relatives along with real relatives have not given us a specific breakdown of how many cases in each category were included in their samples (Gebhard and others, 1965; Peters, 1976). The only exception is Maisch (1972), who reported thirty-four father-daughter versus thirty-two stepfather-daughter cases in his sample of seventy-six.

At first blush, it may seem surprising that more fathers were involved with their real daughters than with step or adoptive daughters, since it is quite widely acknowledged that the intensity of the incest taboo is diminished when a blood relationship does not exist (see Messer, 1969; Maddox, 1975, for interesting discussions of the dynamics of "step-families"). On second thought, however, this result seems very reasonable. Since a psychotherapeutic research setting was used, we may be seeing only the daughters and fathers who are relatively more disturbed by their experience, and these may tend to be cases in which a blood relationship was involved. In addition, there is the simple statistical fact that most daughters grow up with their real fathers (even in southern California), so there are many more potential incest situations involving real relatives. Even given the intense taboo against sexual relations with real relatives, this frequency of opportunity may actually result in there being a larger proportion of real father-daughter cases in the general population.

Note the number of cases of multiple incest in the present study. In thirteen of the fifty-eight cases outlined in Table 3, the patient reported involvement with more than one relative; usually there were two relatives (eleven cases), and rarely there were three or four (one case each). The present study thus found much more multiple incest than did Weinberg's (1955) report of five out of 203 cases, probably due to his very narrow definition of incest (intercourse with a blood relative within the nuclear family). Special features of these cases will be discussed in Chapter Ten.

Since the taboo against mother-son incest is the strongest, one would expect to find the fewest cases of it in a sample that includes all of the possible nuclear family combinations. The present study reports only two such cases, as compared to thirty-eight cases of father-daughter and eleven of brother-sister incest. This result is quite comparable with other findings: Kubo (1959) found one in a series of twenty-nine nuclear family matings; Weinberg (1955), three in a series of 203. Since mother-son incest is often reported to be associated with gross psychopathology (Wahl, 1960), one would certainly expect the use of a psychotherapeutic research setting to maximize the number of cases found. Thus the small number found in the present study reinforces the generally held belief about the rarity of this kind of sexual behavior, even though the importance of more subtle, nonovert sexual interactions between mothers and sons may be much more common and have very important kinds of psychodynamic results (see, for example, Masters and Johnson, 1970).

Brother-Sister Versus Father-Daughter Incest

The most common variety of incest within the nuclear family is generally thought to be brother-sister incest. Although there are exceptions (Fox, 1962), brother-sister incest is less severely taboo than parent-child in most cultures, and it is the only kind of nuclear family incest for which there is evidence (Middleton, 1962) of widespread acceptance in at least one society, Egypt during the Roman era. Weinberg (1955) surveyed public opinion of the types of incest and found that the overwhelming majority (72 percent) of his American subjects thought parent-child incest to be more abhorrent than brother-sister incest. It therefore seems eminently reasonable to suppose that brother-sister incest occurs more frequently than father-daughter incest, which in turn would occur much more frequently than mother-son incest, given its nearly universal rating as the most loathsome kind of incest. This frequency expectation arises quite naturally from the general observation that more severely taboo behaviors tend to occur less frequently than acts that are less severely taboo.

In the psychotherapy sample, a total of thirty-eight cases of father-daughter and stepfather-daughter incest were found, as compared with eleven cases of brother-sister or stepbrother-sister incest. These figures reduce to a ratio of 3.5 to 1 incest cases of a father-daughter variety versus brother-sister, a finding that is obviously very much at variance with the expectation that brother-sister incest would be more common. This finding is, however, congruent with findings of other studies done in psychotherapeutic or social agency settings. Of those studies that included father-daughter and brother-sister incest in their samples and reported the number of cases in each category, the following ratios in favor of father-daughter incest were found: Greenland (1958), 2 to 1 in a sample of six; Kaufman, Peck, and Tagiuri (1954), 5.5 to 1 in a sample of eleven; Sloane and Karpinski (1942), 1.5 to 1 in a sample of five; Schachter and Cotte (1960), 3.25 to 1 in a sample of seventeen; Weinberg (1955), 4.3 to 1 in a sample of 203; and Kubo (1959), 1 to 1 in a sample of thirty-six. Thus no clinical investigator has found more brother-sister cases, and only Kubo has reported an equal number of brother-sister and father-daughter cases. It is especially interesting to note Kubo's observation (1959, p. 128) that many of his brother-sister cases were situations in which an older brother was functioning as the head of a fatherless family and were very much like father-daughter cases. These kinds of brother-sister situations were especially common in his sample because his study was done in postwar Japan, where fatherless families must have been very nearly the norm.

It can still be persuasively argued that brother-sister incest is actually more frequent than father-daughter in the general population but, since it is less intensely taboo, is associated with less psychological disturbance and is therefore less likely to be discovered in a psychotherapeutic research setting. There can be no serious dispute of the contention that the particular research setting has an important influence on the types of incest cases that are found. Adams and Neel (1967), for instance, reported cases of nuclear family incest located through childcare and adoption agencies in which a child was born to the incest participants, and they found twelve brother-sister and six father-daughter cases. However, since brother-sister incest is more likely to result in pregnancy because brothers tend to be less concerned with birth control than fathers (Weinberg, 1955, p. 51), it seems obvious that the research setting determined this result. At the other extreme is the Kinsey Institute study of sex offenders (Gebhard and others, 1965), in which imprisoned fathers outnumbered brothers 147 to 18. This also was a thoroughly predictable result in a prison setting, since the more severe taboo against father-daughter incest would virtually guarantee that more fathers than brothers would be tried and sentenced to prison terms, even if the laws against the two offenses are the same in a formal sense. Indeed, Gebhard and others commented that the imprisoned brothers seemed as a group to be "stupid but well-meaning" persons whose social and legal blundering had landed them in jail and that some members of the group had been so much older than their sisters at the time of the offense that they were really imprisoned for child molestation.

It seems, then, that one must turn to the few samples that have been collected from the general population to get a more accurate idea of the true ratio of these two types of incest. The Kinsey study of males (Kinsey, Pomeroy, and Martin, 1948) found so little incest that no meaningful ratio could be computed; the Kinsey study of females (Kinsey and others, 1953) found twenty-four reports of sexual approaches by fathers as compared to eighteen reported approaches by brothers. However, the latter figures tell only part of the story with regard to incest because the reports were in response to a question about preadolescent experiences with males at least five years older than the subject, so sexual approaches by younger or slightly older brothers would have been omitted. We are therefore left with the control group of 477 noncriminal males who contributed sex histories to the Kinsey Institute study of sex offenders (Gebhard and others, 1965) and who were specifically asked about incestuous experiences. Two recent reviewers (Lindzey, 1967; Lester, 1972) have referred to this study as evidence for estimating that brother-sister incest is about five times more common than father-daughter in the general population. While this ratio was found for some of the groups imprisoned for sex offenses other than incest, the noncriminal control group reported only one case of nuclear family incest (Gebhard and others, 1965, table 63, p. 572). There is therefore no evidence in this study for the preponderance of any type of nuclear family incest in the *general population*.

The question of whether brother-sister incest is more common than father-daughter remains unresolved. Although the present study does nothing more than add to the accumulation of evidence that father-daughter incest is the most common variety discovered in clinical populations, I would like to risk the suggestion that the ratios found in these studies may not be as far off base as has been thought—that father-daughter incest may actually be somewhat more common than brother-sister. The argument rests primarily on an examination of the probable number of *potential* father-daughter and brother-sister matings in the general population. For simplicity, let us assume that the average American family is composed of a mother, a father or stepfather, and two children. In only one quarter of these families will the children both be male, thus eliminating any possibility of father-daughter incest; in the other three quarters, there will be one or more daughters present in the home. However, when we examine the brother-sister combinations a very different picture emerges. In half of the families, the children will either be all male or all female; in the other half (contrasted with the three quarters possibility of father-daughter combinations) the presence of a brother and a sister will make sibling incest possible. The possibilities for brother-sister incest are actually further reduced when one considers that in half of the brother-sister families the sister will be older than the brother, and sibling incest is relatively unlikely in such situations. The present study found only one case out of eleven brother-sister relationships in which the sister was older; similarly, Kubo (1959) found only two out of fifteen, and he speculated that older sisters often develop a motherly attitude toward their younger brothers that makes a sexual relationship between them extremely unlikely.

This speculation—that the relative number of families in which brother-sister incest can potentially occur may make it a less frequent event than father-daughter incest—is not intended to provide a complete explanation of the surprisingly low incidence of brother-sister incest often found in incest research. Surely patterns of family dynamics are important in the occurrence of overt incest. After studying family patterns in thirty-seven cases of brother-sister incest, Weinberg (1955) concluded that it tends to occur in families where the father is absent or present but ineffectual and tends to be rendered very unlikely when a dominant father figure is present, evidently because he can act as an effective restraining agent in the event that his son shows a sexual interest in his daughter. But when a dominant father is also sexually interested in his daughter there is often no other family member who is strong enough to restrain him. Since father-dominant families are the most typical family pattern in our culture, one would expect that the expression of sexual feelings between brothers and sisters is usually restrained despite the fact that the taboo on sibling incest is less intense than that on father-daughter incest.

Even though the factors just discussed may be acting to reduce the incidence of brother-sister incest, there is still a sense in which it is very probably much more common than father-daughter incest. Whenever there is an opportunity for brother-sister incest—that is, a family with opposite sex siblings lacking an effective restraining agent—I would hypothesize that it is quite likely to occur due to the relative weakness of the taboo against it. However, father-daughter incest seems to be quite a rare event when one considers the fact that the majority of families possess the basic characteristics that enable its occurrence —the presence of a father and a daughter and the relatively dominant position of the father. Even when the temptation is strong, the strength of the taboo would almost always restrain the father.

Demographic Characteristics of Female Incest Participants

A control group for the forty-seven female patients reporting incest was obtained by drawing at random fifty charts from the clinic files, with the stipulation that each chart be for a female patient over the age of twelve and that an intake report be contained in the chart. (These stipulations differ from those used when the control group for the entire incest sample was drawn, and these are entirely separate groups.) Careful notes were taken for each of these control subjects, including presenting symptoms, family history, and course of psychotherapy, and these findings will be discussed in Chapters Five and Six. Demographic information for the female incest-reporting patients and their control group is given in Table 4, which shows these groups to be very comparable in most respects. The incest group was significantly younger than the control group (26.1 versus 33.3 years), and one might speculate that patients who have had incestuous experience are more likely to report it in therapy if it was a rather recent occurrence or if they are currently undergoing the kinds of sexual adjustments and marital crises that characterize female patients in their twenties and thirties. It seems far less plausible to think that the incidence of incest has changed, given the lack of variation in the rate of detected incest over time that has generally been found in other studies (Weinberg, 1955).

Table 4. Demographic Characteristics of Forty-Seven Female Incest Participants and Fifty Female Random Controls, in Percentages

Age at Intake

	Incest	Control
60+	0	4
50-59	0	12
40-49	9	16
30-39	26	22
20-29	38	32
10-19	28	14
Mean Age	26.1	33.3

Marital Status of Patients over 18

	Incest	Control
Married	59	63
Single	24	21
Divorced	12	7
Separated	6	7
Widowed	0	2

Religion

	Incest	Control
Protestant	32	50
Catholic	34	20
Jewish	4	18
None	30	12

Education of Patients over 18

Years of Education	Incest	Control
16+	6	0
15-16	15	5
13-14	29	21
11-12	41	67
9-10	9	2
<9	0	5
Mean Years of Education	13	12.1

Table 4 (Continued)

Children of Married Patients over 18				Occupational Group of Female Patients		
	Incest	Control			Incest	Control
7	8	3		Housewife	26	37
6	0	0		Professional	15	0
5	8	9		Skilled labor	21	21
4	4	3		Unskilled labor	3	2
3	19	24		Clerical	18	23
2	27	24		Managerial	0	0
1	4	24		Civil service	9	9
0	31	15		Police, fire	0	0
				Student	0	0
Mean Children	2.2	2.2		Unemployed	9	7

Ethnic Group				Yearly Family Income		
	Incest	Control			Incest	Control
Black	17	26		15+	22	18
Latin	15	8		10-15	42	45
White	66	64		7, 5-10	20	16
Asian	2	2		5-7, 5	8	10
				2, 5-5	5	8
				0-2, 5	2	2

Almost all of the other minor differences between the incest and control groups on these demographic variables are best interpreted as being chance fluctuations. There is a tendency for the incest group to have had more years of formal education, as one,might expect in a group that is younger. There is also a tendency for the incest group to list their religion as "None," thus depleting the ranks of nominal Protestants.

The slight differences observed in the "Ethnic Group" breakdowns in Tables 2 and 4 deserve special attention, owing to the commonly held belief that incest is more acceptable and prevalent in certain minority groups. Few studies have looked specifically at this issue. The Kinsey Institute studies (Kinsey, Pomeroy, and Martin, 1948; Kinsey and others, 1953; Gebhard and others, 1965) have completely avoided it by including only Caucasians in their samples. Weinberg (1955) has assembled the largest sample inclusive of all ethnic groups, and he noted that his sample contained a larger proportion of blacks and of foreign-born whites of Polish and Italian origin than would be expected on the basis of the ethnic composition of the state of Illinois. He went so far as to speculate that these groups "have acquired some tolerance for this form of behavior" (p. 44). In the present study, there was only one patient who was a foreign-born European, so there is no new information about the prevalence of incest in Polish or Italian groups. On the other hand, black patients are slightly *under*represented in the incest group, while patients of Latin American background are somewhat overrepresented. It seems that the disproportionate number of Latin patients reporting incest in this sample may well be an artifact of the high degree of cooperation displayed by the clinic's Spanish-speaking therapist in reporting incest cases. Therefore, unless this finding can be replicated in other research settings, it should not be interpreted as a demonstration that incest is more common in Americans of Latin American background.

Participants in
Father-Daughter Incest

開 開 開 開 開 開 開 開 開 開 開 開 開 開 開 開

Given that the mere thought of incest is repugnant to most individuals and that an actual act of incest is punishable, at least potentially, by a long prison sentence, how can we explain the fact that incest occurs with regularity in our society? Except for the very special aura of forbiddenness that attaches to the term *incest*, one could substitute the name of any other serious crime in this question and have basically the same problem. It is the central question in the study of criminology and social deviance, and the kinds of answers that are regularly proposed fall very roughly into two broad categories: (1) social pathology, such as economic depression, overcrowded living accommodations, and powerlessness and (2) individual pathology, such as mental retardation, psychosis, and alcoholism. Of course, these categories overlap to a large degree, since society is made up of individuals, pathological or not, and individual pathologies do not develop in a social vacuum. In the pages that follow, we will be focusing almost exclusively on aspects of individual pathology that are seen as being contributory to the occurrence of overt incest; although this psychological focus is intentional, the reader should bear in mind that socioeconomic and cultural influences may also be important in incest behavior and have been discussed extensively by other authors (for example, Weinberg, 1955). The goal of this chapter is to describe and discuss the characteristics of father-daughter incest participants as they have been revealed in previous studies and as they appeared in the case histories I have collected.

The Father

When an intensely taboo act occurs, we tend to look for "causes" within the individual who is seen as the perpetrator. More or less constant conditions such as psychosis and mental retardation are seen as interfering with full emotional knowledge of the taboo and the consequences of breaking it or as weakening the individual's ability to inhibit antisocial behavior. Temporary states of derangement brought on by alcohol, drugs, or extreme stress are also invoked as explanations. In an effort to test these obvious hypotheses, researchers have carefully examined the case histories and personality characteristics of incestuous fathers, and there appears to be more information available on these men than on any other kind of incest participant, probably because they are often in contact with social agencies that have the power to strongly motivate their cooperation.

Of the fifty-eight cases I surveyed, thirty-seven were cases of father-daughter incest. In five cases, the father was the identified patient; in twenty of the remaining thirty-two cases, the daughter provided a description of some of her father's characteristics in the course of describing the incest to her therapist or the father was seen briefly in connection with his daughter's psychological disturbance. Some of the daughters' descriptions were very brief; others were augmented by interviews with other family members. Although the primary purpose of the study was to assess the effects of incest on the daughters' lives, information about other members of the incestuous family was collected whenever it was available.

Background of Emotional Deprivation. We would expect incestuous fathers to report less than optimal experiences in their families of origin, but the real question to be answered is how their backgrounds differ from those of other socially deviant groups. For instance, it is frequently found that these men have experienced mild to extreme levels of poverty in their youth (Weinberg, 1955; Kaufman, Peck, and Tagiuri, 1954; Riemer, 1940), but only the Kinsey Institute study of sex offenders (Gebhard and others, 1965) has compared incestuous fathers with other imprisoned sex offenders and thus demonstrated conclusively that economic deprivation is a special characteristic of the incest group.

Riemer (1940) studied a sample of fifty-eight incestuous fathers and reported that these men had typically left home at a very early age and lived by themselves or in a nonfamily environment until they married and founded families of their own. The absence of parent figures at an early age, Riemer believed, may have played an important role in enabling the father to disregard the incest taboo because the father's early life had deemphasized the special value of the parent-child relationship. It was thus possible for the father to think of his daughter as just another female when he approached her for sexual relations. Also, with his severely deprived background the father would have had minimal opportunity to learn about social responsibilities and constraints of all kinds, and therefore, while he certainly knew about the incest taboo on an intellectual level, he would not have strongly internalized it.

American studies done in clinical settings have tended to find that the future incestuous father was emotionally deprived in his family of origin, and even when he came from a middle-class background he had often experienced desertion of the family by his own father during his formative years (Lustig and others, 1966; Weiner, 1962). Weiner (1962, 1964) was particularly impressed by the strong ambivalence displayed by the incestuous father toward his own father, who was most frequently described as being harsh and authoritarian if not absent from the home. As such, he was hated and feared yet also admired and respected by his son, who was left with ungratified longings for an affectionate relationship with a father figure. Weiner hypothesized that these men identified with their daughters in the sexual relationship and received gratification from the fantasy of obtaining paternal warmth and sexual affection, and he presented some evidence for "identity conflicts" and "passive homosexual longings" in the results of projective testing of these fathers. However, Weiner examined only five men. He also did not explain very convincingly why the fathers chose to have sex with their daughters instead of their sons if their incestuous activities were indeed attributable to passive homosexual desires.

The Kinsey Institute study of sex offenders (Gebhard and others, 1965) is the largest American study of the backgrounds of incestuous fathers, and its findings are both confusing and enlightening. Compared with other sex offenders and a normal control group, men who had had sexual contact with daughters under twelve years of age were distinguished by poor relationships with their fathers, as the previous clinical studies would have predicted, and by preferences for their mothers, even though their relationships with them were also unhappy. The maternal preference was so striking that Gebhard and his colleagues commented, "The combination of incest with a young person and the youthful partiality for the mother suggests an oedipal phenomenon that we are not equipped to analyze" (p. 209). Several other researchers (Marcuse, 1923; Cormier, Kennedy, and Sangowicz, 1962; Lustig and others, 1966; Cavallin, 1966) have suggested that the daughter represents the mother in the unconscious mind of the incestuous father, so that it is actually the desire for consummation of a mother-son incest union or for revenge against the depriving mother that motivates the father-daughter relationship.

However, the picture was quite different when the family backgrounds of men imprisoned for incest with "adult" (sixteen years or over) daughters were examined. These men usually had no strong preference for either parent and got along with both of their parents almost as well as did the noncriminal control group. In other words, there was a correlation between the age of the daughter in father-daughter incest and the quality of the father's attachments within his family of origin—the "healthier" his family background, the older his daughter when he initiated incest. It therefore seems that emotional deprivation and very disturbed father-son relationships characterize only one group of incestuous fathers and are not necessary conditions for the occurrence of incest. Whatever psychodynamic explanations have been attached to these factors can therefore be true of only a subgroup of father-daughter incest cases.

Another "family background" factor that is seldom cited in the literature is what social learning theory would call an *incestuous model*. Weiner (1962) reported one such case. Raphling, Carpenter, and Davis (1967) have described an incestuous father who had observed sexual relations between his own father and his older sister on more than one occasion, and they concluded that such experiences were important determinants of this man's choice of incest rather than extramarital relationships as a means of releasing his sexual tension. Observation of incest in one's own family, especially when it seems to have no serious consequences, at the very least would make one aware that family members are possible sexual partners even if they are not socially approved. And learning within the family that incest is at least semiacceptable might well offset signals from peers outside the family that incest is strongly taboo behavior. However, since the Kinsey group did not ask incestuous fathers about observations of incest, we have no way of estimating how frequently father-son modeling occurs in cases of overt incest.

In the sample of psychotherapy patients, information about incestuous fathers and stepfathers was usually limited to descriptions of their characteristics as adults. A few case histories seemed to illustrate the chaotic family life and early emotional deprivation so frequently reported in the past. For example:

> Malcolm began running away from his abusive, alcoholic parents at the age of ten, and during his adolescence he lived in a series of foster homes

and juvenile facilities, where his aggressively antisocial behavior alienated any would-be surrogate
parents. As a young adult, he worked sporadically
and belonged to a delinquent subculture, eventually marrying a prostitute who left him soon
after their son was born.

Rachel's father had been deserted by his parents when he was six years old. During the next six
years, he was placed in at least twenty foster
homes and residential facilities, where his pathological lying and other bizarre behaviors made him
difficult to handle. At twelve, he was formally
adopted by a welfare eligibility worker who knew
his history and made a valiant attempt to provide
him with a stable and loving home; however, at age
fifteen he ran away and married a girl he had impregnated.

Intelligence. Subnormal intelligence could be a factor
that enables fathers to disregard the incest taboo, either by lim-
iting their understanding of what sexual relationships are forbidden or by impairing impulse control through a decreased ability
to visualize the consequences of actions. Indeed, there have
been individual cases reported in the literature (see Bender and
Blau, 1937) in which a mentally defective father engaged in sex
play with his young children as if he were one of their peers,
and some studies with large samples have found a high rate of
subnormal intelligence among incestuous fathers. Weinberg
(1955) classified nearly 65 percent of these fathers as being of
dull normal intelligence or below, while only about 9 percent
had superior intelligence; Kubo (1959) reported that two out of
thirteen fathers were what he called "imbeciles."

However, it had been much more common to find that a
sample of incestuous fathers is quite average with respect to intelligence (Cavallin, 1966; Lukianowicz, 1972), and Weiner
(1962) even found higher than average Wechsler IQ's in most of
his cases, but his sample seems to have been quite unusually
upper-middle class. The Kinsey Institute study (Gebhard and
others, 1965) found that imprisoned incest offenders were very

seldom mentally defective and that as a group they were brighter than most other types of sex offenders. The fathers who had
relations with daughters aged twelve and under were even more
intelligent than the noncriminal control group; fathers of girls
over sixteen were more frequently defective (9 percent) or below average (32 percent) in intelligence, probably because they
often had come from impoverished rural backgrounds. The
brightness of the former group suggests that personal maladjustment is a more important determinant of incest with prepubertal
(under twelve) daughters than intelligence, which may only
serve to allow these fathers to rationalize their sexual behavior
more elaborately. Even in cases where fathers are mentally defective, Kubo (1959) noted that they seemed fully aware that
incest was socially disapproved behavior and that they attempted to conceal the incestuous activity from others.

In the psychotherapy sample, there were no fathers who
were mentally defective and only a few who may have been on
the dull side of normal. None seemed especially bright, either;
there were no fathers who were college graduates, although the
general male clinic population contained about 25 percent college graduates. Intelligence, high or low, seemed to be an unimportant factor in incest behavior in this sample.

Employment History. Some previous authors have emphasized that a history of frequent job changes and periods of
unemployment may be symptomatic of personal maladjustment
in a sample of adult males; it may also provide a father more
time to be alone with his daughter, especially if his wife must
work to support the family. Riemer (1940) described the typical incestuous father as having had numerous unskilled jobs and
eventually becoming unemployed or employed in a marginal,
poverty-level position prior to initiation of incest. Over half of
the fathers in Weinberg's (1955) sample were supported by
other family members or by public agencies. Lukianowicz
(1972) stated that 70 percent of the fathers in his sample were
habitually unemployed in a time of almost full employment in
Northern Ireland, suggesting that these men were somehow personally inadequate despite their average level of intelligence.
Kaufman, Peck, and Tagiuri (1954) also felt that the occupa-

tional histories of the men in their sample reflected a generally irresponsible attitude toward life.

But, as was the case with intelligence, other studies (Cormier, Kennedy, and Sangowicz, 1962; Cavallin, 1966; Weiner, 1962) have described their subjects as having good occupational histories and as successfully presenting a "good family man" façade to the community. It seems that the finding of chaotic employment histories may simply reflect the bias introduced by the use of social agencies that are likely to encounter the unemployed as data sources. In the psychotherapy sample, most incestuous fathers had been reasonably successful, the typical man having held the same blue-collar job for a number of years. Two examples will illustrate the extremes with regard to employment history:

> Valerie's father was very overdependent on his wife for both emotional and financial support. At first he worked at a variety of jobs, but after several years he gave up all pretense of looking for work and had been a "househusband" and part-time student for eight years prior to his daughter's contact with the clinic.

> Carl was described by his therapist as "Mr. Upright Citizen." He had been employed by a law enforcement agency for nearly twenty-five years and had attained a position of authority with responsibility for several other coworkers. He had received various awards for his long record of good service to his department.

Dominance Within the Family. Although it is undoubtedly the norm in our society for husbands and fathers to dominate wives and children, incestuous fathers have often been described as being unusually tyrannical within their families. Weinberg (1955, pp. 63-65) seemed to be especially impressed with the abusiveness of incestuous fathers:

> In the family organization of father and daughter incest participants, the father dominated

and adversely influenced the family by his emotional instability and by his sex attitudes. . . . The
father's dominant family position did not necessarily result from his financial contributions but
from his intimidation and control of other family
members. . . . The father asserted his authority by
customary means and by threats, intimidation, and
physical violence. His beatings were not always intended for disciplinary purposes but for expressing
his hostility, which in some instances was very
sadistic. . . . Many fathers also exploited the family. Indifferent to their needs, they shifted responsibilities to other members, but kept authority. . . . Some fathers of highly ingrown families
became very "possessive" of their children, domi-
nated their personal lives, tried to find out all
about their social activities and their friends—in
effect eliminated their personal privacy.

Case histories involving domination through physical
abuse have also been reported by Rhinehart (1961), Cormier,
Kennedy, and Sangowicz (1962), and Raphling, Carpenter, and
Davis (1967). The latter study described an incestuous father
who was truly sadistic in the sense of deriving sexual pleasure
from beating his wife during sexual relations. Most usually,
however, these men become abusive only in order to impose
their will on other family members or during hostile bouts with
alcohol. At any rate, there is a range of domination patterns. At
one extreme is the father who is sociopathic and is merely treating his family in the same manner as he treats other persons, as
objects to fulfill his desires. At the other extreme is the father
who seems to be overinvested in his family and seeks to control
all aspects of their lives by whatever means he finds effective.
    Lustig and others (1966) were impressed by the fre-
quency with which the incestuous father wanted to be viewed
as a "patriarch" within his family. Having been deserted or
treated cruelly by his own father, he seemed to lack a secure
sense of his masculine identity and attempted to compensate
for his feelings of inadequacy by projecting an image of role

competence. He was perceived by neighbors and colleagues as being a hard-working, respectable family man without any serious behavior problems. However, his lack of experience with a good father figure deprived him of a realistic model for the role of patriarch that he desperately needed to play, and as a result he went too far in imposing authority, in the form of incestuous sexual activity, on his children.

There have been few contradictory findings in this area. In large samples, an occasional father may be described as passive, but mother-dominated families are seldom reported: Maisch (1972) gives a figure of 9 percent for mother domination; Szabo (1962) described about 4 percent of the mothers in his sample as being *les dominatrices*. Some major studies (Riemer, 1940; Cavallin, 1966; Gebhard and others, 1965) have not discussed this aspect of the incestuous father's behavior, and it seems possible that their reliance on the reports of the men themselves left the dominance behavior unobserved. The studies that utilized interviews with other family members discovered much more about the father's behavior at home than his self-report revealed. In the psychotherapy sample, nine of the fathers were reported to have been unusually dominant, controlling, or abusive prior to the initiation of incest, and this number should be taken as an absolute minimum since information was lacking on many of the fathers of female patients. Examples of abusive and overcontrolling dominance patterns follow:

> Vanessa's mother had several children by her first marriage, and her second husband had several children of his own. This huge family lived in abject poverty and was dominated by the brutality of the stepfather, who beat the mother and children with any convenient object—on one occasion he used a baseball bat. Some of the children ran away and told authorities that they preferred to stay in juvenile detention facilities rather than to return to the home.

> Pauline was brought to a child guidance clinic when she was in the fourth grade. She presented

as an extremely anxious child with psychosomatic symptoms that often prevented her attending school. Assessment of the family revealed that her father spent an inordinate amount of time with her, insisting on having long homework sessions in which he oversaw and directed all of her efforts. He put tremendous pressure on her to do better in school than her average level of ability would allow. When her mother separated from her father, he took up residence in an apartment across the street so that he could observe their comings and goings with binoculars.

Alcoholism and Drugs. If paternal dominance gives the incestuous father the intrafamilial power to effect a sexual relationship with his daughter, alcohol very frequently deadens his moral constraints and allows the first act of incest to occur. From the earliest research on incest (Marcuse, 1923), it has been noted that chronic alcoholism, or a drunken episode in a time of stress, is often associated with father-daughter incest. Sometimes the man reaches a state of pathological intoxication —Weinberg (1955) describes one case in which a father threatened to kill his whole family and then raped his daughter in front of his wife. Weinberg also noted that there were often reports that the father seemed more excited (and sexually aroused) when under the influence instead of experiencing the usual sedating effects of alcohol. In the typical case, however, the alcohol functioned as it normally does to lower inhibitions and permit behavior that would be suppressed in a state of sobriety.

It is difficult to give exact figures on the percentage of incestuous fathers who are alcoholics or problem drinkers, because these terms are seldom defined in research reports. Only 15 percent of Lukianowicz' (1972) sample were diagnosed as alcoholics, whereas 73 percent of the fathers studied by Kaufman, Peck, and Tagiuri (1954) were thus labeled. It is more typical to read that somewhere between 20 and 50 percent of a sample of fathers are alcoholic (for example, Cavallin, 1966, with 33 percent; Merland, Fiorentini, and Orsini, 1962, with 47 percent). The most exact information has been provided by

Gebhard and others (1965), who defined as *alcoholic* any man who drank a fifth or more per day or drank to the extent that his social and occupational adjustment was seriously impaired. Using this definition, nearly 25 percent of the fathers imprisoned for sexual relations with prepubertal (under twelve) daughters were alcoholic; the percentage of alcoholic fathers decreased as the age of the daughter involved in the case increased. A much larger number of offenders, although not alcoholics, drank to relieve stress and reported that they had been drinking at the time of the first incest incident. Use of drugs other than alcohol did not seem to have been a factor in any of the incest offenses.

Twelve of the fathers in the psychotherapy sample were reported to be alcoholics or heavy drinkers. Although it was not possible to ascertain how much they drank, it was striking that their alcohol consumption was often the only characteristic that the daughter would describe many years after the incest incident, and it seemed apparent that many of the daughters had seized on alcohol as a sufficient explanation of their father's sexual behavior. Two of the fathers who were alcoholic also used drugs. One took amphetamines and barbiturates, and another had a history of injecting methamphetamine. It is not known specifically whether these men were under the influence of drugs during their incest incidents, but it seems probable that they were, since they both engaged in incest on numerous occasions for at least a year during which there was concurrent drug use. The following examples illustrate how alcohol can play a role in cases that are very different in other respects:

> Malcolm had a long history of arrests for violent crimes and disorderly conduct. His employment record was extremely irregular, and he had recently lost his job because he came to work intoxicated. He was living on the wages that his second wife earned as a cafeteria worker at the time of contact with the clinic. Faced with a possible prison sentence for drunken driving, he had agreed to try Antabuse.

Carl, previously described as "Mr. Upright Citizen," had two arrests for drunken driving but otherwise had succeeded in engaging in heavy drinking at home while continuing to perform well on the job and present a good façade to the community.

Psychopathy. The terms *psychopath, sociopath,* and *character disorder* are employed by many incest researchers to describe an enduring personality pattern of at least some incestuous fathers. Some caution is advisable in the use of these terms, since there may well be a tendency to assume that a person who initiates incest in the absence of psychosis or frankly neurotic symptoms simply *must* be a psychopath, given the heinous nature of the crime in the eyes of most persons. In fact, these labels should be reserved for those who have a history of antisocial behavior other than incest and who display minimal levels of guilt and anxiety in relation to their misbehavior.

If an incest sample is middle class in nature, it is not uncommon to find no cases in which the father is considered antisocial (Lustig and others, 1966). A lower-class sample yields many more diagnoses of *psychopath*, a rather extreme example being Lukianowicz' (1972) sample of twenty-six incestuous fathers, of whom nineteen were considered to be psychopathic (fourteen "inadequate" and five "aggressive" psychopaths). Since only the aggressive psychopaths had histories of criminal behavior other than incest, it seems likely that the inadequate psychopaths were men who would not have received the psychopath label in other studies. Usually men labeled psychopathic are in a distinct minority in incest studies, because the incestuous father is most frequently a noncriminal type who does not often get into trouble outside of the home.

Although he did not state what percentage of fathers belonged to it, Weinberg (1955, p. 98) described a major category of incest offenders as being psychopaths whose sexual behavior was characterized by indiscriminate promiscuity: "The psychopath who was unable to sustain his relations with other persons did not confine his relations to the family. His contacts with women were transient and physical rather than sustained and tender, and he was unable to foster friendships with men. He seemed emotionally retarded and had little or no facility for socially intimate contacts or for appreciating the distress of others, even the members of his family. Such offenders seemed to have no particular preference for their daughters as sexual partners but were willing to settle for them when their wives and girlfriends were unavailable. Some had such a flagrant disregard for family feelings that they offered to share their daughters with other men. Many had criminal records, although few were professional criminals. Prior convictions of incestuous fathers were for "personal offenses," such as wife beating, public fighting, or drunkenness, and occasionally for sex offenses other than incest.

In the Kinsey Institute study (Gebhard and others, 1965), 10 percent of the men imprisoned for incest offenses with daughters under the age of twelve were classified as "amoral delinquents," their term for *psychopath*. The amoral delinquents' offenses were opportunistic, based on "propinquity and ease of access" rather than on any enduring sexual interest in the daughter. They were also domineering and abusive in their home environments, keeping their wives and children subordinate and making them fearful of opposing any of their egocentric desires. More aggressive than other incest offenders, they tended to have longer criminal records, although they were not professional criminals. The incest offenders as a group, however, were the least criminal of all the sex offenders studied, and their previous offenses tended to be "crimes against order," such as vagrancy and disorderly conduct, as opposed to serious crimes against property or other persons.

In the psychotherapy sample, too little was known of the fathers in cases that were reported by daughters long after the occurrence of incest to justify affixing a term such as *psychopath*. In thirteen of the cases of father-daughter incest, the father was either seen one or more times by the therapist or described both by the patient and by other family informants.

In two of these cases, the therapist believed that the father definitely warranted the *psychopath* label:

> Malcolm had juvenile and adult convictions for petty theft and assault, and he displayed minimal anxiety and guilt when asked about his crimes, shrugging off a barroom stabbing by saying that his victim "probably deserved it." He took delight in shocking his therapist with details of his antisocial behavior and seemed to view his sexual relations with his young stepdaughter with amusement. His MMPI confirmed his therapist's perceptions of these psychopathic tendencies.

> Harry was incorrigible in school and spent his adolescent years in forestry work camps with other juvenile delinquents. He became the black sheep of his family and has had no communication with his parents and siblings for many years, even though most of them live less than a mile from his home. As an adult, he was arrested only for drunk driving until his daughter reported incest to the police and he was ordered to undergo a psychiatric examination. He ingratiated himself to the psychiatrist, painting himself as a well-intentioned family man whose temper got the best of him from time to time; however, interviews with other family members revealed a history of desertions, brutality, and extreme callousness in regard to his wife and children. He was also a suspect in several unsolved sex crimes in his area.

Hypersexuality. To suppose that an unusually strong sex drive underlies sexual offenses is generally considered naive. In fact, the opposite idea—that sex offenders require intense or bizarre kinds of stimulation in order to whet a weak sex drive—has often been held more plausible. In general, the Kinsey Institute study (Gebhard and others, 1965) found that sex offenders are not much different from other prisoners or noncriminal controls in their frequency of sexual outlet. But surprisingly, there is some agreement in the literature on the hypersexuality of at least a subgroup of incestuous fathers.

Lukianowicz (1972, p. 307) received an impression of unusually strong sex drives in his sample of twenty-six incestuous fathers and commented that "all appeared to be 'oversexed' males with poor inhibitions and overtolerant wives." Shelton (1975) and Weiner (1962), both of whom studied small samples of fathers intensively, were also impressed by the strong interest in sexual activity manifested by their subjects and their very frequent patterns of masturbation, interest in oral-genital activity, and tendency to get involved in other kinds of sex offenses. Maisch (1972) disputed the hypersexuality of incestuous males by giving a figure of 14 percent of fathers in his sample having five or more orgasms per week, but he seemed to have missed the point that hypersexuality is defined by the strength and nature of the sexual interest and not by frequency of outlet per se.

Weinberg (1955) reported that some incestuous fathers had always been very "loose" about sex, often going nude in front of their children and even having intercourse in their presence. Most of the fathers seemed to go through a period of hypersexuality immediately prior to initiating the incestuous relationship. They became restless and tense as a result of some kind of personal setback and often resorted to alcohol, which excited them—rather than soothed them—even more. Their sexual tension mounted and the sex drive became very intense for a short period of time, owing, Weinberg implied, to a combination of events, which usually included the loss of sexual access to their wives. That the incestuous father can also be characterized by an extremely high level of sex drive over a long period of time is attested to by a detailed case history (Raphling, Carpenter, and Davis, 1967), in which the father was said to have had intercourse with his wife three to four times per day for the first ten years of their marriage despite the woman's frequent protests.

The large sample study by the Kinsey Institute researchers (Gebhard and others, 1965) confirmed the impression of hypersexuality gained by earlier clinical researchers, at least in the cases of men who had incestuous relations with daughters under the age of twelve. Gebhard and his colleagues found that (p. 227, italics added): "In some cases . . . there appears to have developed a *pathological obsession with sex*. This expresses itself in much time spent in sexual fantasy, in talking too much about sexual matters, in increasing or attempting to increase marital coitus markedly, in seeking increased visual stimuli, in unnecessary nudity bordering on exhibition, and in preoccupation with mouth-genital contact. One often gains the impression that these men, frustrated in many areas of life, seek happiness by sexual overcompensation." The Kinsey Institute team found it especially significant that these men placed a great deal of emphasis on sexual foreplay, mouth-genital contact, variety of positions in intercourse, and anal intercourse in comparison with other sex offenders or controls. In another social milieu, their sexual behavior might be commonplace; however, it was atypical sexual behavior for men with their backgrounds and socioeconomic status, and it seemed to suggest a readiness for sexual experimentation that might be rooted in personality disturbance.

Daughters in the psychotherapy sample were unlikely to know anything about their fathers' sexual behavior beyond the incestuous behavior itself. Thus many of the cases may have involved a degree of hypersexuality that went undetected, but one can state that, of the thirteen fathers actually interviewed by therapists, two appeared to have an unusually strong interest in sexuality. One of these men was psychopathic, and it is possible that his boasting about his sexual exploits was an effort to amaze or frighten his female therapist, who did come to view him as a potential rapist. The second case is probably more similar to the cases that impressed the Kinsey Institute researchers:

Carl had only three interviews with a therapist and spent a good deal of that time talking about his second wife's lack of sexual interest as compared with his first wife. His first marriage had lasted twenty years, and he described it as having fulfilled his fondest sexual dreams with very frequent and enjoyable intercourse. Even after his wife had decided to leave him, they went on a honeymoon in order to enjoy each other sexually one last time. His second wife was upset by his emphasis on sex and especially by his interest in reading pornographic accounts of incestuous relationships. The therapist concluded that sexuality was very prominent in the life of this otherwise conventional man.

Psychosis. Given the impulse to initiate sexual relations with a daughter, any circumstance that serves to lower a father's inhibitions and reduce his capacity for exercising self-control may make the difference between temptation and consummation. We have already discussed the role of alcohol in overt incest. Psychosis would seem to be a condition favoring incest because of the breakdown in ego controls that to a greater or lesser extent accompanies a psychotic state. Overt incest, like murder, is one of those human events that is so unthinkable to most people that there is a tendency to suppose that anyone who would do it *must* be "crazy." It is therefore reasonable to expect that many incestuous fathers were psychotic when incest began, but this expectation has generally not been confirmed.

A number of studies have found no instance of psychosis prior to the incest offense (Weiner, 1962; Cavallin, 1966; Lustig and others, 1966; Lukianowicz, 1972). Weinberg (1955) states that "several" of his 159 incestuous fathers were psychotic. Other investigators have found 6 percent (Medlicott, 1967), 12 percent (Merland, Fiorentini, and Orsini, 1962), and 40 percent (Magal and Winnick, 1968). One is left with the impression that the proportion of psychotic fathers is quite low, with the exact proportion found in any one study depending on the research setting in which cases were collected. Studies conducted in prison settings, for instance, usually find very few psychotic fathers because such men are much more likely to be sent to mental institutions if they are convicted in the first place. The Kinsey Institute study (Gebhard and others, 1965) discussed this sample bias as an explanation for their finding only a few psychotic men imprisoned for incest. There is some evidence (Martin, 1958), however, that imprisoned incest offenders display more generalized psychological disturbance on projective tests than men who are imprisoned for sexual relations for young, non-related females.

Kubo (1959) is the only researcher to have noted a pattern in the distribution of the psychotic cases in his sample. He remarked that isolated rural families of low socioeconomic status were often involved with incest in the absence of marked psychological disturbances in the participants. Many of the urban incest cases, however, were characterized by the presence of psychosis, which seemed to have allowed the incest to occur even when the family enjoyed middle-class socioeconomic standing. This pattern suggests that subcultural factors can be important in enabling overt incest to occur, and when these factors are absent the personal disturbance of the participants becomes more important as a causal factor.

Another finding of some interest has been that the father often becomes psychotic after the offense has been exposed, sometimes while serving his prison sentence and sometimes before sentence is imposed. In the latter situation, one suspects a manipulative quality, as in an instance reported by Lukianowicz (1972, pp. 304-305): "Only one of the incestuous fathers twice developed a 'reactive depression' and got himself admitted to a psychiatric hospital—on both occasions when his incestuous activities became exposed and his arrest and prosecution were imminent. Yet his 'depression' did not prevent him from establishing incestuous relations with the third of his four daughters as soon as the danger of prosecution was over." More commonly, the psychosis is schizophrenic in nature and seems to have been developing over a long period of time and to have been precipitated by the turmoil surrounding the public exposure of incest. Weinberg (1955), for instance, found that eleven men in his large sample had become psychotic *after* being imprisoned for incest. Cavallin (1966), reporting on the psychiatric workups of twelve imprisoned incest offenders, found three who appeared to be borderline psychotics and two who were quite definitely schizophrenic but only displayed symptoms after their incarceration. Weiner (1962) reported on five incestuous fathers who were seen at an outpatient psychiatric clinic and given a battery of psychological tests that included the Thematic Apperception Test (TAT) and the Rorschach. Immediately after the testing it was concluded that none of these men had given any of the recognized "schizophrenic signs" or the projective tests. Nevertheless, only two weeks after the testing was completed one of the men was admitted to the hospital in a full-blown schizophrenic state with an elaborate delusional system, hallucinations, and extreme religiosity, which suggested an acute paranoid schizophrenic breakdown in a person who was previously intact enough to function adequately in the community until his early fifties.

In the psychotherapy sample, only one father was reported by a daughter to have been "mentally ill" at the time of incest. It was not possible to ascertain from her report whether he was schizophrenic or psychotically depressed, but a history of several hospitalizations culminating in his suicide almost certainly indicates psychosis. Two other fathers were thought to be psychotic by their daughters' therapists on the ground that their behavior had a bizarre quality to it, but the fact that both of these men had successfully supported families and had never been hospitalized suggests that they were at most borderline cases of psychosis. Since only one father in this group was ever imprisoned for incest and in most cases the incest was revealed to no one outside of the family, the possibility remains that some of these men were latent schizophrenics similar to those found in studies of imprisoned incest offenders.

Paranoid Personality Disorder. When an "official" diagnosis has been made of incestuous fathers who are not psychotic or psychopathic, the term *paranoid personality disorder* has seemed to cover the hostility, suspiciousness, and intellectual defense structure that are frequently described in these cases. Weinberg (1955) was one of the first researchers to comment on the frequency of paranoid thinking patterns. Although most fathers in his sample were nonpsychotic and many had been classified as "inadequate" personalities by court and prison psychiatrists, they often had histories of egocentric, suspicious behavior, such as belligerent attitudes toward employers that frequently caused them to lose their jobs, as well as quarrels with neighbors and family members over quite trivial issues. They had often suspected their wives of infidelity on the flimsiest of grounds and had been extremely suspicious and overprotective their daughters, attempting to monitor all their social activities.

It is significant that three recent studies (Weiner, 1962; Cavallin, 1966; Raphling, Carpenter, and Davis, 1967) in which psychological testing was used to supplement psychiatric evaluations concluded that paranoid trends existed in the thinking of some or all of the fathers. Cavallin reported that all twelve incestuous fathers in his study had paranoid features that were confirmed by results of the MMPI, showing that they tended to use projection as their major ego defense mechanism. Weiner (1962), using projective tests, arrived at a similar conclusion— the fathers he studied manifested several signs of paranoid thinking and appeared to be using their above-average intellectual capabilities to maintain an intellectual defense structure. They also tested as introverted, "closed in" individuals who did not readily express their emotional needs to others. Raphling, Carpenter, and Davis (1967) paint an especially vivid picture of a father who had intercourse with two of his daughters, was sexually sadistic to his wife, and yet was also a prudish man who was heavily involved in his church and attempted to inculcate high moral standards in his family. Projective testing revealed a paranoid defense structure that evidently enabled him to reconcile his activities and beliefs in his own mind, at least enough to prevent his being overwhelmed with guilt.

The finding of paranoid thinking in the preceding three studies was accompanied by findings of "problems with identification" and "unconscious homosexual strivings," but there was no evidence for overt homosexual involvement in the case histories presented by the authors (Weiner, 1962; Cavallin, 1966; Raphling, Carpenter, and Davis, 1967). Gebhard and others (1965) specifically asked sex offenders about homosexual acts and desires and found that incestuous fathers as a group were strongly heterosexual, even more so than their nonprisoner con-

trol group. Of course, it is possible that the incest offender re-
presses his homosexual desires so thoroughly that they are never
allowed any expression other than incest, but it is difficult to
imagine how one could ever prove or disprove such an hypothesis. Perhaps we should consider the possibility that "unconscious homosexual strivings" have been "found" because of the
long-standing belief among clinicians that paranoia and repressed homosexual needs are dynamically linked. In the case of
incestuous fathers, there seems to be abundant evidence for
paranoid thinking but very little convincing evidence for underlying homosexuality.

Among fathers in the psychotherapy sample who were actually seen one or more times by a therapist, the finding of
paranoid thinking was made in ten out of thirteen cases. Two of
these cases were borderline psychotics with prominent paranoid
features of suspiciousness and attempts to completely control
their families. In four other cases, there were both behavioral
indications of paranoid thinking and the results of the MMPI as
interpreted by a computer scoring service (Caldwell Report,
Division of Clinical Psychological Services, Inc., Los Angeles).
In each case, the MMPI-based diagnosis included a mention of
the possibility of paranoid episodes or acute paranoid states, although the primary diagnosis ranged from antisocial personality
to situational adjustment reaction. The tendency to use projection as a defense seemed to be the one commonality in these
cases, which were otherwise very diverse. A case in which the
paranoid trend was quite prominent follows:

> Floyd's father was an abusively alcoholic
> man who inspired great fear and hostility in his
> two sons and simultaneously required them to "toe
> the line" in every respect. As a result of their hos-
> tile relationship, Floyd left home to join the
> service as a teen-ager, finding the exigencies of mili-
> tary life considerably more agreeable than his fam-
> ily of origin. After the service, he found employ-
> ment in a low-level clerical position and married a
> meek, submissive woman with three children from
> a former marriage. He described himself as shy and

having difficulties in approaching women, and it appears that he settled for less than he wanted in choosing this woman as his wife. At any rate, their relationship rapidly deteriorated when he found that her "virtue" was rooted in frigidity rather than moral belief and that her personal habits were slovenly, at least by his high standard of order and neatness. He repeatedly described himself as a perfectionist, but his perfectionism did not prevent him from drinking heavily and physically abusing his wife when she failed to live up to his standards. Nor did it deter him from having intercourse and oral-genital relations with his ten-year-old stepdaughter over a six-month period. When the girl told a neighbor, who reported it to his wife, his initial reaction on being confronted by her was that incest is very much more common than most people think and therefore she should not be so shocked by it. Under duress from his wife, he saw a therapist for an evaluation interview and presented as an anxious, depressed man who made a show of wishing to know what had motivated his behavior. However, he basically seemed to believe that others were responsible for his behavior—his wife for not enjoying sex with him and his stepdaughter for being "tall for her age" and "seductive" in some unspecified way. His MMPI report disclosed a significant level of disturbance, suggesting a diagnosis of "paranoid state, in danger of decompensating." However, when it became apparent that his wife would not press charges, he refused further appointments at the clinic.

Pedophilia. When the daughter is clearly prepubertal —under twelve years of age, let us say—it seems reasonable to hypothesize that the father who approaches her for sexual activity may be a pedophile who is attracted to his daughter as part of a general attraction to prepubertal girls. Marcuse (1923) mentioned pedophilia as a possible factor in incest. Weinberg (1955) stated that pedophiles constituted a distinct category of

offenders within his large sample but did not reveal how many
fathers were thought to be pedophiles. Gebhard and others
(1965) recognized a pedophile variety of incest offenders but
stated that this kind of offender was rare; since theirs was a prison sample, one would actually expect the number of such cases
to be maximized, because a pedophile would be viewed as a
danger to the community, not simply to his own family, and
thus be more likely to be imprisoned.

Clinical studies of incestuous fathers have rarely found
them to be pedophiles, either behaviorally or in their fantasy
lives. The psychotherapy sample also contained no cases in
which it was known that a special desire for young girls had
played a role in motivating the incest behavior. (One pedophile
was found in the sample, but he was not involved in father-
daughter incest, probably because all of his children were
males!) One is left with the impression that the pedophile is a
distinctive type of incest offender but that pedophilia is very
seldom a factor in the occurrence of father-daughter incest.

Classification of Incestuous Fathers. We have reviewed
the factors thought to be characteristic of incestuous fathers at
some length because the incest literature contains a fair amount
of information about such men, subject as they are to psychiatric evaluations during court proceedings and while imprisoned. Some general impressions of the group as a whole emerge
clearly. The typical incestuous father is not mentally retarded,
psychotic, or pedophilic but is characterized by some sort of
personal disturbance that interferes with his ability to control
his impulses in a situation where the temptation to commit incest exists. Abuse of alcohol is very often associated with his
incest offense and is an important factor in weakening his self-
control. Also, although the father has committed an offense
that is viewed as horrendous by his fellow citizens, he is usually
not a generally criminal type who is a danger to those outside
his family. But beyond these general characteristics it is obvious
that men of very diverse backgrounds and social characteristics
are involved in incest with their daughters and that it would be
useful to have a meaningful classification of incestuous fathers.

Typologies of incest behavior have been proposed by

Marcuse (1923), Weinberg (1955), Bagley (1969), and Gebhard and others (1965). Although their terminologies differ, these authors agree on the existence of psychopaths, psychotics, mental defectives, and pedophiles as distinct categories of incest offenders. Usually alcoholism is not treated as a separate category, because many fathers who clearly belong to one of the other categories in terms of prominent personality traits are alcoholic as well. The Kinsey Institute group (Gebhard and others, 1965) suggested the need for a "drunken" category that would include men who committed incest on only a few occasions when they were so intoxicated as to be *non compos mentis*, in legal terminology. The drunken offender need not be an alcoholic.

In most studies of father-daughter incest, the majority of fathers do not fit any of the established psychiatric diagnoses but do seem to share some personality characteristics that could have predisposed them to commit incest. The most prominent characteristic that has been observed is a tendency to limit social and sexual contacts to the family. There are numerous jokes about incest being an attempt to "keep it in the family," the source of humor being that sexual relations are an emphatic exception to the culturally approved goal of mutual activity and "togetherness" for parents and children. The incestuous family has been described as so "ingrown" that the father is unable to seek sexual release outside of it should his marital relationship not provide for his sexual needs, and "keeping it in the family" then loses its humorous connotation, becoming a real motive for incest.

Weinberg (1955) was the first to name this large category of incestuous fathers. Referring to an early psychoanalytic work by Abraham ([1909] 1955) describing "neurotic endogamy" in first-cousin marriages, Weinberg (1955, p. 94) suggested that the term *endogamic* be used to describe a father who is an "ingrown personality type . . . who confines his sexual objects to family members [and who] resorts to incest with a daughter . . . because he does not cultivate and does not crave social or sexual contacts with women outside the family." This endogamic type of father often committed incest with more than one daughter and sometimes seemed motivated by the resemblance of the daughter to his wife as a young woman, a circumstance that Marcuse (1923) has called the "recognition motive." Often raised in an ingrown family himself, the endogamic father never had succeeded in establishing gratifying social relationships outside of the family, and sometimes he was actually seclusive, going so far as to hide when visitors came to see his wife. At the same time, this shy man who was so inhibited in social relationships had difficulty restraining himself from impulsive acts; he often did not respect or esteem the women in his family, "foresaw" that his daughter would become promiscuous anyway, and considered it his paternal prerogative to initiate her sexually. Although he was very dependent on his wife and children, he was at the same time arrogant and domineering in his relations with them, and he tended to be suspicious of their extrafamilial relationships, attempting to control their social lives. This odd combination of dependence, seclusiveness, and domination of family members led to incest when the wife became sexually unavailable and when the husband's self-control was weakened, often through the use of alcohol.

When we review the incest literature, the endogamic father appears in many different studies under different names and with slightly varying descriptions. Riemer's (1940) description of his Swedish sample suggested that many of the fathers were isolated in rural areas and had no skill in approaching the opposite sex; they also sometimes justified the incest or grounds that it was preferable to "frivolous relations with outsiders." In Japan, Kubo (1959, p. 144) found that the largest category of incest offenders consisted of men who have "a strong inferiority complex [and] . . . cannot freely associate with others and . . . are taciturn, melancholy, but earnest in character." And clinical studies done after Weinberg's classification (Lustig and others, 1966; Cavallin, 1966; Weiner, 1962; Cormier, Kennedy, and Sangowicz, 1962) have found endogamic characteristics in most or all of their subjects. Bagley (1969), in a computer analysis of incest cases, discerned a major category that he called "functional incest," and some of the essential features of this category included a patriarchal family structure, either an isolated rural family or an "introverted" family, and poor or nonexistent relations with the surrounding community.

The term *endogamic,* while useful, has been applied to such a wide variety of cases that its meaning is not always clear, and it seems desirable to recognize that there are two reasonably distinct kinds of incestuous fathers who have an essentially endogamic orientation: The first is a father with a personality disorder, and the second is a father who belongs to an isolated subculture that is somewhat tolerant of incest. In other words, the endogamic orientation can arise from disturbance within the individual father, who can isolate himself and his family even in the most favorable kind of social milieu, or it may arise from a subculture in which physical isolation and increased tolerance of incest tend to create "ingrown," endogamic families in the absence of any marked personality disorder in the father.

The Kinsey Institute study (Gebhard and others, 1965), while not using the term *endogamic,* described the two kinds of endogamic orientations just suggested. What I have called a "personality disorder," they labeled the "dependent variety" of incest offenders. Such men made up about three quarters of the incest offenders against daughters under the age of twelve, and the Kinsey Institute group's description of them sounds very similar to Weinberg's (1955) endogamic group. These fathers were generally ineffectual in their social relationships outside of the home, and although they often had irregular employment histories, they usually had no criminal record. Dependent on their wives for emotional support, they were nonetheless domineering in the home and tended to engage in escapist drinking bouts during which they might become abusive. Sometimes there was evidence for an extreme interest in sexuality and unusual sexual practices, and most of the men in this group seemed to have an intellectual defense structure, rationalizing their behavior in various ways and projecting the blame for incest onto others.

The subcultural variety of incest offender described by the Kinsey Institute group was much more frequently imprisoned for sexual activity with an older, definitely postpubertal daughter. Possessed of the "Ozark attitude toward kinship," this offender "was a member of a Tobacco Road type milieu wherein incest was regarded as unfortunate but not un- expected" (Gebhard and others, p. 268). They tended to be devoutly religious, moralistic, intolerant of deviant sexual prac- tices, and very desirous of marrying a virgin; at the same time they had managed to lead disorganized personal lives, alternat- ing periods of drunkenness and violence with open repentance in the context of the fundamentalist religious beliefs that they espoused. They were therefore able to effectively relieve their guilt feelings for all of their transgressions, including incest. This ability, combined with the isolation of the family in an im- poverished rural environment where the incest taboo was somewhat weakened, allowed incest to occur in some situations. And, although phrases such as "Ozark attitude" and "Tobacco Road milieu" may evoke a strictly American image of the incest-prone subculture, it is almost certain that this kind of in- cestuous father has his counterparts all over the world. They have been described in Sweden (Riemer, 1940), Japan (Kubo, 1959), and Northern Ireland (Lukianowicz, 1972), for instance, and no doubt exist in many other cultures where poverty, rural isolation, and lack of effective personal restraints coexist.

The suggested set of categories is summarized in Table 5. The last category is called *situational,* a term already used by Gebhard and others (1965) to designate a variety of cases that do not clearly fit into the other categories. These cases usually consist of a series of stressful events—loss of job, divorce, death of family member, accident, or illness—that temporarily break down the resistance of an otherwise ordinary man who happens to have a tempting daughter or stepdaughter.

In any one study of father-daughter incest, the number of cases that will fall into each of these categories depends on the research setting. In the psychotherapy sample, there were no cases that seemed to fit the endogamic-subcultural category be- cause the cases were drawn from an urban working- and middle- class population. As already mentioned, pedophiles and mental defectives were not found in this group, either. All of the other categories were represented with the following percentages fall- ing into each: 68 percent endogamic-personality disorder, 1

Table 5. Classification of Incestuous Fathers

| Endogamic | • Heavily dependent on family for emotional and sexual needs |
| | • Unwilling or unable to satisfy sexual needs outside the family |

Personality disorder
- Shy and ineffectual in social relations
- Intellectual defense structure and tendency to paranoid thinking
- Intensely involved with daughter, overcontrolling of her
- Sometimes preoccupied with sex
- Often involved with prepubescent daughter

Subcultural variety
- Lives in isolated rural area
- Moralistic, periodically atoning for sins
- Social milieu semitolerant of incest
- Usually involved with postpubertal daughter

Psychopathic	• Criminal history
	• Sexually promiscuous, unrestrained by marital bonds
	• Little emotional attachment to daughter
Psychotic	• Severe ego disorganization of organic or functional origin
Drunken	• Incest occurs only when father is extremely intoxicated
Pedophilic	• Generally attracted to young children as sex partners
	• May lose interest in daughter as she ages
Mental defective	• Low intelligence a factor in reduced ego controls
Situational	• Incest occurring only during high-stress period for father

percent psychopathic, 5 percent psychotic, 5 percent drunken, and 5 percent situational.

Beyond academic curiosity, it may well be asked whether there is any point in setting up a classification for incestuous fathers and attempting to "diagnose" cases of father-daughter incest within this scheme. While the labels themselves are of no importance, it does seem desirable to assess the pattern of motives in each case and to recognize that incestuous behavior can arise in a variety of personality types and social settings. In Chapter Six, we will discuss the significance of the father's motives as perceived by the daughter; some of the obvious implications of the typology of incest offenders for public policy and psychotherapy will be treated in Chapter Eleven.

The Mother

The mother, of course, is not usually a participant in father-daughter incest in the sense of joining in the overt sexual

activities. Cases of direct participation are extremely rare (fc
example, see Weiner, 1962; Maisch, 1972). The mother ha
however, frequently been of prominent interest to researche
as the third party in the father-daughter incest relationship be
cause of her perceived collusive role and because she is ofte
available for interviews during court proceedings or in the co
text of psychotherapy.

In incestuous families, the mother has often been pe
ceived as the family member who "sets up" the father an
daughter for the incest relationship, usually by withdrawin
from her sexual role in the marriage and ignoring the speci
relationship that may then develop between husband an
daughter. Less frequently, she is seen as actively promoting th
relationship, even though she seems capable of massive denial c
the consequences of her actions. Lustig and others (1966) pr
vide an illuminating example in their description of a moth
who often rejected her husband's sexual advances. According t
the husband, incest began on a night when he arrived hom
from work to find his wife dressed seductively and acting flirt;
tious while mixing him cocktails. However, when he made se
ual overtures she suddenly withdrew from him, saying that sh
disliked to have sex when he had been drinking and also th;
she had to go out to a meeting. Before leaving, she placed the
ten-year-old daughter in his lap, saying, "You two take care c
each other while I'm gone."

Even when the mother has played no demonstrable rol
in setting the stage for incest, she is thought to be partially r
sponsible for the inception and continuance of the incestuou
relationship through her failure to take any action that woul
prevent or terminate it. In many cases, the signs of unusu
paternal behavior are present long before sexual activity occur
Obvious preincest paternal behavior includes an insistence o
sleeping near the daughter, efforts to see her in the nude or t
exhibit himself to her, and an unusual amount of physical co
tact with her. For example, one father in the psychotherap
sample engaged in "wrestling matches" with his fourteen-yea
old daughter, causing his wife considerable consternation. I
some cases, the father begins to act like an adolescent suitor i

his daughter's presence; he may actually insist on holding her hand or putting his arm around her while watching television, like a young couple at the movies. Obvious jealousy of the daughter's friends, both male and female, or an inclination to fantasize about her sexual feelings and activities are other, more subtle signs of incestuous feelings that may be exceeding the usual, well-repressed sexual possessiveness that a father may feel for his daughter. At any rate, there are often indications that incest may occur, and a mother may react to them in numerous ways that will increase or decrease the likelihood of incest.

Weinberg (1955) maintained that father-daughter incest is less likely to occur if a "restraining agent" is present in the home. Such a person, not necessarily the mother, is strongly opposed to incestuous behavior and has the intrafamilial power to restrain the father or to insulate the daughter from his attentions. Although this role is sometimes assumed by older siblings or in-laws, there is a societal expectation that a mother will protect her children from abuse of all kinds even if her protective role requires her to behave in ways that are inconsistent with her passive, acquiescent role as female partner in a male-dominant, "patriarchal" family. Therefore, if she does not restrain the father in an incest situation, she is seen as having failed in a very important aspect of her maternal role, and efforts are made to explain her failure. Although research on the role of the mother does not approach the volume of work that has been done on the incestuous father, several current hypotheses about her characteristics will be surveyed in this chapter.

Background of Emotional Deprivation. As was the case with incestuous fathers, the mother in an incestuous family has often been deprived of a normal family life as a child. Maisch (1972) found that 10 percent of the mothers in his sample has spent all or part of their childhood in orphanages, and other researchers (Eist and Mandel, 1968; Lustig and others, 1966) have published case history material showing experiences of institutionalization or desertion by parents. While we lack conclusive evidence that these experiences are more frequent in the histories of these mothers than in other women of comparable socioeconomic background, it seems that at least some mothers

in incestuous families have been deprived of the opportunity o
learning the maternal role from their own mothers. As we have
already observed in the case of the fathers, lack of family ex
perience in childhood could also serve to weaken the strength o
the internalized incest taboo in addition to creating various
kinds of personality disturbance.

More frequently it has been found that the mother's rela
tionship with her own mother (the maternal grandmother) has
been characterized by rejection and hostility. Kaufman, Peck
and Tagiuri (1954) gave a composite case history of the mothers
they studied that began with the grandmother's desertion by
her husband and her consequent hostility to her daughter (the
mother), who resembled her father in appearance and personal
ity. The grandmother, while continuing to care for her physi
cally, had deprived her not only of affection but also of the op
portunity to learn to function adequately as a wife and mother
The mother therefore entered on adulthood with a fathomless
feeling of inferiority and with a continuing need for the good
mothering she had missed as a child. As a result, she continued
to be emotionally tied to the grandmother with the vague hope
of receiving love and approval from her. But the relationship
was miserable and futile, and she eventually began to displace
her ambivalent feelings for her own mother onto her own
daughter as the daughter assumed the "little-mother" role. Thus
the process that made the daughter especially vulnerable to in
cest had been unfolding over three generations.

Other clinical researchers have found similar patterns o
emotional deprivation in the maternal branch of incestuous
families. Lustig and others (1966) remarked on the same odd
destructive combination of ambivalence and overdependence
Observing a mother over three years of psychotherapy with her
family and finding a very similar pattern, Eist and Mandel
(1968, p. 219) gave the following example of the mother's des
perate need for affection from her own mother:

> During the early part of treatment . . . a sit-
> uation arose which exemplifies Mrs. T.'s frenzied
> attempts to obtain maternal approval. Mrs. T.'s
> mother wrote, mentioning she would be coming

into town for a visit on one of several consecutive days. No specific time of arrival was provided, but it was clear that either bus or airplane would be the alternatives as far as her mother's choice of transportation was concerned. For several days, Mrs. T. darted back and forth between the air terminal and bus depot, meeting all planes and buses arriving from her mother's place of residence. She did manage to meet her mother and was very disappointed that her mother had decided to go on rather than stay. This was a chronic and frequently exacerbated disappointment.

As with the incestuous father, a family background of incest can weaken the mother's internalized incest taboo and thus reduce her ability or inclination to serve as a restraining agent. Such cases have occasionally been reported in the literature. Raphling, Carpenter, and Davis (1967) describe a case of father-daughter incest in which both the father and mother came from incestuous families in an isolated rural area of the Midwest, and while the mother did not seem to have actively promoted incest, she may have been more tolerant of it because of her own experience. In the psychotherapy sample, one of the mothers had had incestuous experience with her stepfather during adolescence, and it seemed quite probable that she was at least semi-tolerant of her husband's advances to their daughters. After incest was revealed, she decided to leave her husband, but there was considerable doubt that her leaving was motivated by a horror of incest, since she married her former stepfather within a year.

Since the mothers in father-daughter incest cases were not usually the identified patients, their backgrounds were seldom explored by therapists, and thus we cannot know the true proportion of backgrounds of emotional deprivation and incest in the sample. One example of severe deprivation of early family life was found:

Valerie's mother brought her to the clinic to be hospitalized for her latest schizophrenic episode. Since the daughter was incoherent, the mother was interviewed at some length to obtain a family history. The mother described herself as the fifteenth of seventeen children in a Mexican family that lived in grinding poverty in a border town. At the age of five, she was diagnosed as having active tuberculosis, which required her to be hospitalized in a sanitarium some distance from her home. Her family more or less forgot about her over the years, and she remained institutionalized until she was fifteen. Almost as soon as she was discharged from the hospital, she married a teen-age boy whose mother she greatly admired, in order to create a family life for herself. Since the couple lived close to the mother-in-law and had little competence to handle the rearing of the children that quickly followed their marriage, the older woman fell into the role of directing their lives and taking primary responsibility for raising the children from them. Valerie's mother felt incompetent and childlike in the presence of the mother-in-law, soon began to resent her competence, and became increasingly hostile to Valerie because she seemed to resemble the mother-in-law. After a few years, the marriage began to deteriorate, and the mother refused to continue sexual relations with her husband. The fact that the mother condoned the rather open incestuous relationship that developed between Valerie and her father led Valerie's therapist to believe that her concept of family life had been seriously distorted by her severe emotional deprivation experience in early life.

Absence or Incapacitation. Sometimes the mother's fail ure to act as a restraining agent is a simple matter of her no being present in the home when the incestuous situation is de veloping. Occasionally incest occurs in a situation where the mother has died, leaving the father and daughter alone in the home. This situation can be complicated by the daughter's re semblance to her mother, which may cause her father to dis place his feelings for his deceased wife onto her. Marcuse (1923

p. 279) used the term *recognition motive* to describe such cases and gave the following case history as illustration: "A man, aged fifty-one, had lived for a number of years in incestuous union with his daughter, aged twenty-six, and begotten five children. In court, he stated Augustine was his extramarital daughter from his intended wife, who had died shortly before her marriage. She had received a careful education. After her return to him, he had fancied to see in her the deceased mother, whose exact likeness she was. The idea entered his head to continue with her in the interrupted relations of his idealized bride. The girl consented—'and thus our family originated.'" Such cases are extremely rare in the literature. More usually, the wife's death contributes to incest simply by ending her role as sexual partner to the father and protector of the children.

A serious illness, mental or physical, can remove the mother from the home for a long period of time, and even if she remains in the home her presence can become a source of psychological stress for the father and daughter while her weakness prevents her from intervening when the signs of incest appear. Weinberg (1955), for instance, describes a case in which an incestuous father literally kept his wife, a chronic schizophrenic, in the kitchen most of the time, depriving her of all social contacts either with outsiders or with her own children. Psychotic mothers are the exception, however, and are probably not more frequent in incestuous families than in the general population of a similar socioeconomic background.

Some of the largest studies (Weinberg, 1955; Gebhard and others, 1965) have not reported the percentage of mothers who were absent or incapacitated. Kubo (1959) reported that, out of thirteen cases of father-daughter incest, four mothers had died, one had deserted the family, four were "in sick bed," one was feeble-minded, and one was schizophrenic. But his sample seems to be an extreme case, and we may speculate that it reflects the health standards in rural Japan twenty years ago. Closer to home, Maisch (1972) found nearly 20 percent of the mothers in his German sample to have been seriously ill at the time of the onset of incest, and Cavallin (1966) found one deceased and one psychotic mother in twelve father-daughter

cases. Also of interest is Gligor's (1966) report that in 16 per
cent of her sample of incest cases the mother was pregnant at
the time the incest began, suggesting that pregnancy, although
not a "desertion" of long duration, may function like an illness
in its effects on the family role structure.

In the psychotherapy sample, there were six cases in
which the mother's desertion, death, or serious illness prior to
the incest probably played a significant part in the developing
incest situation. Two mothers were deceased, two mothers were
psychotic and had been intermittently hospitalized prior to in
cest, and in the other two cases the mother in a large, poverty
stricken family deserted her children, thus leaving her husband
in a state of severe psychological and economic stress.

Passivity, Dependency, and Masochism. Given that the
mother is present in the home and is opposed to the occurrence
of incest, there are certain personality characteristics that would
make her acting as an effective restraining agent more difficult.
Especially in families where the father is extremely dominant
and insists on playing the role of patriarch, we would expect to
find a wife who is willing to play the complementary passive
role, and she would have to break out of this role in order to
seriously question her husband's behavior with her daughter. If
the husband were reasonably discreet in his incest behavior, it
would require active initiative on the wife's part to prevent or
terminate the relationship. Probably the rarest kind of "incest"
case history in the literature is one in which incest is prevented
by the mother's strong and assertive reaction to the father's
behavior, although this kind of private solution to an incipient
incest situation must surely occur from time to time. An example of incest "nipped in the bud" is given by Cormier, Kennedy,
and Sangowicz (1962), who describe a case in which a mother
insisted that her husband enter psychotherapy because of the
unusually intense relationship between him and their adolescent
daughter, and incest was averted when the father seriously
examined his feelings toward his daughter.

A woman's passivity and meekness require no special explanation in cases where her husband is dominant in a benign
way and provides both financial and emotional support to her.

However, in many incestuous families the husband is over-controlling, emotionally cold, and even physically abusive in a manner that verges on overt sadism. We then assume that the woman must be extremely dependent on her husband and tend to attribute immaturity to her since her dependency needs exceed the adult norm, even for women. In extreme cases, especially when physical abuse is involved, the concept of masochism is invoked, evidently because it seems as if the woman must positively enjoy physical and emotional pain in order to remain in the marital situation. The term *masochism* is not generally used in its narrow meaning of deriving sexual pleasure from pain or humiliation; in this context, it denotes a kind of satisfaction gained from being a virtuous victim who suffers endlessly for her family and actively seeks to perpetuate her victim role in the face of well-meaning attempts by others to help her to escape from her miserable situation.

The three characteristics that we have been discussing —passivity, dependency, and masochism—appear repetitively in descriptions of the wives of incestuous fathers. Weinberg (1955) mentioned masochism as a frequent characteristic of these women. Cormier, Kennedy, and Sangowicz (1962) found a number of mothers in their sample to be so passive and submissive to their husbands that they were unable to protect their daughters from them. Lukianowicz (1972, p. 305), whose sample of incestuous fathers was largely composed of men diagnosed as psychopaths, reported that most of the mothers, "appeared to be 'normal,' hard-working, and much-suffering women, usually with large families, and either a habitually unemployed, inefficient, 'good-for-nothing' husband (in fourteen cases), or an aggressive and demanding husband (in twelve cases)." One may perhaps speculate that a masochistic orientation is required for marriage to a psychopath. Kaufman, Peck, and Tagiuri (1954) describe the mothers seen in their clinical study as being very needy in an emotional sense and constantly fighting off their feelings of worthlessness. Extremely dependent on their husbands, they seemed unable to assume the role of adult woman and not only were passive but also gave the impression of being incompetent. Sloppy in dress and appearance, appearing to be intellectually dull (when, in fact, they scored in the average range on intelligence tests), "most of them were poor housekeepers, panicky in the face of responsibility, and seemed on the surface to be satisfied to live in disorder and poverty" (p. 269). Browning and Boatman (1977) have recently asserted that such women are found to be chronically depressed when seen in psychotherapy.

Of the thirty mothers in the psychotherapy sample who either were seen by the therapist or were well described by their daughters, thirteen were passive-dependent and possibly masochistic. The following two case descriptions will illustrate the diversity of such cases:

> Pauline's mother had been dominated by her first husband and finally sought a divorce from him with the emotional support of her therapist, even though she reported again and again that she feared him. She remarried within a short time. Her second husband was an arrogant, swaggering police officer who insisted that she quit her job because he felt that a working wife would be an embarrassment for him. She acquiesced.

> Harriet's mother worked long hours in a cafeteria in order to support her daughter, husband, and his son by a former marriage, despite the fact that she was in poor health and had had several operations within the past two years. Her husband's alcoholic binges and antisocial behavior made it difficult for him to hold a job for more than a few months at a time; he also became violent during his drinking bouts and on at least one occasion had threatened to kill her with a knife. In the course of family therapy, it came to light that her first husband had also been an alcoholic psychopath who had been flagrantly unfaithful to her while he depended on her for financial support. While drunk on an extramarital date, he crashed her car into a telephone pole and received a spinal injury that paralyzed him for several months. She

patiently nursed him, feeding him with a spoon, bathing him, and cleaning up excrement. He gradually recovered and left her. Her therapist concluded that she "had a need to be a martyr"!

Promiscuity. Especially when studies of father-daughter incest have been done in public agency settings or through court referrals, it has been found that a significant number of the mothers (although still a minority) had histories of sexual acting out that caused them to be labeled *promiscuous.* Unfortunately, researchers have seldom defined promiscuity, and one therefore has the uncomfortable feeling that its meaning is quite different in various times and places and also that the qualifications for promiscuity are grossly unequal for males and females. The term still retains a certain degree of usefulness, however, if one thinks of it as merely designating a level of sexual activity that is unacceptable in a certain culture at a certain point in time—in some places, sexual relations with more than one partner before marriage may be considered promiscuous, while a long series of "one-night stands" might be required somewhere else.

Lukianowicz (1972), who had an unusually large number of psychopathic fathers in his sample, found that the wives of such men were either masochistic or psychopathic and promiscuous themselves; eight of the twenty-five mothers in this study were thought to be promiscuous, and some of them went so far as to bring men home for sexual activity while their husbands were out. Kaufman, Peck, and Tagiuri (1954) mentioned that half of the mothers in their clinical sample had gone through periods of promiscuity earlier in their lives, presumably before their marriages. Of studies with larger samples, Maisch (1972) gave a 22 percent figure for promiscuity in his German sample and implied that many of these women remained promiscuous after their marriages. Szabo (1962) found 15 percent of the mothers in his French sample to be of "doubtful morality." Gligor (1966), defining parental promiscuity as "extramarital sexual activity or random mating" that became known during the adjudication of the incest case, found that 16 percent of the

mothers in her sample were promiscuous and also demonstrate
that mothers in incest families were more likely to be labele
promiscuous than mothers of adolescent girls coming before th
juvenile court for nonincestuous sexual activity.

When the mother is promiscuous in the sense of violatin
the sexual norms of her community, we may well ask what rol
her sexual behavior plays in laying the groundwork for a father
daughter incest situation. It is possible that her extramarita
behavior plays no specific role but is simply one aspect of wha
Weinberg (1955) called "families with loose sex cultures." B
this somewhat dated phrase, he meant that both parents an
children were unusually tolerant of sexual activity and mini
mized the importance of sexual privacy, such that the childre
often had the opportunity to witness the "primal scene." I
such a family setting, Weinberg thought that the strength of a
sexual taboos, including incest, was diluted. It has also been sug
gested by Lukianowicz (1972, p. 306) that the mother's extra
marital affairs serve to distract her from her husband's behavio
with her daughter and that these mothers "were apparentl
quite happy to tolerate their husband's 'unfaithfulness' wit
their own daughters, as long as their husbands did not object t
their own promiscuous behavior."

Another connection of the promiscuity of the mothe
with father-daughter incest in some cases may be the passive
dependent, masochistic personality traits discussed previously
The image of a promiscuous woman as being a "hard," psycho
pathic type is accurate in certain instances and completely mi
leading in others. She is often an emotionally needy person wh
gives herself to men as the price for being held and cuddled ten
porarily. Or she may not be assertive enough to turn men dow
effectively. Or she may derive masochistic pleasure from bein
"used" by men and from repeatedly demonstrating wha
"beasts" they are. The point is that promiscuity can be the r
sult of the same set of inadequate personality traits that allow
mother to abdicate her family role and fail to restrain her hu
band from initiating father-daughter incest.

In the psychotherapy sample, only three out of the thirt
mothers who either were seen in therapy or were well describe

by their daughters were known to have been promiscuous. Promiscuity was considered to be present when the woman carried on one or more extramarital affairs so indiscreetly that her husband and children knew about it or when she had had premarital intercourse with many partners outside the context of enduring love relationships. It is probable that the daughters or husbands often did not know about her premarital promiscuity and thus there were no reports of it. An example of extramarital promiscuity follows:

> Rachel's mother was forty years old, and her face was prematurely wrinkled, making her look more like fifty-five. Perhaps in an attempt to compensate, she dressed like a college girl in "miniskirts," platform shoes, and frilly blouses that were evidently supposed to give her a helpless, little-girl look. The result was grotesque. Her husband, a borderline psychotic, allowed her to entertain men at home, feeling that she was "going through a stage" and would get over it if he were sufficiently tolerant. At the time of contact with the clinic, she had a twenty-year-old boyfriend who had recently been discharged from the Navy and was living with her in the family home. During his stay with them, he also slept with her sixteen-year-old daughter and then bragged about this conquest to the rest of the family. Mother and boyfriend would leave on trips from time to time but return when they ran out of money. When seen in connection with her daughter's bizarre behavior, she insisted that the family had no special problems and that her daughter's problems were all of an organic nature.

Aversion to Sexuality. A constant finding in studies of father-daughter incest has been that the father has lost sexual access to the mother in many if not most cases. Riemer (1940, p. 571) is often quoted as saying of his large sample of fathers that "With almost no exceptions the patient, shortly before the incestuous relationship begins, finds himself barred from sexual intercourse with his own wife." He mentioned absence from the home or serious illness as reasons that the wife would be sexually unavailable, and one wonders if, forty years ago in rural Sweden, it was unthinkable for a wife to deny sex to her husband simply because she disliked it. Since that time, denial of sex because of the wife's aversion to it has been mentioned in the literature with increasing frequency.

Of the larger studies, only Maisch (1972) has given a percentage of the sample in which the wife was averse to sexual relations. Of his incestuous fathers, 26 percent stated that they had been having relations with their wives only on rare occasions, because the wives were "frigid." The Kinsey Institute study (Gebhard and others, 1965) also gives indirect evidence that the wife was denying her husband in a significant number of cases, since the incest offenders as a group reported that the high rates of marital intercourse they had had as young men had dwindled to very low rates, compared to other groups, in the years before the incest offense. In addition, they reported a low rate of orgasmic response from their wives, but questions were evidently not asked about the wives' general attitude toward sex and the role it may have played in their increasingly sexless marriages.

Clinical studies of father-daughter incest have given us some more qualitative information about the lack of sexual response in the wives of incestuous fathers. In Weiner's (1962) study, four out of five wives were reported to have been sexually frigid. One of these women had had intercourse with her husband on only one occasion and found it so distasteful that she refused to sleep with him for the next seventeen years, although she did consent to masturbate him, sometimes in the presence of their daughter. Lustig and others (1966, p. 35) described the wives in their sample as sexually rejecting and depreciating their husbands while often being simultaneously sexually provocative. Although the mother had a "good wife" façade, when it came to participation in the sexual aspect of the relationship the "husband was made to feel guilty about placing sexual demands on her, and typically she was 'too tired' or too overwhelmed, armed always with an unassailable excuse to reject sexual relations." Cormier, Kennedy, and Sangowicz (1962) reported that many of the mothers whom they studied were sexually nonresponsive. Some were "frigid" in every sense of the word in that they were hostile and unloving in both sexual and nonsexual situations; others were loving wives in a non-sexual context and never denied sex to their husbands, but their husbands were extremely frustrated by their wives' total inability to respond in the sexual relationship. Since female sexual response is increasingly emphasized in our society and males are inclined to think that they are responsible for bringing it about, the wife who is merely doing her "conjugal duty" in allowing sexual relations is no doubt much less satisfying to her husband today than she was in former times.

Outright denial of sexual relations or the unsatisfactory relationship often resulting from a lack of sexual response leaves the husband without a socially acceptable sexual outlet. Various masculine "proving" behaviors may also be elicited in response to the element of sexual and personal rejection that would not be present if sexual relations were discontinued for more understandable reasons, such as the wife's serious illness. Many non-incestuous fathers, of course, are somehow able to endure the frustrations of such a marital situation. Whether a father will be strongly tempted to commit incest will depend on his personality makeup; whether he will actually succeed in carrying out incestuous activities will also partially depend on the attitudes of his wife and daughter.

In the psychotherapy sample, daughters who described incestuous experiences that had occurred many years ago seldom reported any information about their parents' sexual relationship, no doubt because they knew little or nothing about it. Some did recall, nevertheless, their mothers' general attitude toward sexuality. One woman commented that "Mother always made it perfectly clear that sex was a drag." Another described her mother as having a "cold, Victorian" attitude and as being so naive about sexual matters that she believed her daughter to be virginal after the daughter had been in a detention facility for juvenile delinquents several times. Of the ten wives of incestuous fathers who were actually seen at the clinic, four described extreme aversion to sexuality or denial of sex to their husbands. Their attitudes ranged from indifference to revulsion, as in the following example:

> Floyd's wife had been in individual and group psychotherapy at the clinic for over a year before it was discovered that her husband was having sexual relations with his ten-year-old stepdaughter. Prior to the incest revelation, his wife had complained of depression and anxiety stemming from chronic difficulties in her five years of marriage to Floyd. She felt herself constantly criticized by him on account of her low standards of housekeeping, her inability to lose weight, and her frigidity in their sexual relations. On at least one occasion, he beat and kicked her in addition to his usual verbal abuse. Although her therapy group initially was very sympathetic to her, her inability to take any assertive action or to express anger directly eventually inspired a great deal of criticism from group members, who called her a "doormat" on several occasions. The therapist also eventually lost patience with her "complaints" about her lack of sexual response. When she would bring up the topic of sexuality, the therapist and group members would eagerly offer suggestions about how she could improve her sexual functioning, but there were always a dozen reasons why she could not follow through on them. One day a group member asked her if she could reach a climax through masturbation, and her response to this idea was so filled with horror and revulsion that it became obvious to all present that her aversion to sex was a powerful and deeply rooted attitude that was unlikely to be changed by suggestions of the "Masters and Johnson" type. Thereafter, the group did not take her very seriously when she said she would like to be sexually responsive, as it appeared to them that she was only giving lip service to the new cultural ideal that a good wife *should* be orgasmic.

Role Reversal with Daughter. It should be obvious from the characteristics already discussed that the mother in a father-daughter incest family is not very successful in fulfilling the role requirements of "adult woman." Thus far we have been examining her behavior mainly in relation to her husband; now we shall ask how her perceived inadequacies affect her daughter.

Kaufman, Peck, and Tagiuri (1954) did the first in-depth clinical study of mothers and daughters in incestuous families. Although their sample was very small, their description of the dynamics of the mother-daughter relationship has been quoted frequently in the incest literature and deserves our special attention here. Essentially, their formulation states that the mother develops a very special, conflict-laden relationship with one of her daughters long before incest occurs. The chosen daughter is initially treated very well, even being overindulged in comparison with her siblings, and she is encouraged to assume the responsibilities of an adult woman very early in life. At first, mother and daughter are allies and workmates in the care of younger siblings and the performance of household tasks, but gradually the mother relinquishes her responsibilities to the daughter and allows her to play the role of "little mother" in the family. This role reversal implies a special, wifelike relationship with her father. Although encouragement of incest is not on a conscious level, the mother is assumed to have backed out of her sexual role in the marriage and been relieved when her husband directed his sexual attention to the daughter.

Having succeeded in setting up the daughter as "little mother," the mother gradually becomes dependent on her in a childlike fashion and begins to displace her feelings for her own mother (the daughter's maternal grandmother) onto her daughter. The quality of the relationship then changes, with the mother expressing hostility to the daughter in direct and indirect ways while still remaining dependent on her. At the end of the preincest process, therefore, the daughter has been thrust into a premature adult role, rejected by her formerly loving mother, and somehow expected to be responsible for the needs of other family members.

The incest scenario proposed by Kaufman and his colleagues (1954) has been repeatedly found in subsequent clinical studies of father-daughter incest (for example, Heims and Kaufman, 1963; Rhinehart, 1961; Machotka, Pittman, and Flomenhaft, 1967). Lustig and others (1966, p. 34) claimed to have found this mother-daughter pattern in all of the six families studied by them. "In all cases [the daughters] had become the female authority in the household by the age of eight. Their advice was sought by the mothers on topics from groceries to sex. In addition to this, the daughters had much more responsibility for the care of the house than would normally be expected." They also described cases in which the daughter's responsibilities included acting as an intermediary between her parents when marital conflicts arose. And finally the case history descriptions from abroad often contain the same pattern of dynamics within the incestuous family. For instance, Magal and Winnick (1968, p. 181), reporting on an Israeli family, observed that the mother "was a woman of weak character who lived in permanent fear of her drunkard husband. Ever since [the daughter] was a little girl, her mother preferred her to all other children and put her to various tasks. . . . [The daughter] used to go marketing, she managed the money, took care of the smaller children. When she was twelve years old, [she] had to take care of the household and she alone could calm down her drunk father by talking to him kindly. She induced him to go to bed and sat by him all night."

Given that the pattern described by Kaufman and his colleagues (1954) occurs in many cases of father-daughter incest, it is by no means universal. As we have seen, there seem to be several distinct types of fathers who commit incest so there surely must be several patterns of family interaction that precede its occurrence. Most of the cases in which the mother has foisted her responsibilities on a daughter seem to have been of the "endogamic" variety, described previously. If the father were psychopathic or psychotic, quite a different pattern of dynamics might be observed, but case histories of this type, which examine the role of the mother, are lacking in the literature. It should be emphasized that the collusive type of mother who "sets up" the incest situation through role reversal and denial of sex is only the most studied type, and her well-documented existence in some incestuous families should not lead to the assumption that the mother *must* have played a "setup" role in every case of incest that is encountered in clinical practice.

Another consideration to bear in mind is that the role reversal of mother and daughter may be prevalent in many other kinds of disturbed families; we do not have evidence that the pattern is especially prevalent in incest families. Indeed, parts of the pattern are probably very common in nondisturbed families, especially the assumption of the "little-mother" role by the daughter. As we shall see, incest usually occurs with the oldest daughter who is present in the home, and it is very common in our society for the oldest daughter to be entrusted with household duties and the care of younger siblings. We would therefore expect to find a certain number of "little mothers" in a sample of incestuous daughters even if their roles had nothing to do with the genesis of incest. The "little-mother" role only becomes a symptom of family disturbance at the point where the real mother relinquishes her authority as female head of the family and takes actions that increase the probability of incest—most commonly, denial of sex to the husband and the provision of opportunities for incest to occur.

In the psychotherapy sample, none of the daughters suspected that she had been "set up" for incest by her mother even though the daughters were frequently hostile to their mothers and blamed them for various consequences of the incest, as will be discussed in the next chapter. The mothers who were actually seen with their daughters did not seem to have foisted undue responsibility on their daughters, and two of them seemed to be infantilizing their daughters rather than pushing them into an adult role. Nevertheless, four daughters reported that they had been given premature household responsibilities *and* that their mothers were very dependent on them; it is possible that these represent situations in which the daughter was "set up" for incest but that the daughter never gained awareness of what was happening. Typical of these cases was the following:

Sabrina described her mother as having been
a neurotic type of woman who had used frequent

illnesses to induce guilt in family members and manipulate them in an indirect way. Since her mother worked evenings, Sabrina was expected to be in charge of feeding and caring for three younger siblings and her father on a regular basis. Even after incest was revealed, her mother continued her evening work schedule and expressed little concern for what had happened. Many years later, Sabrina complained to her therapist that she felt she had never had mothering for herself but had been required to mother the rest of her family, including her mother.

The Daughter

We have already learned a certain amount about the incestuous daughter in our discussion of the father and mother. If she resembles other family members, her appearance may be a lure to incest. If she is playing the role of "little mother," she may be initiated into the role of "little wife." And, as with her mother, the more passive, dependent, or masochistic she is, the more likely it will be that a dominant father can succeed in establishing a sexual relationship with her if he is so inclined. A number of other attributes have been discussed in the literature and will be treated here insofar as they are traits that precede incest and may contribute to its occurrence. The issue of the daughter's "seductiveness" or willingness to enter the incestuous relationship will be raised in the next chapter.

Intelligence and School Performance. Part of the popular "Tobacco Road" stereotype of incest participants is that they are often of low intelligence. We have seen that the stereotype is only partially true for fathers, in that the endogamic-subcultural type tends to be of dull normal or marginal intelligence (Gebhard and others, 1965). The only study with a heavily rural sample to list the characteristics of daughters was Kubo (1959), and he reported that two out of fourteen daughters were "imbeciles" and several more were considered to be "feeble" intellectually. Neither Kubo nor the Gebhard group provide any evidence as to whether these fathers and daughters were duller than the norm within their own subcultures, so it may be that lower intelligence simply goes along with rural isolation and semitolerant attitudes toward incest and does not play any specific role in the causation of incest.

In primarily urban incest samples, low intelligence is usually present only in a small minority of daughters. Weinberg (1955) did not give a percentage of daughters who were considered dull but did observe that some feeble-minded daughters were very dependent on their fathers and had had such difficulty adjusting to the demands of life that they had retreated into their families and offered little resistance to their fathers. Gligor (1966) is the only American researcher to provide IQ test data for a large sample of daughters—a mean IQ score of 93 for the thirty-seven Caucasian daughters in the sample. Their performance as measured by school grades was also slightly below average, about 37 percent being classified as "poor" and only 17 percent as "good" students. Similar figures were given by Maisch (1972), who shows a distribution of scores on the German version of the Wechsler intelligence scale that is normal in every respect with the exception of having no scores that are extremely high or low. While about 31 percent of the daughters were rated "inadequate" in their scholastic performance, this percentage was typical of the schools that they attended, and Maisch concluded that the group of incestuous daughters was quite ordinary in this regard.

The overwhelming majority of the thirty-eight incestuous daughters in the psychotherapy sample were described as having average intelligence by their therapists, who included a rough estimate of intelligence in their intake reports on the basis of the patient's verbal behavior and reported educational achievement. Only two daughters (5 percent) impressed their therapists as being brighter than average. Three daughters (8 percent) were rated below average in intelligence: One was diagnosed "mild mental retardation"; another, "borderline defective"; and the third, "dull normal." In two of these cases, the therapist believed that the daughter's low intellectual level played a significant role in the incest situation. The mildly retarded daughter was described as being naive and very passive in her relationships with men and as being very dependent on her family for emotional and financial support even though she was in her mid twenties at the time of incest. The "borderline defective" daughter was also epileptic and had been infantilized by her parents, who believed her to be of even lower intelligence than the therapist's estimate. In her case, her father used her perceived dullness as a rationale for incest, stating that she had a woman's body with the brain of a small child and thus required careful sex education from him lest she get into sexual difficulties.

Sexual Attractiveness. An attractive daughter would seem to be at increased risk for incest, especially when her secondary sexual characteristics begin to develop. One sometimes pictures a "nymphet" type of girl who poses a temptation to her father and to other men as well. An early clinical study of incest and other adult-child sexual relationships (Bender and Blau, 1937) remarked that the children studied were unusually attractive, but subsequent authors have not mentioned the physical appearance of the daughter very frequently. Occasionally the daughter is described as being physically unattractive and therefore especially in need of physical affection from her family (Magal and Winnick, 1968; Woodbury and Schwartz, 1971). On balance, therefore, it seems that attractiveness plays a rather unimportant role in predisposing the daughter to incest; at least in the case of highly taboo sexual activity such as rape and incest, the personality of the male participant and the stresses acting on him at the moment seem far more important in determining the occurrence of the offense than any characteristic of his female partner.

As a rough measure of the attractiveness of incestuous daughters, therapist descriptions of girls who had recently had incestuous experience were examined. In nine cases, there was an intake report in which a brief description of the daughter's appearance was included, and in four of these reports she was specifically described as being attractive. In a random sample of intake reports on girls of a comparable age, 43 percent were described as attractive. The incestuous daughter is quite like the "typical adolescent" in her physical attractiveness.

Precocious development of secondary sexual characteristics has been mentioned as an occasional characteristic of the daughter that could serve to increase temptation for a predisposed father. A very young girl with obvious breast development can inspire sexual curiosity and approaches from males before she is mature enough to handle them, and in the case of her father she may interpret sexual overtures as being simply a new variety of parental affection. Since incestuous fathers frequently stress the physical maturity of a young daughter in explaining (or rationalizing) the incest offense (Gebhard and others, 1965), perhaps it is not unreasonable to expect to find many cases of early sexual development in a sample of incestuous daughters. There is some evidence presented by Maisch (1972) that the average age at menarche of incestuous daughters is earlier than for girls in the general population and that the onset of the incestuous relationship is closely linked with the early signs of sexual maturity. However, the difference from the general population was slight and most of the sample was probably well within the normal range for development. Similarly, the occurrence of early puberty was rare in the psychotherapy sample. In one case, the daughter reported that she had had to wear a "Size 34 C" bra when she was only nine years old and that several men, including her father and brother, had insisted on touching her breasts. In another, a stepfather described his daughter as being "very well developed for a ten-year-old," but his wife contradicted this description and considered her daughter to be quite typical of her age group.

A third way in which the sexual attractiveness of a young daughter could be enhanced is what has been called *pseudomaturity*. Even if she is not unusually pretty or prematurely voluptuous, a girl can seem to be a more appropriate sexual object if she behaves in a manner that strongly suggests that she is a mature woman, as she does when she takes on the role of "little mother" already discussed. Some authors have described such pseudomature girls as having a few ego functions grossly overdeveloped while others remain at an infantile level. Kaufman, Peck, and Tagiuri (1954) give as an example a case description of an eleven-year-old girl who was sent to a children's camp after incest was discovered in her family. Her behavior was so mature in some areas, such as caring for the younger children, that the camp counselors swiftly forgot her age and were assigning her the responsibilities of a sixteen-year-old. However, it soon became apparent that her maturity was only skin deep when she threw tantrums typical of a five-year-old on occasions when she was frustrated.

Pseudomature behavior was not observed in any of the girls who were seen for psychotherapy soon after the occurrence of incest, nor was it reported by their mothers. However, as related previously, several of the older women in psychotherapy had had adult responsibilities thrust on them in childhood, so it is possible that pseudomaturity was a factor in their incestuous situations in a way that is difficult to assess from a description given many years later.

Promiscuity and Delinquent Behavior. Weinberg (1955) noted that the daughter's preexisting sexual experience could influence a father who was predisposed to incest. Promiscuity in the daughter in some instances was sexually arousing to the father who engaged in fantasies about her sex life, and it served as the basis for rationalizing incestuous behavior on the grounds that the father was trying to "correct" the daughter by reducing her need for sexual contact with other men. The father could also cite the fact that his daughter was not a virgin as a mitigating circumstance and claim that the daughter was only trying to gain freedom from him to pursue a wayward life if she reported incest to authorities. As an illustration, Weinberg described a case in which father-daughter incest took place only after the daughter had run away from home with the intention of becoming a prostitute. On her return, the father insisted on having intercourse with her, ostensibly because he thought that sexual satisfaction would curb her willingness to have sexual relations with other men.

Although Weinberg (1955) cited promiscuity and submissiveness as characteristics of daughters that increased the probability of incest, he found that daughters were promiscuous before incest in only a small minority of cases, and this finding has been repeated by other researchers. Gligor (1966) defined adolescent promiscuity as the indiscriminate acting out of sexual impulses or sexual involvement with two or more males simultaneously, thus excluding long-term sexual relationships with boyfriends from her definition. Under this definition, only 4 percent of a sample of fifty-seven incestuous daughters who went through juvenile court proceedings were promiscuous before or during the period of father-daughter incest. Maisch (1972) also obtained his sample from court proceedings and found that 13 percent of the girls were known to have had "undesirable sexual relations," prior to incest. (It is not completely clear what sexual relations were "undesirable" in West Germany at the time of the study, but Maisch was probably referring to something akin to Gligor's definition of promiscuity.) Many of these girls gave other evidence of a developing delinquent orientation, such as frequent lying, truancy, running away, or habitual stealing.

Therapists of daughters in the psychotherapy sample were asked whether there had been sexual experience prior to the incest and whether the patient had ever been promiscuous. The judgment of promiscuity was made only if the girl or woman had reported having sex on a very casual basis or changing her sexual partner very frequently—say, every few weeks or months. Long-term "love" relationships thus did not qualify as promiscuity, no matter how much sex was involved. Under these criteria, there was only one case in which a therapist thought that a daughter had been promiscuous *prior* to the incestuous relationship. She had had a number of sexual relationships before the age of thirteen with both males and females, and her psychopathic stepfather then had intercourse with her "to save her from the girls." Her sexual behavior had both excited him and provided him with an excuse to engage in incest. In one other case, the father denied incest and accused his daughter of fabricating the charge so as to free herself from his strict supervision. According to him, she had had sexual relations with an uncle, a cousin, and numerous unrelated boyfriends; according to her, she had had sex with two or three boyfriends with whom she had lasting relationships, and the incestuous relations had begun long before that. The therapist believed not only that incest had actually occurred but also that the girl had had numerous sexual relationships that she was unwilling to reveal while court proceedings were imminent. In two other cases, the daughter had had sexual relations prior to an incestuous incident but was not thought to be promiscuous under the definition given earlier.

Maisch (1972) emphasized that promiscuity was only one aspect of a generally antisocial attitude toward life that was displayed by 25 percent of his court-referred sample before the occurrence of incest, and he presented illustrative case histories of girls who had been in trouble with one authority or another since earliest childhood. In such cases, it is easy to believe that the so-called victim of incest behaved in a provocative, aggressive manner toward the father or stepfather and may have also lacked any real feelings of relationship that would tend to make her resist incestuous approaches. In the psychotherapy sample, however, there were only two cases in which there was evidence for other kinds of antisocial behavior *prior* to incest. Again, the disparity between these findings and Maisch's illustrates the importance of the research setting in determining results in that a sample collected through courts or social agencies is likely to contain more individuals who are generally delinquent than is a sample obtained in a psychotherapy context. Daughters in the psychotherapy sample had to have health care coverage either through their place of employment or through a parent or spouse who belonged to a covered employee group. Thus the individual with a lifelong antisocial orientation was unlikely to be included in the clinic population from which the sample was drawn.

Previous Incestuous Experience. In discussing the role of promiscuity, we have omitted mention of the possibility that the daughter's prior sexual experience might have been with another family member. Since incest is a relatively rare occurrence, it seems extremely unlikely that such cases would occur very often just by chance. However, since incest is the product of a disturbed family that usually remains disturbed over a long time period and since the daughter at least sometimes encourages incest by her passivity or her sexually suggestive behavior, a combination of father-daughter and stepfather-daughter incest might be expected occasionally. Rhinehart (1961) has given a detailed case history of a young woman who had had sexual intercourse with her father for several years before moving in with her mother and stepfather at age eighteen. She then seduced her stepfather, and her therapist suspected that the seduction had been motivated by her unconscious wish for revenge against her mother, who had abandoned her as a child. Machotka, Pittman, and Flomenhaft (1967) have presented a similar case history of sequential father-daughter incest.

There were two cases in the psychotherapy sample in which a daughter was sexually approached by a stepfather some years after father-daughter incest had occurred. In one of these cases, the mother may have set up the daughter for another incest situation by marrying a man who was similar to her first husband in his insistence on playing the "patriarch" role and by allowing her daughter to dress in sexually suggestive clothing at an early age. No revenge motive was detected in this case. In the second case, it would seem that the daughter's disturbance about sexual relations with her father either brought about relations with her stepfather or caused her to imagine that sexual advances were made to her, as it was uncertain whether the stepfather actually approached her:

> Ida's mother and father were never married to each other; both of them married after she was born, and she was shuttled back and forth between their households during most of her childhood. Whenever she was staying with her father, he would enter her room in the middle of the night and fondle her genitals while she pretended to remain asleep. As time went on, she became increasingly frightened and disturbed by these experiences, and at age twelve she pleaded with her mother to care for her on a permanent basis. When she moved into her mother's house, she became very seclusive and phobic about having anyone else enter her room. For several months, she barricaded herself in her room every evening after dinner by pushing furniture up against the inside of the door

and refusing to leave the room even to accept
phone calls. Although her phobia subsided within a
year, she experienced intermittent periods of disturbance throughout her adolescence. At age fifteen, she made a suicide attempt by slashing at her
wrists and had several months of therapy with a
psychologist but refused to tell her about her father's incestuous behavior. During this time, she
accused her stepfather of entering her room at
night, pulling down the bed covers, and fondling
her breasts while she pretended to be asleep, but
the stepfather vehemently denied that any such incident had occurred and her mother believed him.
While Ida firmly believed that the stepfather had
made sexual advances, her incestuous background
and neurotic symptoms suggested the possibility
that she experienced dreamlike states in which incest was reexperienced with her stepfather.

Position in the Family. It is well established that the eldest daughter is more vulnerable to becoming a participant in
father-daughter incest. In Weinberg's (1955) large sample, 64
percent of the daughters were the eldest daughters in their families, and many more were the eldest daughter present in the
home at the time that incest began. Most of the remaining cases
were situations in which the father had attempted incest with
an older sister and then shifted his attention to a younger sister
when his first incest choice rejected him or left the home. Very
occasionally, a younger daughter had been chosen for incest because she was more promiscuous or more docile than an older
sister.

In thirty-two of the father-daughter incest cases in the
psychotherapy sample, the sex and birth order of siblings living
at home at the time of incest was known. In 31 percent of
cases, there was only one daughter at home, and thus the incestuous father had no choice of partners. In 34 percent of the
cases the daughter chosen for incest was the eldest of two or
more daughters living at home, and in 25 percent of the cases
she was a younger daughter. Over half of the cases involving

younger daughters were instances of the father's "moving on" from an incestuous relationship with an older daughter who was withdrawing from him even though she was still in the home, and in the remaining cases there were rather clear reasons why a younger daughter was singled out. For instance, one daughter was mentally dull and emotionally immature, while her older sister was an intelligent, assertive girl. The father justified incest on the grounds that the younger girl required special protection from predatory men outside the family, and it seemed obvious that her mental debility had made her more vulnerable to incestuous approaches than her sister would have been.

Selection of the eldest available daughter for incest would be expected on the basis of the role reversal between mother and daughter, since she would be in the most natural position for caring for the other siblings. If the "little-mother" role actually encourages incest, then the eldest daughter is much more at risk than younger daughters. However, an even more plausible explanation, which would probably apply to a larger number of father-daughter incest cases, is that the father is seldom a pedophile who would have an active sexual interest in prepubertal girls. If the father prefers adult, or at least adolescent, females as sexual partners but is desperate or uncontrolled enough to initiate sexual contact with a daughter, he would tend to choose the daughter who is most physically developed, because her secondary sexual characteristics would be arousing to him. He might also be able to rationalize that at least he is not breaking *two* taboos, since the prohibition against sex with children is almost as strong as the incest taboo.

The
Father-Daughter "Affair"

■ ■ ■ ■ ■ ■ ■ ■ ■ ■ ■ ■ ■ ■ ■ ■

The three main characters in the plot of father-daughter incest have been described at some length in the previous chapter in order to maximize the reader's understanding of the actual occurrence of incest. Most incest situations have been brewing for many years before an overt act takes place. The father's personality disturbance generally precedes incest and may in fact extend back to his childhood; the mother's overt encouragement of incest or her failure to restrain the father is often rooted in her relationship with her own mother; and the daughter's preexisting characteristics can affect both her vulnerability to being sexually approached and her reaction when the incest attempt occurs. No single personality disturbance or pattern of family dynamics is *the* cause of father-daughter incest, but some commonalities have emerged over many studies of incest in different research settings and in different societies. Each incest situation, like each human being, is absolutely unique in its details and yet can be validly seen as

140

representative of types of incest situations that have no doubt been recurring almost universally since the inception of the taboo.

A composite description of the emergent findings on incest participants will serve as a review, although grossly oversimplified, of their characteristics. At center stage stand the father and daughter. He is usually quite an average sort of man, neither very bright nor mentally defective, sometimes chronically unemployed but frequently having a run-of-the-mill work record. However, he often bears the scars of a childhood in which he was deserted or mistreated by his own father and thus formed a distorted concept of family life, particularly of the father's role in it. As an adult, he is seldom psychotic, but may be seen as a psychopathic personality or, more commonly, as a paranoid personality disorder. Rarely a pedophile, he is sometimes a man with a strong interest in sexual activity, and very frequently his tendency to abuse alcohol weakens his self-control and enables him to use his dominant, sometimes "patriarchal" position in the family to intimidate his wife and children. His daughter is also seldom psychotic or mentally defective; she may be a docile, obedient girl who would not oppose her father's will, or, in a minority of cases, she may be sexually promiscuous in a way that arouses and tempts her father. She may also seem to be mature beyond her years because of the housekeeping and childcare responsibilities that she has assumed and occasionally because she is an "early developer." Her mother, although not at center stage, often plays a role by allowing or even covertly fostering the incestuous relationship. The mother has sometimes withdrawn from her role as female head of the household and as her husband's sexual partner and depended on her eldest daughter to substitute for her. Occasionally she is sexually promiscuous, but much more often she is a passive, dependent, "beaten down" wife who is not capable of protecting her children from the abuse of her domineering husband. Sometimes, also, her "failure" to protect her daughter is simply the result of her absence from the family due to her desertion, serious illness, or death. There are usually other siblings, neighbors, and members of the extended family waiting in the

wings to participate in the incest drama, but they are too variable to be characterized adequately in a composite description
of this type.

In this chapter, we will concentrate on sketching the sequence of events in the actual occurrence of father-daughter
incest, from the situation of the family just before the initiation
of incest through the immediate aftereffects of disclosure. Various aspects of the incest incident, such as seductive behavior of
the daughter, kinds of sexual activities, and reaction of the
mother, will be discussed more or less in chronological order, as
they would occur in a "typical" case of incest.

Conditions in the Home

Early studies of incest used court and prison settings to
obtain case samples and found, not surprisingly, that incest participants were usually of the lowest socioeconomic class and
that their housing conditions were very poor. Large families
were often found to be occupying a small number of rooms and
beds, requiring parents to sleep with children and opposite sex
siblings with each other. The factor of overcrowded housing was
therefore thought to be important in enhancing temptation and
providing the opportunity for incest. Weinberg (1955) devoted
an entire chapter to this theory and gave statistics on persons
per room in his large urban sample. While the majority of incest
participants did live in overcrowded homes, at least 36 percent
of the sample lived in conditions above the standard of one person per room, and a close examination of the families who were
overcrowded revealed that alternative sleeping arrangements
were possible in almost all cases in which fathers and daughters
were "forced" to sleep together. It appeared to Weinberg that
these fathers were predisposed to incest and used overcrowding
as an excuse to sleep with their daughters. In some cases, the
crowded home may have contributed to incest by reducing the
sexual privacy of the family, but Weinberg concluded that in
general the interpersonal relationships within the family were
much more important than the physical setting in causing incest.

Estimates of persons per room were not obtained for the

psychotherapy sample, but questions about the manner in which incest began revealed only one case in which sleeping arrangements played a role in the initial occurrence of incest. A teen-age daughter reported that she slept on a king-sized water bed with her mother, stepfather, a younger half-sister, and a toy poodle, and that her stepfather molested her on occasions when she rolled over her mother, who usually slept between them. This bizarre sleeping arrangement occurred in a middle-class family in which the children had their own bedrooms, so the overcrowded bed was created for reasons other than necessity. The therapist suspected that the resultant incest accusation was used by the mother and daughter as grounds for expelling the stepfather from the home, as they had wished to do for some time. The arrangement also provided the mother with an excuse to refuse sex to her husband, whom she considered physically repulsive.

Studies of incest done in court and prison settings have given the impression that most incestuous families live in extreme poverty and have reinforced the cultural stereotype of incest as an event that occurs only in families like those of the Jukes and the Kallikaks. A few studies (Weiner, 1962; Lustig and others, 1966) have upset this notion by obtaining samples of middle-class incestuous families, and recent reviewers (Weiner, 1964; Henderson, 1972) have concluded that most studies obtain results that simply mirror the particular population from which the sample was drawn. While one might expect incest to be somewhat more common in lower-class families due to the increased incidence of alcoholism, social isolation, and personal disturbance that is often associated with poverty, the association between incest and poverty is not as strong and absolute as most people would believe. As we have already observed in Chapter Three, the psychotherapy sample of incest cases appeared to be a cross section of the clinic population with regard to income, education, and employment. Patients' reports on the economic standing of their families of origin also seldom revealed impoverished families, with the exception of Mexican-American patients, who had often been raised in very large families in settings of rural poverty.

Any condition that leaves the father and daughter alone

together for long time periods provides the opportunity for incest in predisposed individuals. In the previous chapter, we discussed the frequency with which the mother is deceased, incapacitated by serious illness, or away from the home to pursue her extramarital affairs, noting that the father is sometimes unemployed while his wife works to support the family. A frequent finding (at least five cases in the psychotherapy sample) has also been that the father and mother both work and have radically different work schedules. Numerous other circumstances have been noted. For instance, in rural areas the father and daughter sometimes find themselves together in an isolated work place (Riemer, 1940). The circumstances may be truly accidental, or they may be planned by the father, who contrives to send other family members away under various pretexts or to take the daughter on vacation trips alone.

Finally, the recent occurrence of stressful events in the family has often been associated with the onset of incest. Riemer (1940) emphasized that almost all of the fifty-eight cases that he studied revealed some serious disruption of the family's well-being in the last year or two before incest began. Economic crises, diseases or accidents, and loss of employment because of alcoholism were often the stressful events. Weinberg (1955) asserted that all of the fathers in his sample had gone through a period of restlessness and tension just prior to resorting to incest. Injuries, diseases, financial setbacks, and other kinds of personal losses or conflicts had often left the father in a state of anxiety and depression that he exacerbated by increasing his alcohol consumption, and his distress was accompanied by increasingly impulsive behavior and often by intensification of his sexual desires.

Having now surveyed a large number of personal characteristics and situational factors that tend to be associated with the onset of father-daughter incest, it is appropriate to emphasize that none of these factors is specific to incest. Even in situations where all of the factors coexist, incest is probably a rare occurrence. As Cormier, Kennedy, and Sangowicz (1962) carefully point out, many men are subjected to all of these circumstances and yet do not give in to temptation but keep their incestuous feelings repressed, perhaps displacing them to other women in extramarital affairs or combatting them by being overly severe with their daughters. Gebhard and others (1965, p. 227) make much the same point in an interesting way: "The 'normal,' or at least the 'nonincestuous' male, when fed up with his life and unhappy marital state, seeks and usually obtains relief from stress in a number of ways that society deplores yet tolerates: He gets drunk; he discharges his aggression in barroom or party brawls; he finds heterosexual gratification either from prostitutes, pickups, or a more stable affair or with a mistress. The incest offender seems unable to utilize these time-honored methods effectively."

Initiation of Incest

In the vast majority of father-daughter incest cases, the first move is made by the father. (Here we are discussing active initiation—seductive behavior on the part of the daughter is another issue and will be discussed later.) In large samples collected through courts or public agencies (for example, Riemer, 1940; Weinberg, 1955), the father is nearly always described as taking the initiative, even in cases where the daughter was thought to have been "seductive." Maisch (1972) repeated this finding and described two exceptions to this rule. In both of these cases, a teen-age daughter had fallen in love with a stepfather and actively provoked the sexual activity in the same manner as she would approach a boy of her own age. Yet Gligor (1966) found no cases in which the daughter directly initiated sexual activity in a court-collected sample of fifty-seven father-daughter incest cases (no stepfathers included).

In clinical studies of incest, a few daughter-initiated cases have been reported, but they stand out as the exceptions. Magal and Winnick (1968) have described a family in which the father was so violently alcoholic that he had been repeatedly institutionalized for beating his wife and children. One of his daughters had assumed the "little-mother" role and took responsibility for protecting the rest of the family by calming him down when he was drunk. By talking kindly to him, she would persuade him to go to bed, and she gradually began to lie down with him, kiss him, and introduce genital fondling as a continuation of her efforts to soothe him, at least in the beginning. Another case of daughter-initiated incest has been reported by Machotka, Pittman, and Flomenhaft (1967). During an acute psychotic episode, the eighteen-year-old daughter got into bed with both of her parents in a childlike way and then requested that her father have intercourse with her "in order to help her." The father, a bit befuddled but wanting to help, might have complied had his wife not intervened and prevented incest. Again, such cases are extremely unusual, even in clinical samples, so it comes as no surprise that none of the daughters in the psychotherapy sample was thought to have overtly initiated incest. Of course, it is possible that some daughters were actively provocative at the time of incest and later repressed their part in the incest affair or consciously withheld such information from the therapist. If so, it seems rather incredible that none of these women attained insight into their active role during the course of psychotherapy, which sometimes lasted for years.

The most common way in which the father initiates sexual activity is to begin genital petting, while lying in bed with the daughter, which may or may not progress to intercourse. Riemer (1940) reported that about 30 percent of his cases began when the father and daughter happened to be in bed with each other. More recently, Maisch (1972) found that about 20 percent of his sample in West Germany had been sharing the same bed just prior to the onset of incest, although other sleeping arrangements were possible in most instances. We have already mentioned that only one case in the psychotherapy sample involved a father and daughter sharing the same bed prior to incest, but in 43 percent of the cases in which the manner of initiation was known the father had entered his daughter's bed by stealth while he believed her to be asleep. Weinberg (1955) also found such approaches to be common, although he gave no percentage. One suspects that living accommodations in the United States are generally less crowded than in Europe and that American fathers cannot take advantage of overcrowding as an excuse to sleep with daughters. However, in American homes an adolescent daughter very frequently has a room of her own, where incest can be kept from the eyes of the mother and other siblings.

The typical report in the psychotherapy sample was to the effect that the daughter woke up to find her father in bed with her, fondling her breasts or genital area. She felt frightened and confused and most often pretended to remain asleep and hoped that her father would go away. One case will illustrate this common scenario:

> Deanna's stepfather was her mother's third husband with a drinking problem. The divorce from Deanna's father had taken place shortly after her conception, and she had been told that the stepfather was really her biological parent. When she was thirteen, she awoke one night to find her stepfather in bed with her, and he was petting her genital area. It seemed so unbelievable to her that several seconds elapsed before she was certain that the sexual activity was not a realistic dream. At that point, she experienced a conflict between directly confronting him and allowing the activity to continue, and confrontation seemed very difficult both because she believed him to be drunk and unpredictable in his behavior and because she feared the effects that such a confrontation might have on her family. She therefore pretended to be asleep for another minute and then gave very obvious signs of beginning to wake up, whereupon he left the room. She locked her door after this single incident, and no further attempts were made, although she was bothered from time to time by what she perceived as a smirk on her stepfather's face when he looked at her.

Once incest has been initiated in this manner, the father may continue to make sexual approaches in other settings, or the stealthy, middle-of-the-night approach may be repeated over a long period of time, with the daughter continuing to pretend to be asleep so that she will not have to confront the reality of the situation. One daughter who had frequently experienced these approaches over a period of years told her therapist that she wanted the activity to stop but was afraid that she would be sent to an orphanage if she made her father angry, since she had no mother or other relatives to live with.

Incest rarely begins with an actual rape. In court-collected samples, we would expect the incidence of rape to be maximized, because the use of force would surely increase the chances of formal charges being brought against the father. Szabo (1962) reported that 42 percent of his sample of father-daughter cases had begun "with violence." However, the typical finding is that physical violence occurs in only a small minority of cases. For example, Maisch (1972) found that 6 percent of his cases began with rape, Gebhard and others (1965) discovered only two instances of "major physical force" in 147 cases of father-daughter incest, and Weinberg (1955) gave a few examples of daughters who were beaten into submission but no statistics on how frequently major or minor force was involved in the cases in his sample. In the psychotherapy sample, six daughters used the word *rape* in describing their sexual experiences with their fathers, but in four of these cases the therapist did not think "rape" was the most accurate description of what had occurred. When further details about the incestuous activities were elicited, it appeared that "rape" usually meant that the father had insisted on the sexual relations and not that direct physical force had been used. In one of the true cases of incest rape, the father was psychotic and suicidal at the time of the offense, and the rape was part of a desperate outburst of anger and aggression directed toward his family.

Threats or duress are much more common than physical force but still do not apply to the majority of incest cases. The daughter is often threatened to prevent her from revealing the incestuous relationship after it has begun, but threats are seldom necessary at the beginning. Gebhard and others (1965) found that only about 15 percent of their sample of imprisoned fathers had specifically threatened their daughters in order to initiate sexual activity and that there was a clear relationship between duress and the kind of sexual activity sought. The offender who wanted oral-genital relations issued threats to the daughter in over one third of the cases, and threats were also relatively common when intercourse was attempted with a young child. The offender who began the relationship with genital fondling very seldom had to use force or threats. In the psychotherapy sample, specific threats were also rare, except for later attempts to prevent the daughter from telling anyone. One father who had been practicing genital manipulation with his daughter for some time threatened to get rid of her English sheep dog if she did not submit to his attempts at intercourse. Many more daughters, however, reported that they had *felt* threatened even though the father said nothing about the consequences of refusing to cooperate.

The lack of force or specific threats in father-daughter incest should not lead to the conclusion that the daughter is actively cooperating in the activity. On the contrary, the daughter is generally passive because of her perception of the father's authority and because of all of her past experience with failures to obey him. Gebhard and others (1965) found it impossible to assess the extent of the daughter's willingness because the authoritarian position of the father in the family made it extremely difficult to distinguish between real willingness and submission to authority. As we have already emphasized, the incestuous father is most likely to be a man who is very dominant within the family and who may even be tyrannical enough to inspire real fear in his wife and children. A girl who is accustomed to obeying such a father is most likely to go along passively with his demands for sexual activity, for physical resistance is unthinkable to her and leaving the home is a very frightening prospect. Sometimes, as was reported by many daughters in the psychotherapy sample, they were afraid to offer any resistance because of an implied threat to themselves. Occasionally, they saw themselves as protecting other family members from the father, as in a case reported by Yorukoglu and Kemph (1966) wherein the father got drunk and physically abusive with the mother and younger brother whenever his daughter would try to stop his progressively more demanding sexual advances to her. The authoritarian father-passive daughter combination is the most common incest initiation pattern when the daughter is very young; an adolescent daughter is more likely to rebel and to see leaving the home as a real alternative to submitting to incest.

Thus far we have spoken only of the negative incentives provided by the father. In many instances, he attempts to obtain his daughter's cooperation by rewarding her in various ways. Cormier, Kennedy, and Sangowicz (1962) remarked that the incestuous father often behaves as if he were an adolescent boy making his first clumsy attempts at courtship behavior in relation to his daughter, giving her presents of money and clothing, guarding her jealously from the approaches of other men, and yet invoking his position as the all-powerful father at the same time. Many fathers were genuinely more loving and attentive toward the incestuous daughter than toward their other children and thus had even more leverage in inducing her cooperation. Weinberg (1955) also noted that the daughter who allowed or encouraged sexual advances sometimes became her father's favored child and enjoyed privileges that were denied to the rest of the family, whereas daughters who resisted incest were often rejected and repudiated by their fathers. In the psychotherapy sample, there were three cases in which it was known that the father had courted the daughter with special attention, but only one case in which the daughter received money or gifts specifically for performance of a sexual act. There was also one report of non-specific material rewards for incest:

> Vanessa was approached by her stepfather on only one occasion, while she was in bed pretending to sleep. She was very afraid of him, both because he frequently beat the children and because his stepchildren knew that he was having intercourse with at least two of his natural daughters who lived with him. These daughters were perceived by the other children as receiving higher-quality food, better clothes, and more privileges than the rest, although they were restricted to the home and not allowed to date boys their own age.

There are numerous other ways in which the incestuous father makes his approach. Sometimes the normal expressions of physical affection between father and daughter grow more intense and sexual in nature over a long period of time, and the young child then perceives the sexual activities as merely another kind of parental affection, at least until she begins to wonder why she is supposed to keep it a secret. Sometimes the sexual activity begins abruptly, but the father gives the child some sort of explanation for it that induces cooperation. A very young child can believe that sexual activity is a new kind of game and may be easily deceived, especially if her mother provides no sex education and she is isolated from her peers. One woman in the psychotherapy sample recalled that when she was five years old she thought that her father was urinating on her, and she did not like getting wet but had no clear idea of the sexual significance of ejaculation.

A somewhat older daughter can be persuaded that sex with her father is proper for any of a number of reasons. Some daughters are told that it is their duty to replace their mother because she has died or left the family or been hospitalized for an illness. Some daughters are given a "sex education" rationale, which is the most common single deceptive technique reported in the literature. Karpman (1954) has presented a very thorough, first-person account of a daughter who was introduced to sexual activity through a graded series of "lessons." Only one case in the psychotherapy sample had involved an outspoken pretext of sex education accompanied by fatherly warnings about predatory men outside the family. In this case, already mentioned briefly, the father used the daughter's borderline intelligence as an excuse for initiating sexual activities, telling her that she required special instruction in order to function well sexually. However, although such pretexts may serve the purpose of quieting the daughter's objections at the beginning, she is seldom convinced of the rectitude of her father's behavior for very long because she gets very different messages about sexual behavior from her peer group and from other family members.

Kinds of Sexual Activity

Some studies, notably Weinberg's (1955), have set up research definitions of incest that have insisted that intercourse between father and daughter be involved in order to include a case in the sample. When all types of sexual contact are included in the definition, a study's findings about incest tend to be slightly different because incest consisting only of genital manipulation has distinctly different characteristics from incest involving genital intercourse. Daughters who experience only genital manipulation tend to be younger. Gebhard and others (1965) found that only 9 percent of men imprisoned for incest with daughters under twelve years of age had performed genital intercourse as part of the incest offense; when the daughter was between twelve and sixteen, the comparable figure was 72 percent; and when the daughter was sixteen or older, it was 91 percent. Maisch (1972) also presented detailed evidence that the incidence of intercourse with the daughter rises sharply after the twelfth birthday and tends to coincide with the age at which the girl is developing secondary sexual characteristics. It appears that the difficulty of attempting intercourse with a prepubertal child as well as the protests that such an attempt might elicit from an otherwise acquiescent partner serve as deterrents to intercourse in lieu of the father's self-control. If he insists on having intercourse, the father must either introduce it very gradually or resort to force or severe threats.

A similar pattern of sexual activity was found in the psychotherapy sample. In cases where the sexual activities were clearly reported by the daughter, there were five daughters under twelve at the time of incest who had had sexual intercourse with their fathers, and two of these cases involved physical force. Seven of the daughters over twelve at the beginning of incest had had sexual intercourse with their fathers, and none of these cases involved physical force. These figures tend to confirm the difficulty of effecting genital intercourse with prepubertal girls but do not adequately convey the psychological trauma that such attempts can entail. One woman used terms like "really revolting," "disgusting," and "unbelievable" to describe her father's attempts at intercourse. Two other women (not included in the figures just given) thought that intercourse had taken place but could not remember that part of the incest incident, although they could recall many other details of their family circumstances and of the father's approach and initiation of sexual activities. One of these patients, now in her forties, had repressed the memory of the incestuous relationship for over thirty years; when the memory became conscious, there was still a "blank" following the scene in which her stepfather fondled her genitals and got on top of her, but she "supposed" that intercourse had then occurred.

In the majority of incestuous relationships with daughters under the age of twelve, the father was content with simple genital fondling or oral-genital relations. Gebhard and others (1965), who specifically asked imprisoned fathers about their sexual techniques, found that 39 percent had oral-genital relations with daughters under twelve, and we might suppose that these techniques were used as a substitute for intercourse in this young age group. However, Gebhard and others also report that these men had tried oral-genital techniques with their wives much more frequently than had other prisoners or their non-criminal control group, so it appears that these fathers may have been displaying a generalized willingness to engage in taboo sexual behavior, including incest. A few other reports tend to confirm the father's emphasis on "deviant" techniques. Weiner (1962) noted that two of the five fathers in his clinical sample were intensely interested in sex and emphasized oral-genital techniques. Gligor (1966) defined "deviant sex activity" as oral-genital relations, anal intercourse, or sexual activity with two or more partners simultaneously and found that 20 percent of a court-collected sample of white incestuous daughters had engaged in such activities with their fathers. This percentage was significantly greater than the percentage of cases of deviant sexual activities in a control group of sexually acting-out girls. In comparable groups of black girls, no deviant sexual activities were reported, so it appears that an emphasis on such activities is conditioned by subculture as well as by the personality characteristics of the incestuous father.

Relatively few of the patients in the psychotherapy sample reported that oral-genital relations had occurred in the context of their incestuous situations. Only 22 percent of the cases in which the sexual activities were described involved such relations. Although this percentage is lower than the 39 percent found by Gebhard and others (1965), it confirms their finding that these techniques are especially common when the daughter is under twelve, since all of the daughters involved in oral-genital relations were under twelve when the incest began. It is also probable that many more cases actually involved oral-genital relations that were not reported to the therapist, since this behavior seems to inspire more sex guilt than does genital intercourse. Patients seldom talked about it spontaneously. One woman reported it indirectly by saying that "my father did *everything* except for penetration." In another case, the girl was specifically asked about it by law enforcement officers in connection with a formal charge of incest. In yet another case, the daughter was psychotic at the time that the therapist asked her about the incest incident, and one would expect her ego defenses to be low. Whatever the reason, female children tend to view such activities with such strong aversion that force or threats are often required to secure their participation (Gebhard and others, 1965), and thus we might expect that psychotherapy patients would be especially likely to repress or distort their memories of such incidents.

Rationalizations of Incest

Few men are so lacking in conscience that they feel no guilt during and after an incest affair. Especially when incest is with a natural daughter who is still a child, the father is well aware of the intensity of the taboo he has broken and attempts to assuage his guilt by concocting reasonable-sounding explanations for his behavior. These rationalizations may be given to the daughter in order to enlist her cooperation in the sexual activity; they may also be revealed to the wife or to various societal agents after disclosure of an incest affair, in an attempt to minimize the consequences. Many years ago, Riemer (1940) discussed the rationalizations used by men in his rural Swedish sample. While some fathers accepted their culpability, many more attempted to defend their behavior with statements that revealed "an absurd mixture of surviving values of family solidarity and lack of responsibility." Some used the "keep-it-in-the-family" rationale, maintaining that incest was at least preferable to adultery. Occasionally, a father said he believed that the daughter would get pregnant very soon anyway so she might as well have his child since he would have to support it. At times, incest was justified as being some kind of vague protest against an unjust society or as being compelled by romantic love. And, finally, some of these fathers and their families subscribed to the folk belief that incest would cure the father's venereal disease.

As times have changed, so have the rationalizations used by the incestuous father. Weinberg (1955) found an occasional case in which the "curative" value of incest was cited, especially by recent immigrants from Europe, and he also found incest to be justified by fathers on grounds of fulfilling the sexual desires of an already promiscuous daughter so that she would not have to seek sex outside the family and of providing a virtuous daughter with an essential "sex education." (Probably sex education was not viewed in a positive light in Riemer's rural Sweden and thus could not be used by his fathers to rationalize incest.) Cormier, Kennedy, and Sangowicz (1962) cited the expressed belief of some fathers that their wives' frigidity explained and excused their incestuous behavior. Weiner (1962) commented that all of the five incestuous fathers whom he studied had an unusual ability to rationalize the incest, usually by insisting that the daughter must learn the facts of life and that it is a good father's *duty* to teach her. One father added that his sex education program for his daughter would prevent her from becoming frigid, like his wife, when she grew up. Another said he thought that sexual relations would improve the relationship between himself and his daughter and make her less hostile toward him! Most recently, Gebhard and others (1965) have noted that imprisoned incest offenders assuaged their intense guilt feelings by use of the sex education rationale and by pointing out that "things could have been worse" had they not avoided the use of force or of certain sexual techniques. They also tended to attribute a very active, seductive role to the daughter and to emphasize her physical maturity.

The sex education premise was explicitly invoked by only one father in the psychotherapy sample, but there may well have been many more fathers who, after the fact of incest, used this method of rationalization without revealing it to their daughters. One father, who had evidently read up on the subject, cited evidence from the literature that incest is not as rare as commonly thought as partial justification for his own incestuous behavior. He also explained that his ten-year-old stepdaughter was tall and well developed for her age and had acted in a seductive manner. There was also a case in which the father, who was very concerned about his daughter's psychological problems, came for an interview with her therapist and fully admitted the incest without attempting to justify it; he confessed that he had been personally "messed up" and was drinking too heavily at the time of incest. In all of these cases, the father was of the "endogamic" or "situational" variety, and guilt was a prominent feature in these cases. In the few cases where the father was considered psychopathic, there was little or no guilt, and the rationales given for incest seemed more casual. In a case already mentioned, the father expressed no guilt or misgivings about relations with his twelve-year-old stepdaughter and said that he began the relationship to save her from becoming a lesbian. A second father of the psychopathic variety simply stated that he had a tendency to be rough on his children and to lose his temper, just as his father had before him—he seemed to be shrugging off responsibility for incest on genetic grounds!

The Daughter's Reaction

The subject of the daughter's reaction has already been given partial coverage in our discussion of the manner in which incest is initiated. Here we shall focus more specifically on the daughter, the degree of resistance or acceptance that she displays, and the possibility of her obtaining sexual gratification from the incest affair.

Most large sample studies have given the overall impression that the daughter is usually resistant, at least in a passive manner, although active participation occurs in an unspecified minority of cases. Riemer (1940, p. 575) described the average daughter as remaining passive because "she is too afraid of the father to scream or to ask her mother for protection." Weinberg (1955, p. 53) generalized that the daughter, "having been coerced in the incest act . . . was usually the passive participant." Although stating that "the daughter was intimidated and kept silent about the affair until desperate" (p. 123), Weinberg did allude to finding some cases in which daughters actively reciprocated their fathers' sexual feelings and participated willingly in the sexual activities. Szabo (1962) also concluded that passive resistance was the most common reaction of the daughter in a large, court-collected sample.

Some of the more recent studies have set up several categories of responses and have given the percentage of daughters in each. In cases where an opinion was given, Gebhard and others (1965) noted the court's opinion on the role of the daughter. Daughters in their three age categories were combined; 45 percent were thought to have been either encouraging or passive during the affair, while 55 percent had actively resisted the father's attentions. There was a definite tendency for the older daughters to have been more cooperative in incest, probably because girls over sixteen who do resist can often resist so effectively that the incest affair never goes beyond an unsuccessful attempt. A girl in late adolescence is less economically helpless and thus has a realistic option of leaving the home if sexual advances are made. Gligor (1966) also has given us data on the reactions of daughters recorded in court records of incest cases. In her sample, 12 percent of the daughters were believed to have participated in a willful or encouraging manner, 32 percent were passive and displayed no resistance, 35 percent were passive out of fear of punishment by the father but definitely attempted to avoid sexual activity with him, and 21 percent overtly resisted the father and were defiant in the face of his sexual overtures. Maisch (1972) similarly gave percentages of reactions in a sample of court-collected cases. While only 6 percent of the cases involved unequivocal cooperation on the daughter's part, there were even fewer cases in which the daughter showed active resistance. In the overwhelming majority of cases, the daughter was described as passive at the beginning of the incest affair.

In twenty-seven cases in the psychotherapy sample, the daughter provided enough information about the onset of incest to permit assignment to categories. In five (19 percent) of these cases, the daughter physically resisted the incestuous advances, and two of these daughters fought so furiously that their fathers discontinued their attempts at incest. In only one case was the daughter known to have been actively cooperative, and in all the remaining cases (77 percent) the daughter was more or less passive. The word *passive* describes a large variety of incest situations and reactions to them. Most passive of all was the strategy of daughters who pretended to be asleep when they were approached in their beds during the night. Very young children may also be passive in that they at first construe sexual activity to be a game. A woman who recalled sex play with her father between the ages of five and seven had offered no resistance to the "new game," although she felt vaguely "bothered" by it. An eight-year-old girl was "terrified" of her father when he played with her in a drunken stupor, but she offered no overt resistance. Older girls were also afraid to oppose their fathers openly and were threatened when they showed signs of resistance. In one case, a girl had passively submitted to the sexual demands of her father for over two years, fearing an abusive outburst if she resisted because of his generally self-centered and violent behavior within the family. When she was fifteen, the "enormity of the incest situation dawned," and she mustered the courage to tell her father that their relations must stop, whereupon he beat and assaulted her. Another adolescent girl was not physically threatened, but her father attempted to cut off all her social contacts with boys and girls her age and allowed her to leave the house only after submitting to sexual relations with him.

It is well established, then, that the majority of daughters are passive at the beginning of the incest affair and often remain passive as the affair continues over a period of years. In some cases, this passivity may mean that the child is receiving sexual

gratification from the father. There has been a tendency for researchers (for example, Weiner, 1962; Weiss and others, 1955)
to infer that such gratification must have been obtained because
the child allowed the relationship to continue; however, such
inferences ignore the subjective realities of the daughter's situation within the family. To truly understand the passivity of the
daughter, one needs to imagine the situation as it is perceived
through the eyes of a child. Especially in a paternalistic family,
the daughter has been taught to obey her father in all situations,
to anticipate punishment for any show of defiance, and to believe that what her father does is unquestionably in her best
interests. As we have already mentioned, the father may actually convince the daughter that it is his duty to teach her about
sexual relations or her duty to provide satisfaction in the absence of her mother. But even if she knows that incest is socially reprehensible, the real and implied threats in the situation are
often sufficient to secure her passive cooperation in the absence
of any reasonable alternatives. It must be remembered that leaving the home is a tremendously frightening alternative for most
children and young adolescents. Telling the mother is usually a
reasonable alternative, but it may not be so reasonable if the
father has issued specific threats about the consequences of
doing so. And, even if the mother is told, her reaction is far
from predictable, as will be discussed hereafter.

There are nonsexual kinds of gratification in an incest affair that may also contribute to the daughter's passivity. Material rewards and "favored-child" status have already been noted.
Some clinical researchers (for example, Rhinehart, 1961) have
observed that sexual activity may be pleasurable for the daughter because it satisfies pregenital needs to be held and cuddled
in a child who has often been severely deprived of physical
affection. Finally, the daughter often loves her father as a
parent despite his lapses in self-control and may be extremely
reluctant to betray him to others in order to end the relationship. The presence of some or all of these positive, nonsexual
gratifications creates an ambivalence that makes it even more
difficult for the daughter to actively resist the initiation of incest or to take steps to end it.

The report of truly sexual pleasure on the part of the

daughter in father-daughter incest has been rare in the literature. Rascovsky and Rascovsky (1950) described at some length
a case in which a daughter in her twenties at the time of the
affair with her father relished the sexual relationship. Weinberg
(1955), Maisch (1972), and other researchers with large samples
have discovered sexual motives in daughter participants in a
small minority of cases, especially when the father was actually
the girl's stepfather. Similarly, in the psychotherapy sample
there was only one case in which the daughter definitely derived
sexual satisfaction from the relationship, and this case seemed
unusual in that it involved a sixteen-year-old daughter and a
thirty-year-old stepfather. While the daughter reported that she
had resisted the sexual advances when she was twelve years old,
she had come to enjoy sex with the stepfather over the next
four years to the extent that the family's therapist thought she
"craved" it. The therapist attributed her pleasure at least partly
to the circumstance that the stepfather was a very handsome,
young-looking man while the daughter was too homely to attract the attention of her age peers. Also, both of them were
dependent on the mother for financial and emotional support,
so that their relationship was more like that of brother and sister than of father and daughter.

The psychotherapy sample also contained two cases in
which the inconsistent behavior of the daughter gave the therapist cause to wonder what kinds of unacknowledged "payoffs"
the daughter might be getting from incest. In both cases, the
daughters were fifteen or sixteen when seen in therapy, and
they presented psychotic symptom pictures. Both appeared at
first to be extremely hostile toward their natural fathers, with
whom they had had intercourse over a period of several years.
One of them referred to sexual intercourse as "that terrible
thing" and said she thought that her father had singled her out
for incest because she was "bad." The other spewed out obscene language when asked about her feelings toward her father
and threatened to kill him if he dared to touch her again. Yet
independent sources of information indicated that both of these
young women had actually insisted on living with their fathers
when alternative arrangements were possible. One had been

placed in a series of foster homes by a child protection agency, but she continually ran away and went back to her father's home. In cases such as these, one is certainly justified in inferring a deep-rooted ambivalence—the openly expressed negative feelings are perfectly real, but they may be underlaid by unconscious needs for the father as a parent or as a sexual companion.

There were also cases in which the daughter found continued sexual relations with her father distasteful but was reluctant to disclose the relationship or to leave the home because she loved her father and was protective of him. These girls were not psychotic. The mother was usually either out of the home or so cold and rejecting that the child had to rely on the father for parental affection. While they remembered the incest affair as a generally negative experience, they had compassion for the father and were able to understand and partially excuse his behavior as an expression of his personal unhappiness. One of these daughters had told a social worker about the incest when she was twelve years old and then felt extremely guilty when her father was jailed for child molestation. Again, it is not necessary to infer that the child likes incest in cases of this sort —only that she had positive feelings for her father in addition to the negative feelings that led to the disclosure of incest.

The Issue of Seductiveness

In the crime of incest, as well as in the crime of rape, the female participant was formerly thought to be a helpless victim, a totally innocent object of a deranged or immoral man's lust. With the increasing recognition of sexual feelings in women and children and development of the concept of "victim proneness" in criminology, the pendulum has swung very far in the other direction. The attitude of many mental health professionals and law enforcement personnel may now be stated succinctly (if crudely) as "She probably asked for it!" The recent incest literature reflects and perpetuates this kind of skepticism. Some researchers have emphasized the culpability of child participants. An example would be Lukianowicz (1972, p. 309), who described two cases of child rape and then went on to state that

"all other children, male and female, were far from being innocent victims; on the contrary, they were willing partners and
often provocative seductresses." In the 1975 edition of the
Comprehensive Textbook of Psychiatry, Henderson (pp. 1533,
1536) informs mental health professionals that "In father-
daughter incest, for example, the father is aided and abetted in
his liaison by conscious or unconscious seduction by his daughter and by his wife's collusion related to her hostility toward
her daughter. . . . The daughters collude in the incestuous liaison and play an active and even initiating role in establishing the
pattern. . . . The incestuous activity often continues until it is
discovered, and the girls do not act as though they were injured." From statements such as this, a naive reader could easily
get the impression that the incestuous father is the helpless victim of his wife and daughter! The lack of such qualifiers as
sometimes or *often* strongly implies that the daughter always
plays a seductive role, and use of the term *unconscious seduction* suggests that the clinician should discount the daughter's
protests of innocence and even attempt to convince her that she
was responsible for the incest affair. The implications of this
"guilty until proven innocent" stance for clinical practice are
important and warrant our careful examination of the concept
of seductiveness and the evidence for it in incest cases.

As evidence for the daughter's seductiveness, an early
clinical study by Bender and Blau (1937, p. 514) is often cited;
they concluded that:

> This study seems to indicate that these chil-
> dren undoubtedly do not deserve completely the
> cloak of innocence with which they have been
> endowed by moralists, social reformers, and legis-
> lators. The history of the relationship in our cases
> usually suggested at least some cooperation of the
> child in the activity, and in some cases the child
> assumed an active role in initiating the relationship.
> . . . It is true that the child often rationalized with
> excuses of fear of physical harm or the enticement
> of gifts, but these were obviously secondary rea-
> sons. Even in cases in which physical force may

> have been applied by the adult, this did not wholly account for the frequent repetition of the practice. . . . Furthermore, the emotional placidity of most of the children would seem to indicate that they derived some fundamental satisfaction from the relationship. These children rarely acted as injured parties . . . and were distinguished as unusually charming and attractive in their outward personalities. Thus it is not remarkable that frequently we considered the possibility that the child might have been the actual seducer rather than the one innocently seduced.

Portions of the preceding quotation have been repeatedly cited as evidence that daughters are not generally innocent victims. However, the statements have been taken out of context—a complete rereading of the Bender and Blau article reveals that their clinical sample consisted of sixteen cases of adult-child sexual relationships, four of which were incest cases, and only two of these were father-daughter incest. Moreover, their statements about the child's seductive role seem to be referring primarily to the nonincestuous cases, since they specifically note elsewhere that the children involved in incest *were* disturbed about their experiences: "Anxiety states with bewilderment concerning social relations occur especially in children who are seduced by parents. Such incest experiences undoubtedly distort the proper development of their attitude toward members of the family and, subsequently, of society in general" (Bender and Blau, 1937, p. 516).

Some clinical studies have concluded, on the basis of seductive behavior of the patient years after the incest incident, that daughters seduced their fathers. Lukianowicz (1972) cited cases in which the adolescent daughter became sexually promiscuous and preferred adult males to adolescents as sexual partners. Howard (1959, p. 224) seemed to infer, on the grounds that they were hostile toward their parents *after* the conclusion of incest, that the daughters he studied seduced their fathers as a hostile, vengeful act: "The girl does not consciously accept the responsibility for the situation, instead being content to project the responsibility for the situation onto [the] father, to express hostility to the father and mother both and, in some situations, to attempt to invite the sympathy of the examiner." While such post hoc observations of seductiveness or hostility may be suggestive, it is also possible that the behavior of the postincest daughter resulted from the incest situation rather than being the cause of it.

The impression of seductiveness may have also arisen from the father's tendency to rationalize incest by emphasizing his daughter's physical maturity and provocative behavior. Cormier, Kennedy, and Sangowicz (1962) stressed that the fathers in their sample usually told the police that the daughter had been provocative while the daughter told them that she had been coerced. Gebhard and others (1965) also noted the frequent disagreement between the court's assessment of the daughter's role and the imprisoned father's perception of it. Judgments of what is "real" in such contradictory testimony are extremely difficult, since both father and daughter are motivated to downplay any evidence for their own responsibility. Nevertheless, it should be noted that studies that have surveyed court records have found evidence for seductive, provocative behavior on the part of the daughter in only a minority of cases (for example, Gligor, 1966, 12 percent; Maisch, 1972, 6 percent).

In the psychotherapy sample, it was impossible to evaluate the seductiveness of daughters who were reporting on incidents that occurred many years ago. Nevertheless, after long periods in psychotherapy three of these daughters admitted the possibility of their having been seductive; in none of these cases, however, could the daughter recall anything specific about how she might have provoked her father's sexual interest. In the large majority of cases, the therapist's "best guess" was that the incest had occurred very much as the daughter described it. In the eleven cases of daughters who were seen shortly after incest had occurred, one was thought to have dressed in a sexually stimulating manner that was quite inappropriate for a girl in early adolescence. Ten of the girls were hostile toward their fathers during the interview and displayed no obviously seductive behavior at that time. While it is possible that they acted seductively in the home, there were no definite reports from mothers or other relatives of such behavior.

A final point should be made about the concept of seductiveness. When we say that an adult woman is *seductive*, the term implies that her behavior is willful and that she can foresee the consequences of it. If an eighteen-year-old daughter is observed to sit in her father's lap while dressed in a bikini, we may be justified in assigning the *seductive* label to her. But what if an eight-year-old daughter does exactly the same thing? Is it really accurate to describe her behavior as seductive, or are we being "adultomorphic" (ascribing adult motives to a child's behavior) in doing so? This point is made especially well by Peters (1976) in his report on a large number of sexual assaults on children. In cases of incest, he observed that children under thirteen had frequently engaged in "affection-seeking" behavior with their fathers, and the fathers, while in a state of reduced ego control, introduced sexual activities in response to what they perceived as seductiveness. Peters strongly suggested that we not "indict" these children for their naive, affection-seeking behavior and stressed that it was nearly always the adult who introduced the specifically sexual behavior, having misperceived the child's motives in an adultomorphic manner.

Course of the Incest Affair

In a certain number of cases, the first incest incident is the last, either because the father does not succeed in establishing a sexual relationship or because he regains his self-control or is restrained by others. About 25 percent of the cases in the psychotherapy sample were of this limited nature; other studies have found roughly similar percentages. What is surprising, however, is the frequency with which the incest relationship continues over a period of several years. If one eliminates the "one time only" cases from the psychotherapy sample, the average affair lasted about three and one half years. Gebhard and others (1965) and Weinberg (1955) have pointed out that it is the dependent, endogamic type of father who is likely to prolong the incest affair as long as possible. When the father is drunk or acutely psychotic, he engages in incest only in that state of mind; the psychopathic father may engage in incest repeatedly but loses interest in his daughter as soon as other sex objects become available. The father in an ingrown family who has been cut off from sex with his wife may become extremely dependent on the incest relationship, and the literature contains frequent references to the occasional "husband-wife" relationship that develops (for example, Marcuse, 1923; Riemer, 1940; Weinberg, 1955). Weinberg found three cases in which the father seriously contemplated attempting to marry the daughter, but Weinberg did not tell us the daughters' reactions to these plans. Far more commonly, the father tries to prolong the sexual relationship for as long as he can by dominating the daughter, jealously guarding her from other males, and, if he becomes sufficiently desperate, by threatening and abusing her. Weinberg termed this kind of unilateral, possessive relationship "incest attachment" and distinguished it from the much less common "incest love," in which the father's feelings are fully reciprocated by the daughter.

In the psychotherapy sample, there were no cases of "incest love"—even those few daughters who admitted that they may have derived some satisfaction from the relationship denied feeling any sort of romantic, sexual love for their fathers. There were daughters who continued to love their fathers as parents and forgave them for the incest, but this does not fall within the definition of incest love. In all, there were sixteen cases where the incest affair continued over some period of time and where enough was known to make a judgment of the nature of the relationship; seven of these cases appeared to be instances of incest attachment. The following case example is rather typical:

> Dawn's father had had an extended incest affair with her older sister. When the sister left home, he turned to Dawn for sex play, which progressed to genital intercourse gradually, although she had begun to resist his sexual advances, and he found it necessary to threaten to sell her dog unless she tol-

erated his attempts at intercourse. Every show of independence on her part was challenged by him, and his propensity to fly into a rage generally kept Dawn and the rest of the family at bay. Dawn's girlfriends who visited the house were all found to be bad influences on her and banished one by one, but the father's most acute anger was reserved for the boys who began to pay attention to Dawn. When she was fifteen, she became infatuated with a twenty-one-year-old man who lived in their neighborhood and whom she was forbidden to see. Their running away together was the occasion of the family's first contact with the clinic, since the father became so desperate that he called on Sunday and told the psychiatrist who was on duty to handle emergencies that his daughter was about to be introduced to "drugs" by her boyfriend. The entire family was seen the next day, including Dawn, who had reluctantly returned after her father promised not to molest her again. The father appeared "vague and paranoid" to the therapist and was evidently making a desperate bid to retain some control over his daughter by convincing the therapist that Dawn would be in terrible danger from men if she defied him. The father seemed to have built up a rich fantasy life revolving around Dawn's supposed sexual activities with other men, and half the time he believed that his worst fantasies were true and acted as if he truly thought himself to be a supremely virtuous father whose point of view the therapist would surely support. After a few months of steady pressure from the therapist and other family members, he grudgingly accepted the end of the incest affair and allowed Dawn to move to her older sister's house for the duration of her high school years.

If the incest affair is generally one-sided, what keeps the daughter in the incest relationship over a long period of time? Does not her failure to end the affair signify a conscious or unconscious satisfaction with the sexual relationship? In a few cases, this seems to be true, but generally the incest continues because the daughter perceives it as less undesirable than the other options that are available to her. If the family is mother- less and the child has no relatives to depend on, her choice is between the incest affair and a foster family or children's home. No great effort at empathy is required to imagine the child's perception of this situation and the possibility that the incestu- ous activities constitute a "known evil" that is preferable to the unknown. This situation was true in three of the cases in the psychotherapy sample and seemed to account for the daughter's remaining in the incest situation for some time, although these daughters did leave home on their own initiative before the age of sixteen.

In an intact family, the daughter's obvious recourse is to tell her mother and rely on her to do whatever is necessary to end the incest. Some daughters are prevented from telling for some time by specific threats issued by the father. Even though threat is seldom necessary to initiate the affair, the father soon realizes that he must rely on a child to keep a secret the disclo- sure of which might subject him to divorce, humiliation in the eyes of the community, or even a prison term, and he usually begins to warn her about the things that could happen if she tells her mother. Most of the large incest samples in the litera- ture (Riemer, 1940; Weinberg, 1955; Gebhard and others, 1965; Maisch, 1972) have remarked that the daughter is generally very afraid of the consequences of telling and that fathers quite com- monly employ specific threats. In the psychotherapy sample, six daughters told their therapists that their fathers said some- thing such as "I'll kill you," which they often interpreted as a threat of serious punishment rather than a real murder threat. Daughters who were approached in their beds at night while pretending to be asleep were not so specifically threatened, no doubt because the father did not want to destroy the mutually agreed-on fiction that the daughter was unaware of incest.

During the incest affair, the mother frequently uses de- nial as a mechanism to protect herself from recognizing and cor- rectly interpreting the behavior of her husband and daughter (Kaufman, Peck, and Tagiuri, 1954; Machotka, Pittman, and

Flomenhaft, 1967; Weiner, 1962). Sometimes she may be motivated to deny the reality of incest because she herself has had a
hand in unconsciously setting up the incest situation and wishes
it to continue to relieve her of her sexual role in the marriage.
Although this positive motivation for continuation of the incest
affair is present in some cases, it is probably more common that
her denial is the simple product of the very real difficulties she
will have to face if she discovers that incest is actually occurring. Divorce, loss of financial support for herself and the rest of
her children, humiliation in the community, and the possibility
of legal proceedings against her husband give her ample reason
to attempt to avoid recognition of the situation. Like the majority of persons in our society, she probably believes that incest is
a one-in-a-million event that is mainly limited to families of the
Jukes and Kallikaks type, and thus very definite, undeniable evidence may be required for her to even begin to believe that it is
occurring in her own family. Denial of incest clues by mothers
in the psychotherapy sample was difficult to assess, because it
was usually impossible to know how many clues the mother had
been exposed to. Nevertheless, it is significant that there was
not a single case in which the mother actively discovered incest
by questioning her daughter or husband about their unusual behavior, and there was one case in which the daughter described
the mother's denial of evidence in detail:

> Marcia's father began genital manipulation
> and oral-genital relations with her when she was
> five years old and continued these activities on a
> regular basis for nearly two years. She thinks that
> she must have known there was something wrong
> with the relationship because she was afraid that
> her mother would find out about it. The father,
> who was alcoholic and amoral to the point of
> bringing prostitutes home with him from time to
> time, once insisted that she go to bed with him
> while her mother was in the same room. When he
> asked her to get under the covers with him, her
> mother laughed and thought it was "very cute" to
> see them in bed together. While her mother stood

by, greatly amused, her father began to fondle her, and she became so disturbed by the situation that she ran from the room in tears. Her mother never did realize that incest was occurring. However, an older sister who had also had an incest affair with the father recognized the clues to incest and ordered the father to stop it, threatening him with disclosure to legal authorities.

And so the incest affair continues over time, with the father's incest attachment, the daughter's fear and ambivalence, and the mother's denial enabling the family to attain a semipermanent state of equilibrium. However, despite the father's effort to continue it, the affair nearly always ends during the daughter's adolescent years when she begins her struggle for independence from him and seeks to establish close relationships with her peers (Riemer, 1940; Weinberg, 1955; Cormier, Kennedy, and Sangowicz, 1962; Molnar and Cameron, 1975). The daughter may feel increasingly depressed as she realizes how strongly incest behavior is condemned by others. Kubo (1959) has reported an extreme case in which the daughter attempted to murder the father because she came to believe that the incest had deprived her of the possibility of marrying in the future. The daughter may also become guilt ridden as the relationship with her mother deteriorates. More typically, however, a boyfriend enters the picture and causes the father to escalate his jealous efforts to restrict the daughter's social life; the daughter then becomes increasingly rebellious and more willing to take the risks involved in breaking out of the relationship. If the distance and animosity between the girl and her mother are not too great, she attempts to tell her mother about the incest.

Once told, one would expect the mother to react with shock and horror, express hostility toward the husband, and somehow rescue the daughter. And sometimes she does just that. Weinberg (1955) and Shelton (1975) have given detailed descriptions of cases in which the mother and daughter joined forces and expelled the father from the family, at least temporarily. In five of the twenty cases in the psychotherapy sample in which the mother was told by the daughter or an intermediary, the mother acted promptly and effectively to end the incest. This outcome seemed especially likely when the mother was very dissatisfied with her marriage and the incest disclosure simply proved to be the "last straw." Some brief examples illustrate this situation:

> Pamela was molested by her stepfather over a period of several months, and although she disliked being touched by him she did not tell her mother immediately because she "didn't want to upset Mom." When she did tell, the mother insisted that her husband leave the home and moved swiftly to get a legal injunction to keep him from harrassing them. Since he was unemployed and had been living on her earnings, she was in a position of considerable power in the home. When seen in therapy, the daughter seemed to idolize her mother and spoke of her as if she were a movie star, and the mother was relieved that the marriage had ended.

> Floyd's wife had been acutely unhappy in her marriage for at least two years but could not gather up the courage to leave him. Finally, her ten-year-old stepdaughter told a neighbor about the incest, and the neighbor insisted that her mother be told. Although she had previously been unable to assert herself and had been considered "masochistic" by her therapist, she convinced her husband that she would bring charges against him if he did not leave immediately. He went to live with his mother.

> Una was ten years old when she was raped by her father while he was acutely psychotic. Her mother arranged for his hospitalization and provided comfort and emotional support to her daughter, carefully explaining to her that her father was not himself when the rape occurred. She credited her mother with helping her to understand and forgive her father, thus diminishing the traumatic effect of the incident.

However, these reports of maternal support are in the minority in clinical samples of incest cases. As we have already emphasized, the discovery of incest puts the mother in a very difficult position, so perhaps it should not be too surprising to find that she often fails to act according to the social prescription. In those cases in the psychotherapy sample where the mother's reaction was known, 75 percent of the mothers did not act effectively to end the incest situation. In some cases, the mother continued her pattern of denial and simply refused to believe that incest was occurring; in others, she believed the daughter but failed to take any action; and in extreme cases she punished the daughter for the confession.

Continued denial in the face of mounting evidence of incest creates an especially confusing situation for the daughter. She has often tried on several occasions to tell her mother about the incest, only to be cut off abruptly before the confession was completed and to be given the definite impression that the mother did not want to hear it. If the daughter is persistent and makes the confession anyway, the mother may become very upset and often replies with some variation of the following: "I don't believe it. I *can't* believe it! If it were true, I'd have to get a divorce, and I can't stand to do that!" Machotka, Pittman and Flomenhaft (1967, pp. 106-107) have published a recorded dialogue between a mother and daughter in a conjoint psychotherapy session that illustrates the extreme frustration and anger on both sides:

> *Daughter:* (raising voice) You don't see how we could have done it . . . .
>
> *Mother:* No, un-unh. No.
>
> *Daughter:* (angrily) We went to the dump! We went out into the sticks! Right out there in the cow pasture! OK, you went away! Everybody was away from the house! We've had it in your bed! We've had it in *my* bed! We've had it in the bathroom on the floor!
>
> (Mother utters a loud moan.)

Daughter:	We've had it down in the basement! In my bedroom down there, and also in the furnace room! ...
Mother:	(shakily) I just can't believe it, I just can't, just can't ....
Daughter:	Mom ....
Mother:	(with a trembling voice) Just can't see how anything like this could possibly happen and how you could treat me this way.
Daughter:	Because ....
Mother:	(shouting and weeping) After all I've done for you! I've tried to be a mother to you, I've tried to be a respectable mother, and you accuse your father of something that's so horrible, that's....
Daughter:	(shouting) Mother, it's true! You've got to believe it....
Mother:	She's my daughter, and I love her, but I cannot [to therapist] believe this!

The message that the mother seems to convey to the daughter is "If you love me, don't tell me about this." The effect of the message in some cases is to cause the daughter to alternate between insistence on confession and retraction of it when her mother's reaction makes her feel too guilty, and this may be the situation that is responsible for instances in which the daughter convinces a social agency that incest is occurring and then denies it in court. In one case in the psychotherapy sample, a daughter who was borderline psychotic became so desperate that she went up and down her street ringing doorbells and telling her neighbors about the incest, but then abruptly denied it when a child protection agency sought to press charges against her father. The daughter's attachment to her mother is the key to her reaction to the mother's insistence that knowledge of incest be suppressed, as the following two case excerpts illustrate:

Pauline had a close, loving relationship with her mother, who was a genuinely caring, if non-assertive, parent. She was fifteen years old when her new stepfather made sexual advances to her, and she told her mother about it soon after the incidents occurred. Her mother cried and accused her of trying to break up her marriage but despite her denial gave Pauline a new lock for her bedroom door "just in case." Pauline, in individual therapy, came to the conclusion that it would be cruel for her to force this knowledge on her mother and decided to drop the subject and avoid the new stepfather as much as possible.

Kathleen said that she used to be close to her mother but that she became gradually estranged from her during early adolescence. She tried on several occasions to tell her about the ongoing incest affair, but her mother cut off the attempted confession each time. Finally, on an occasion when her father was out of town, she showed her mother pornographic pictures that her father had taken of her, and the mother was shocked into belief, at least temporarily. Since she did not want to leave her husband, plans were made to have Kathleen live with other relatives. On the father's return, his denial of incest was immediately accepted by the mother, and both of them hostilely rejected Kathleen, branding her a "traitor to the family." Kathleen adamantly insisted that incest had occurred, and she was placed with a foster family.

In cases where the mother believes her daughter's confession of incest, she does not necessarily take effective action to end the incest affair. In many incest families, the mother is a weak figure and finds it impossible to be assertive with her husband, although she may try indirect methods of influencing him. Lukianowicz (1972), in his clinical sample of twenty-six father-daughter cases, found ten cases in which the mother knew about the incest for some time before the affair ended but

had adopted a "peace at any price" attitude and not seriously
tried to oppose her husband. The mother may promise her
daughter that she will do something in her behalf, but her efforts are so brief and feeble that the daughter feels disappointed
and betrayed. She then typically leaves the home if she is old
enough. Examples of this pattern can be seen in the following
cases:

> When Dawn told her mother about the in-
> cest, her mother believed her and revealed that
> Dawn's older sister had had the same experience
> with her father. The mother promised to speak to
> her husband about it, and thereafter she made an
> effort to ensure that the father and daughter would
> not be left alone in the house together, but the fa-
> ther's sexual advances continued. Dawn finally re-
> ceived permission to go to live with her older sister.

> Harry's wife, described as "beaten down"
> and masochistic, had meekly endured his abuse for
> many years and had had occasional depressions se-
> vere enough to require hospitalization. When her
> sixteen-year-old daughter told her of the incest, she
> readily believed it and attempted to bar Harry
> from the home, but he frequently managed to
> threaten or "sweet-talk" her into allowing him to
> return. Since the daughter despaired of her safety
> at home, she arranged to live with an aunt and
> uncle.

A final way in which the mother reacts to the daughter's
disclosure is with hostility. Kaufman, Peck, and Tagiuri (1954)
found hostile reactions in their clinical sample and interpreted
them as evidence that the mother actually wanted the incest
affair to continue because it relieved her of her marital responsibilities. Malmquist, Kiresuk, and Spano (1966) noted in their
interviews with five sexually promiscuous women with incest
histories that all of them had tried to tell their mothers about
the incest but had been scolded or physically beaten for making
the accusation. Two mothers in the psychotherapy sample re-

acted with hostility when told of incest, and both daughters reported that their mothers had told them never to talk about it again. It appeared that the mother's hostility was an expression of her desperate need to keep denying the reality of the incest affair, and she did indeed manage to keep her daughter from making further attempts at confession, at the expense of the daughter's feeling betrayed by her. In both cases, the daughter felt that her mother's reaction to their plea for help had been a more shocking experience than the incest itself.

The End of the Affair

Very occasionally, the daughter ends the incest affair herself by simply refusing to go along with the sexual activities any longer. Two daughters in the psychotherapy sample terminated ongoing incest affairs by directly confronting their fathers with their unwillingness to continue. One of these daughters, with her father's help, arranged to be placed in a foster home for three years until he remarried and felt that the temptation to incest was over. As already mentioned, the daughter's revelation of incest to the mother sometimes brings about an immediate end to the affair when the mother bars her husband from the home and seeks a divorce; more frequently, however, confession to the mother does not bring about the end of the affair.

In other times and places, the daughter's pregnancy and the resultant scandal in the community often ended the incest affair. In Riemer's (1940) Swedish sample, 12 percent of the cases were revealed in this fashion; Kubo (1959) reported that more than half of the daughters in his Japanese sample gave birth as a result of incest and that two of them had then committed infanticide; Merland, Fiorentini, and Orsini (1962) found five incestuous pregnancies in a French sample of thirty-four cases; and in West Germany Maisch (1972) reported that 20 percent of the daughters in a court-collected sample were pregnant by their fathers. In the United States, Weinberg (1955) gave a figure of 20.6 percent for daughter pregnancies, although a much smaller number actually gave birth. In the 1960s, however, Gligor (1966) found only four pregnancies in a sample of fifty-seven cases that were brought to court, and in the present psychotherapy sample there was only one case in which the daughter had become pregnant as a result of incest, and that pregnancy had been terminated. It seems, then, that incest is now seldom revealed and terminated as a result of the daughter's pregnancy and that the rate of incestuous pregnancies may have declined, at least in this country. Given Weinberg's (1955) finding that incestuous fathers were quite anxious about the possibility of getting daughters pregnant, perhaps we can speculate that an increased sophistication in the use of contraceptive techniques has been responsible for this change. However, other factors, such as teen-age daughters being able to leave home more easily, could very well be responsible for reducing the number of incestuous pregnancies.

Report of the incest affair to legal authorities is often an important event in the termination of incest. Since most studies with large samples (for example, Weinberg, 1955; Gebhard and others, 1965; Gligor, 1966) have been done through courts or child protection agencies, there has usually been no way to assess how frequently such proceedings mark the end of incest, although authors have commonly hinted that their cases represent only the "tip of the iceberg." Just how big the remainder of the iceberg may be is suggested by examining the proportion of officially reported cases in the psychotherapy sample. In 72 percent of the cases, the incest was never reported to any kind of law enforcement or social agency; in 11 percent, the daughter or mother reported the incest to a social worker or some other representative of a social agency, but no legal proceedings were instituted; and in 17 percent the case reached at least the preliminary stages of a trial. Thus our best estimate from this data would be that for every case of incest reported to police or social agencies there are at least three cases that are never reported to authorities. None of the fathers in the psychotherapy sample spent so much as a day in jail for incest per se. One father went to prison for several months after being convicted of child molestation, and another was convicted on incest charges but placed on probation immediately. The other cases never came to trial. Such a finding strongly suggests that imprisoned incest offenders are unusual in some way, since they are paying a penalty that has been avoided by the overwhelming majority of incestuous fathers.

By far the most common way for an incest affair to end is for the daughter to leave the home. Weinberg (1955), although stating no percentage, recited numerous case histories in which the daughter left home with the aid of a boyfriend or other relative, and it was often the father's jealous attempts to get her back that precipitated her report of incest to authorities. Of the twenty-six continuing incest affairs reported by daughters in the psychotherapy sample, twenty-two had lasted until the father and daughter were living separately; in seven of these cases, the father had left the home, while in fifteen it was the daughter who departed. The younger daughters usually went to live with another relative, while the older daughters ran away or eloped with their high school boyfriends, making very early and precipitous marriages in order to free themselves from the incest situation. One of these daughters remarked ironically to her therapist that although she had had intercourse with her father hundreds of times she and her boyfriend had waited until their wedding night! The impression that the daughters involved in father-daughter incest were especially likely to leave home prior to the age of eighteen was confirmed by comparing the father-daughter incest group with the random control group of women in psychotherapy. Of the incest group, 50 percent had left home before age eighteen, while only 20 percent of the control group had done so. Since the control group was very similar to the incest group with regard to age, socioeconomic status, and other factors that might contribute to leaving home, it seems likely that this behavior is specifically linked to incest.

The Father's Reaction

Once the incest affair has run its course, the father has to cope with the loss of his daughter both as his sexual partner and as his child, since she usually rejects him as a parent as well. He may also have to face his wife, family, and members of the larger community, depending on the manner in which his daughter has ended the affair. If a significant degree of incest attachment was present in their relationship, the father expresses hurt and anger, just as a more traditional abandoned suitor would. Shelton (1975) describes a case in which the father, who was actually in love with his daughter, behaved like a broken-hearted teen-ager after his arrest. In one of the psychotherapy sample cases, the daughter had eloped at the age of seventeen, and when she returned from her honeymoon the rejected father phoned her new husband and told him about the incest, probably hoping to disrupt their marriage. Fortunately, she had confided in her husband about her incestuous experiences prior to their marriage.

How much guilt the father will feel after the affair will depend to a large extent on his personality type. Psychopathic fathers, who engage in incest rather casually and without conscience anyway, display minimal levels of guilt when the incest is exposed. They may, nevertheless, be shamed or embarrassed by public knowledge, since incest is an extremely low-status crime within the criminal community. The majority of incestuous fathers are not psychopathic, however, and are capable of feeling intense guilt both during and after the incest affair. Cormier, Kennedy, and Sangowicz (1962) studied twenty-six fathers of the endogamic type and were impressed by the high levels of guilt, anxiety, and depression that characterized these men after the incest revelation. The typical father in this group was overwhelmed with the feeling that he had betrayed his wife and sought her forgiveness like an anxious child imploring his mother to return him to her good graces. In cases where his wife did reject him, the father often experienced severe depression. Guilt also centered around the daughter herself and the possible harm that the incest might have done her; also, considerable remorse was sometimes felt in relation to the other children in the family as the father began to see how he had failed to fulfill a normal parental role. Occasionally, these feelings were somewhat relieved by religious confession and repentence. Gebhard and his colleagues (1965) noted that many imprisoned incest offenders of the subcultural variety were members of fundamentalist sects that allowed them to publicly ventilate their

guilt feelings, and Weinberg (1955, p. 154) quoted a prison official as saying, "Experienced guards who see a 'fish' (a new-
comer) come through the gate carrying a Bible know he is an
incest offender."

The incestuous father generally tries to alleviate his guilt
and anxiety by reiterating to others the rationalizations that he
has been employing during the affair—his wife is frigid, his
daughter is precociously developed and seductive, it is his duty
to provide sex education, better him than another, and so forth.
In trying to minimize the offense, he may insist that there was
only "sex play" as opposed to intercourse and that it happened
far less frequently than the daughter contends. But careful
assessment of these men usually reveals that their attempts to
defend themselves from guilt are quite unsuccessful. A case in
point would be the following:

> Floyd recited all of the usual rationalizations
> to the clinician who evaluated him. His wife *was*
> sexually frigid. His stepdaughter was probably *not*
> as precocious and provocative as he described her.
> Behavior observations during the interview indi-
> cated high levels of anxiety, manifested in postural
> tension, chain smoking, and trembling of the
> hands. He also intermittently portrayed himself as
> a helpless, dependent man whose wife was rejecting
> him cruelly. He stated that he was the "married
> type," that he was at a complete loss emotionally
> without his wife, and that he wished to remarry
> soon if she carried through with her plans for di-
> vorce.

Some fathers react to the incest revelation with a strong
denial of the offense, directed to their wives, outside authorities, or both. When this reaction occurs, the daughter is por-
trayed in the vilest of terms, both because of the hostility elicited by her betrayal and as part of the father's attempt to explain why she would make such an accusation against him. If his
wife wishes to continue their marriage, she joins him in repudia-
tion of the daughter. In many cases, this process occurs within

the family and never comes to public attention. The daughter then feels alienated and resentful toward both parents and often leaves home at her first opportunity. Frequently, however, the denial is made in the context of a public accusation of incest, and then vituperation of the daughter can become particularly intense as the father tries to defend himself against the possibility of a criminal charge, as in the following case:

> Kathleen reported incest to her psychotherapist when she was fifteen years old. At first she attempted to enlist her mother's aid in ending the situation, and the mother appeared to believe that the incest had occurred but was ineffective in her attempts to persuade her husband to allow the daughter to live with other relatives. She had made it clear from the beginning that she was not interested in a divorce. The psychotherapist then reported the case to a child protection agency, which placed Kathleen in a foster home and sought a court injunction to prevent her parents from easily regaining custody of her. The parents were interviewed by a court investigator, and they vehemently denied that any of Kathleen's charges was true. When asked why they thought she would tell the incest story, they contended that she had had sexual relations with a large number of boyfriends, was also taking various kinds of narcotics, and had proved to be completely incorrigible. They therefore attributed the incest accusation to her desire to get away from their attempts to supervise her social activities and indicated that they had no desire to be reconciled with her unless she accepted their view of the situation. The investigators concluded that the enmity between Kathleen and her parents was so great that there was little hope of their being reunited.

Even when the father is tried, convicted, and imprisoned, the denial stance is frequently maintained. Weinberg (1955) commented on the frequency of complete denial in the face of rather overwhelming evidence of incest, and Gebhard and his colleagues (1965) found that about one third of imprisoned incest offenders persisted in denying incest, while many others gave only qualified admissions or claimed not to remember the offense. Of course, there is always the possibility that incest did not really occur and that the man has been falsely accused by a daughter who is sufficiently believable to have convinced a jury of his guilt, and in any individual case this possibility must be carefully weighed. However, the high proportion of public denials of incest does suggest that many of these denials are conscious or unconscious attempts by the fathers to defend themselves against the censure of society and their own consciences. Kubo (1959) did independent investigations of individual cases in which the incest charge was strongly denied and found that there was convincing evidence that incest had indeed occurred in most of these cases.

When the incest affair ends, the father may simply displace his sexual attention to a younger daughter, if he has one. This displacement is particularly easy for him if the mother is absent or has refused to acknowledge the occurrence of incest with the older daughter. Nearly every published study has reported such cases. Gligor (1966) has given specific figures on this phenomenon, having found that 31 percent of a sample of fifty-seven father-daughter cases had involved sexual relations with more than one daughter in the same family. Only 19 percent of the psychotherapy sample fathers were known to have been sexually involved with more than one daughter, but this is no doubt an underestimate, because the sisters would not always have confided in each other. We have already mentioned that an older sister previously involved in incest successfully ordered her father to stop molesting a younger sister in one of these cases. Usually, however, the older sister had left the home before the father began his second incest affair.

Despite the acknowledged frequency of "moving on" to a younger daughter, some authors (Cormier, Kennedy, and Sangowicz, 1962; Shelton, 1975) have argued against imprisonment of incestuous fathers on the grounds that either "moving on" or continued involvement with the original incest partner is very unlikely. Once there has been a full disclosure of incest within the family, according to this theory, the other family members are then on their guard, and the father is shamed into examining his motives. While there are many good arguments against imprisoning fathers for incest, it does not seem that recidivism is as rare as these authors have claimed. Weinberg (1955), for instance, gives an extended case history in which a father was tried for incest and acquitted for lack of evidence only to resume his incestuous relations with his oldest daughter and make approaches to his other daughters. And in the psychotherapy sample there were at least two cases in which the father either resumed incest or "moved on" following a full disclosure. In one of these, the father and daughter were caught in the act by the mother, who expressed considerable anger and made her husband promise never to do it again; however, the sexual relationship between this father and daughter continued for at least six more years. Therefore, it would seem to be quite unwise to assume that disclosure automatically terminates the incest affair or prevents another one from occurring.

Effects on the Family

Some clinical researchers have seen the continuing father-daughter incest affair as a sort of family defense mechanism that preserves an imperfect equilibrium to which the family members cling desperately (Lustig and others, 1966). Whether or not the incest has in some way helped to keep the family together, its disclosure tends to shatter family relationships. Weinberg (1955) has presented the most extensive data on the effects of public disclosure on families, having in some cases conducted interviews with family members in the home after legal proceedings had been instigated against the father. He concluded that the effects of incest on the family depended largely on the attitude of the mother toward the father, the daughter, and the concept of incest itself. If the mother wished to preserve the family unit either out of love for her husband or financial dependency and if she was semitolerant of incest, she became very hostile toward the daughter and sought to expel her from the family. If the father denied incest, she believed him; if he admitted it, she tended to blame the daughter for seducing him into the relationship. The opposite outcome—expulsion of the father from the home—tended to occur when the mother had a close relationship with her daughter, strongly opposed incest, and was not too dependent on her husband. The mother, daughter, and other siblings then became closer than ever in their unity against the father.

Remember that Weinberg studied only families that came to the attention of legal or social agencies because of the disclosure of incest, and such public disclosures no doubt force the mother to take some action for or against the daughter and husband. In contrast, daughters in the psychotherapy sample most frequently described their mothers as taking no action at all— the family simply drifted along, with the daughter becoming increasingly alienated from both parents. In only three cases was there a definite expulsion of the father by the mother and daughter; in only one case was the daughter rejected by the father and mother; and in the remaining cases the mother was not present in the home, was never told about the incest, or took no action against the father or daughter when she was told. Many of the incestuous families eventually broke up, but the divorce was usually not the direct result of an incest disclosure. In other cases, the parents remained together, and the daughter simply left home as soon as she was able, although she was not specifically expelled.

It thus appears that incest is often associated with the disintegration of the family unit or with emotional estrangement of the daughter from her parents. Reports of families in which father-daughter incest appeared to be acceptable and desirable to all family members have occasionally appeared but are quite rare. Judging from the cases in the psychotherapy sample, when the family stays together it is in spite of the incest and not because of it. However, the damage done to family relationships by incest is not always irreparable. There are several reports (Eist and Mandel, 1968; Cormier, Kennedy, and Sangowicz, 1962; Kates, 1975) in the clinical literature describing successful psychotherapeutic interventions with incestuous families, and there were at least two instances in the psychotherapy sample where family therapy helped to alleviate the hostility and tension that followed the disclosure of incest.

Immediate Effects on the Daughter

The rearrangement of family relationships brought about by incest and its disclosure often means that the daughter must face hostility and rejection from other family members in addition to having sustained any trauma that the incestuous activity itself may have involved. Small wonder, then, that some authors (for example, Halleck, 1962; Szabo, 1962; Shelton, 1975) who have studied incestuous daughters shortly after the end of the incest affair have emerged with the impression that incest had affected them very seriously and had invariably been a damaging experience. Other authors, however, have concluded that incest often seems to have no particular effect on the daughter (for example, Henderson, 1972; Lukianowicz, 1972). How have such disparate points of view emerged?

As with the question of seductiveness, many authors have quoted the clinical study done by Bender and Blau (1937) as a source of evidence for the opinion that incest has little or no effect on children. In the summary of their presentation of sixteen cases of adult sexual contact with children, they stated that "The most remarkable feature presented by these children who have experienced sexual relations with adults was that they showed less evidence of fear, anxiety, guilt, or psychic trauma than might be expected. On the contrary, they more frequently exhibited either a frank, objective attitude, or they were bold, flaunting, and even brazen about the situation. . . . The probation reports from the court frequently remarked about their *brazen poise*" (pp. 510-511, emphasis added). However, as we have already pointed out, there were only four incest cases in the Bender and Blau sample, and only two of these involved father-daughter incest, so we should not infer that this statement refers to incestuous daughters. Also, later in the same article Bender and Blau speculated that the lack of immediate disturbance might have been due to the fact that the adult had

convinced the child that the sexual activity was proper; many of
the children manifested delayed guilt reactions when the meaning of the behavior dawned on them. They also specifically
stated that children involved in incest were noticeably more disturbed than children who were sexually involved with unrelated
adults.

When a child is observed to react blandly or "with brazen
poise," a complete lack of disturbance should not be inferred.
Peters (1976) reported on a large number of children seen at a
rape crisis center and observed that child victims were less ex-
pressive of their fears and concerns than were adult victims.
While he thought that this difference might be due in part to
the less brutal and life-threatening nature of sexual approaches
to children, he concluded on the basis of his clinical experience
with them that the bland-looking child is simply less able to express his or her reaction openly and has retreated into a protective state of emotional withdrawal, which is then misinterpreted
as a lack of effect. Peters therefore stressed the need for professionals who come in contact with such children to calmly and
patiently help them to talk about the experience and get them
to ventilate the fear and anger that is often concealed by their
"brazen poise."

There is evidence from at least three studies that incestuous experience is more disturbing to children than sexual experience with an unknown adult. Bender and Blau (1937), as
previously mentioned, observed more anxiety and confusion in
incestuous children, but their sample was much too small to be
convincing. Landis (1956) did a retrospective study of the effects of sexual approaches by adults in childhood by surveying
nearly 2,000 college students with an anonymous questionnaire
form. About 80 percent of the women who remembered such
an experience said that they had been frightened or emotionally
upset by it, but, more importantly, the degree of emotional upset was significantly related to the nature of the sexual approach and the extent to which the child knew the adult. Not
surprisingly, much more emotional upset was associated with
sexual intercourse or attempted rape than with exhibition, but
more significant for our present purposes was the finding that

more emotional upset was reported when the child knew the offender than when the offender was a stranger. Landis did not report how many of the known offenders were relatives. Also of interest was the finding that the more serious the offense, the *less* likely that the child had told her parents about it, because she feared their reaction.

Peters (1976) was the third researcher to address this question. In comparing his subjective impressions of a large number of cases of adult-child sexual activity, he concluded that the most acute emotional problems occurred when the adult was the child's father, and he attributed the confusion and bewilderment observed in these cases to the conflicts created in the family by the incest revelation. The mother was often observed to vacillate between protection of her child and defense of her husband, and when she chose to side with her husband the child was isolated within the family and tended to assume that she (the child) was entirely to blame for the family's difficulties. When the child had been approached by a stranger, the situation was far less ambiguous; the family was usually united in its support for the child, and she was not made to feel guilty about the incident.

By the very nature of the psychotherapy sample, the girls who were seen soon after the incest incident or affair were disturbed by it and usually expressed considerable anger and resentment toward the father or stepfather and also toward the mother if she had refused to help her daughter end the incest. In one case, the daughter was enjoying the sexual attention of her handsome young stepfather at the time she was seen in therapy and appeared at the time to be none the worse for the experience. However, according to the stepfather, she ended their relationship a few months later by running away with her lesbian lover and leaving her room strewn with pornographic pictures of women, which were predictably found by her mother; she obviously departed with a gesture of hostility. In cases where adult women reported incestuous incidents in their childhoods, the patients were unanimous in their opinion that the event had been a negative one in the sense that they were unhappy about it at the time it had happened and that they often attributed various kinds of symptoms to it. Interestingly, the one patient who tended to minimize the effects of the incest incident explained that her mother had been very supportive of her and had allowed her to express her feelings about it at the time so that she felt she had "worked it through."

A large variety of neurotic, psychosomatic, and behavioral symptoms have been reported in conjunction with incest cases. As is the case with any other stressful event, it is impossible to prove a cause-and-effect connection between incest stress and any of these symptoms, but their appearance in close temporal association is suggestive of a causal relationship. As always, it is important to keep in mind the research setting where cases were studied when evaluating reports on the immediate effects of incest.

Kaufman, Peck, and Tagiuri (1954) made an intensive study of a small number of cases referred to the Judge Baker Guidance Center in Boston for treatment following the disclosure of incest. All of the daughters were depressed to some degree, and a few had made attempts at suicide. Psychosomatic complaints characteristic of depression were common in these girls, as were learning disabilities although all of them were average or above average in intelligence. In various ways, they acted as if they wished to be punished for the incest and earn their mothers' forgiveness, even though most of their verbalized hostility was directed toward the mother who had failed to protect them. A few turned to religion to assuage their guilt.

Molnar and Cameron (1975) reported on ten daughters who were in-patients in a Canadian psychiatric hospital shortly after incest affairs that ended in mid adolescence. These girls were characterized by depressive-suicidal reactions that had often been associated with their running away from home and that had brought them into contact with the psychiatric clinic. In fact, at that particular facility it was estimated that nearly 5 percent of the admissions of girls between the ages of fourteen and seventeen were cases in which the girl was fleeing from an incest situation, and Molnar and Cameron suggested that the "incest syndrome" is common enough to have its own name. Most of these girls had disclosed the incest when they became fully aware of the community's moral code or when they acquired a boyfriend their own age, and the stresses surrounding disclosure seemed to be responsible for their depressive reactions. Cowie, Cowie, and Slater (1968) have also commented on the frequency of sexual advances by male relatives as a causative factor in teen-age runaway cases in Great Britain.

Two other clinical studies of small groups of postincest adolescent girls should be noted here. In Canada, Bigras and his colleagues (1966) found that seven out of the nine daughters they saw in psychiatric treatment manifested a "compulsive masochistic reaction," characterized by self-destructive sexual acting out, runaway behavior, and attempts at suicide. The remaining two patients became psychotic. Browning and Boatman (1977), working in an American in-patient psychiatric setting, also found sexual acting out, running away, and depression to be common postincest symptoms in their group of nine daughters.

In nonclinical incest samples, one can get a more accurate idea of the proportion of neurotic symptoms following incest because a court- or public agency-collected sample has the possibility of including cases in which the daughters are not psychologically disturbed. Unfortunately, some of the largest studies have not included any precise data on such aftereffects (Weinberg, 1955; Gebhard and others, 1965; Gligor, 1966). Maisch (1972), who has done the most meticulous study of the symptoms manifested by daughters before and shortly after incest, reported that over 70 percent of them were characterized by some sort of personality disturbance. About 28 percent were definitely depressed, and one third of these made attempts at suicide; 25 percent were described as character disorders who displayed various forms of antisocial behavior; 12 percent appeared to be suffering from traumatic neuroses with prominent anxiety, phobias, or compulsions; and 17 percent had various kinds of psychosomatic symptoms. While the antisocial behavior and psychosomatic symptoms had occurred as frequently before incest as after it, the neuroses and the depressive reactions, which were similar to those described by Molnar and Cameron (1975), often seemed to have resulted from the stresses of the incest situation. Some of the neurotic symptoms seemed, at least on the surface, to be rather obviously linked to incest, and Maisch (1972) saw them as being essentially similar to attempts to "relive" the traumatic experience that are often observed in neuroses caused by wartime experiences. For instance, one girl had repeated night terrors in which she thought that a man was entering her room intent on murdering her; another had suddenly developed a compulsion to talk about "that terrible thing"—her incest experience. Maisch concluded that the incest stress probably caused personality disturbance in 35 percent of the cases, exacerbated preexisting symptoms in 27 percent, and had no traceable relation to personality problems in the remaining 38 percent.

The psychotherapy sample sheds little additional light on the immediate reactions to incest, since most of the daughters were seen in therapy long after the incestuous experience. Of the eleven daughters who were interviewed during the incest affair or within a year of its termination, three were psychotic, three were character disorders, two were severely neurotic, and three presented mixed pictures of depression, anxiety, and antisocial tendencies. In at least half of these cases, the symptoms were thought to have been present prior to the incest, although the stress of the incest and its disclosure was usually thought to have aggravated them. Sometimes, however, it did seem very likely that the incest had precipitated new symptoms. For instance, a mentally retarded young woman whose stepfather had approached her sexually became severely anxious and depressed when her mother insisted on bringing the topic up time after time and teasing her about it; she was admitted to a psychiatric hospital as a result and spent a good deal of time in group therapy ventilating her anger toward her mother.

In addition to the widely varied symptom pictures in patients who had recently experienced incest, there were two cases of acute neuroses in mid adolescence that the patient described to her therapist some years later and that appeared to have been related to the incest. In one of these, the daughter went to live with her mother and stepfather after years of incest with her natural father and almost immediately developed a fear that someone would break into her room at night; somewhat later, she accused her stepfather of making incestuous approaches to her on what seemed to be very flimsy evidence. In the other case, a girl who had been sporadically approached by her father on occasions when he was drunk experienced a severe anxiety neurosis in mid adolescence in which she locked herself into her closet to sleep every night for many months. Although these cases can hardly be said to be typical, they do resemble some of the traumatic neuroses described by Maisch (1972), and they serve to illustrate the extent to which incest can undermine the daughter's feelings of personal security and privacy in her own home.

Sexual problems are also reported to be common after-effects or side effects of incest. In particular, researchers have noted that samples of sexually promiscuous girls yield a high proportion of reports of incestuous backgrounds and that samples of incestuous daughters yield many cases of promiscuity. The most common finding (for example, Kaufman, Peck, and Tagiuri, 1954; Weinberg, 1955; Kubo, 1959) has been that a minority of incestuous daughters go through a period of sexual acting out after the incest affair. Molnar and Cameron (1975) found no cases of promiscuity; at the other extreme, Lukiano-wicz (1972) described eleven out of twenty-six daughters as promiscuous, as might have been expected, since he drew part of his sample from a home for delinquent girls. Maisch's (1972) finding of 13 percent in a court-collected sample is much more typical, and he was also able to obtain information on the time of onset of the sexual acting out and of other kinds of antisocial behavior, such as lying and stealing. He concluded from the patterns of symptoms that the sexual promiscuity was part of a larger pattern of character disorder that had been developing prior to the incest in most cases. When the family backgrounds of these girls were examined, it was found that the incest and sexual promiscuity were both products of extremely disturbed family relationships, desertion, and downright brutality.

Although the psychotherapy sample was obviously biased toward finding psychological disturbance, it is interesting to note that only 25 percent of the daughters were known to have been sexually promiscuous as adolescents. A few of these girls had also been arrested for shoplifting and other minor crimes and were considered to be character disorders. In three cases, placement in a facility for juvenile delinquents had been necessary for short periods of time. It therefore seems that incest cases that are found in such facilities are atypical and could have given some researchers (for example, Howard, 1959) the misleading impression that incestuous daughters are generally promiscuous and hostile.

An unanticipated finding in the psychotherapy sample was that in at least three cases the incestuous daughters had molested other children during or shortly after their incest experience. The term *molested* is used advisedly here, since the girls went much further in their initiation of sex play than was the norm in their neighborhoods and thus drew the attention of the parents of their playmates and were punished for their activity. In one of these cases, the woman told her therapist that she had introduced oral-genital techniques to her girlfriends in the first and second grade because she was imitating what her father was doing to her at home. In another, the girl had manipulated the genitals of a younger boy in her neighborhood. And in the third a thirteen-year-old daughter had initiated a brief lesbian affair with a little girl for whom she babysat. It seemed in all three cases that the girl's premature experience with adult sexual techniques had led her to misjudge the appropriateness of such activities with other children. In another case, a sixteen-year-old daughter who was borderline in intelligence became so obsessed with talking about sex in school that her teachers and classmates became very anxious about her behavior, and she was finally expelled from school. Here, too, it seemed as if the sexual stimulation received at home were "spilling over" into her interactions with peers.

Kaufman, Peck, and Tagiuri (1954) and Heims and Kaufman (1963), reporting on clinical samples, mentioned that an unspecified number of daughters sought out homosexual relationships as a result of their need for a more nurturant mother figure and the fear of heterosexual experience that had been inspired by the incest affair. However, it is not clear from their presentation how frequently this occurred or whether the homosexual relationships were actually consummated in sexual activity or were the more usual kinds of same-sex attachments that adolescent girls experience. Homosexual activity is not mentioned as an immediate aftereffect of incest by any of the previous large sample studies in the literature. In the psychotherapy sample, there were two cases in which young girls experimented with homosexual behavior during the incest affair. One of these girls continued to have sexual activity with her girlfriends throughout adolescence. In a third case, the daughter was already involved in lesbian relationships when her stepfather began their incest affair; her homosexual orientation continued after the incest affair ended but could hardly be considered an aftereffect. All in all, it appears that homosexual experimentation is occasionally associated with father-daughter incest but is far less common, at least as an immediate aftereffect, than old-fashioned heterosexual promiscuity.

6

Long-Term Aftereffects in Father-Daughter Incest

Incest is a stressful life event. In the previous chapter, we focused on the event itself, reviewing the family setting in which it occurs, the nature of the initial approach by the father, the sexual activities involved, the response of the daughter, and the immediate or eventual end of the incest affair. The most immediate effect of incest was found to be the further disruption of a family that was disturbed to begin with. Sometimes the daughter became emotionally isolated from both parents although she remained in the home for some time following the incest disclosure; in other cases, she was rejected and denounced by both parents and may have been forced to leave the home; and occasionally she was supported by her mother and the father was expelled from the family unit, although he was seldom imprisoned as a result of the incest. Pregnancy as an outcome of father-daughter incest is now infrequent and can usually be safely and quietly terminated with a legal abortion, so that there is no longer need to reveal incest in

194

order to end a pregnancy. The daughter is nevertheless often depressed and guilty at the end of the incest episode, her specific reaction no doubt depending on her underlying personality structure. Suicide attempts, acute traumatic neuroses, school problems, delinquent behavior, and sexual acting out have been reported, and the kinds of problems found are importantly associated with the research setting in which incest is studied. In some cases, also, the effects of incest seemed very minimal or nonspecific.

The focus now shifts to the long-term effects of father-daughter incest, and we shall ask how father-daughter incest changes (or does not change) the course of the daughter's life. In an absolute sense, the question is unanswerable for several reasons. It refers to the effects of "incest"—specifically, a sexual event or series of events between a father and daughter—and there is no way in which the effects of these sexual events can be separated from the family pathology that surrounds them, both before and after the incest itself occurs. The kinds of disturbed family backgrounds that are conducive to the occurrence of overt incest are almost certain to produce developmental difficulties, even if incest never occurs. When parents are severely disturbed, when a child is deserted by one parent or shuttled back and forth between divorced parents, or when a daughter has been forced into a role reversal with her mother, the resultant stress can influence adjustment in adult life. Also, when incest does occur, it brings about important changes in the family role structure that may have long-term aftereffects of their own. It is therefore extremely difficult to isolate the effects of incest from those of the family milieu, and occasionally authors have commented that a patient seemed more disturbed by the reactions of adults and the larger community than by the sexual activity per se. One way out of this dilemma is simply to recognize that incest is by its very nature not a strictly sexual event and that it is absurd to try to see it in isolation from its family context. Therefore, when the aftereffects of incest are discussed in this chapter, the reader should understand that the family dynamics both before and after the sexual relationship are included in the term *incest*.

Even when incest is defined broadly, how can a cause-and-effect relationship be established between the experience of incest and symptoms or personality traits observed in the daughter years after the incest situation? It is certainly naive to take at face value the daughter's perception of the role of incest in her life. If she perceives that incest *caused* some later difficulty, she may be simply selecting a dramatic event in her past on which to blame her own failures as an adult or she may be unconsciously avoiding the recognition that some other childhood event is at the root of her problems. Similarly, her denial of the impact of incest may also be defensive in nature. Psychotherapists are generally well aware of the possibility of such distortions of recall and interpretation and thus shy away from absolute cause-and-effect statements in a case history. Nevertheless, it is possible to make relatively objective observations of various patient characteristics, such as appearance, presenting problems, and degree of disturbance in the present, and to determine whether these characteristics are associated more frequently with incest case histories than with other typical case histories. If there is a significant association between the report of incest and the presence of some characteristic, we have not *proved* a causal relationship, but such a relationship is at least suggested. The situation is analogous to the evidence for cigarette smoking as a cause of lung cancer in humans—the high rate of lung cancer in heavy smokers versus the low rate in nonsmokers is not absolute proof of a causal relationship, but it certainly suggests one.

In a sample of incest cases collected through the reports of psychotherapists, one is assured of finding psychological disturbance of all kinds, as we have previously discussed in Chapter Two. The ideal solution would be to do a longitudinal study in which incest cases were followed up at long intervals so that one could discover what happens to those women who do *not* seek psychotherapy as adults and how frequently nondisturbed women are to be found in the "true" population of women with incestuous experience. But, since incest is frequently not revealed to anyone outside the family at the time of its occurrence, a sample of current incest cases is already somewhat atypical, and the problems of doing an adequate follow-up are enormous. Some previous researchers (Kubo, 1959; Shelton, 1975) have specifically commented on the fact that former incest participants do not wish to be reminded of their incestuous history and are thus very uncooperative when approached for an interview. The "ideal" study may therefore not be possible if the privacy of incest participants is to be respected.

Rasmussen (1934) attempted to follow up 105 children who had come before Norwegian courts in cases of adult-child sexual relationships, and she succeeded in getting some information about their adult adjustment in only half of the cases. These included twelve cases of father-daughter or stepfather-daughter incest in which the daughter's mental status some twenty years after the court appearance was noted. Much of the evidence seemed to be "hearsay" reports, and often very little was known about the daughter beyond the fact that "She is married and has a pretty home" or "She married and went to America," for example. In a few cases, the daughter was institutionalized for mental disturbance, but, short of this extreme, there was very little basis for judging adult psychological adjustment in this follow-up study.

Several previous clinical studies of father-daughter incest have provided information on long-term aftereffects by reporting very thoroughly on from one to three psychotherapy cases. Five studies (Herman and Hirschman, 1977; Lukianowicz, 1972; Medlicott, 1967; Molnar and Cameron, 1975; Vestergaard, 1960) have given us brief reports on somewhat larger samples. All of these researchers have, of course, found various degrees of psychopathology, sometimes more and sometimes less than they had expected to find. None, however, has answered the crucial question, "To what extent does the psychopathology differ in intensity or kind from that in nonincestuous psychotherapy cases?" This question can be answered through the use of an appropriate control group, and some of the focus on pathology that characterizes clinical studies can be attenuated in this manner.

The information to be reported in this chapter is based on twenty-six cases of father-daughter and father-stepdaughter incest in which at least three years had elapsed since the incest occurred.) All but three of these women were over eighteen when seen in psychotherapy, and most were currently in their twenties or thirties. There was, in addition, (a control group of fifty female patients who had sought psychotherapy after age thirteen and had received at least an initial evaluation in the clinic such that an intake report was available.) The reader is referred to Table 3 for further details on the characteristics of the control group. Preliminary comparisons of women involved with natural fathers and stepfathers or adoptive fathers revealed no differences on the major characteristics to be studied, so these groups have been combined for the purposes of the discussion that follows.

Presentation in Therapy

The physical appearance of a female patient is considered to reflect her self-esteem and sex role appropriateness, as well as her assets or handicaps in heterosexual relationships, and thus it is usual to find a brief description of the patient in an intake report. It was not surprising to find that about 31 percent of the incestuous daughters were described by their therapists as being attractive; only one daughter was specifically called unattractive, the others having elicited no specific comments from the therapist who evaluated them. About 24 percent of the women in the control group were also called attractive in their evaluations, so it would seem that the attractiveness of the daughters was cited roughly as often as one would expect in a group of psychotherapy patients. The slightly higher percentage for daughters could be due to chance or to the fact that they were somewhat younger than the average woman in the control group.

It was somewhat more surprising to find that 31 percent of the daughters were described as obese at the time of intake or as having a history of obesity during adolescence. This seems, at first blush, to be a high incidence for a characteristic that is strongly disapproved from both a medical and an esthetic point of view, especially in young women, and the temptation is to offer interpretations of how obesity could be connected to the history of incest. Since many therapists believe that fat serves the female patient as protection against the sexual advances of men, which are unconsciously feared, it is not difficult to find a rationale for the daughters' being obese as a result of the trauma of overt incest, and some of the daughters' therapists did attempt to make this connection, as in the following case example:

> Olivia was described as "obese, but mildly attractive" when she was referred for a psychiatric evaluation at the age of twenty-five. The therapist also noted that she was subject to other kinds of symptoms of a psychosomatic nature, such as heart palpitations and hives, and that she was experiencing extreme mood swings and outbreaks of hostility toward her coworkers on a factory assembly line. These symptoms, plus the presence of blunted affect during the intake interview, led the therapist to see her as being borderline psychotic with a tendency to "somatize." Since she gave a history of incestuous activity with a stepfather whom she hated and feared at age twelve and also said that her obesity dated to that period of life, the connection between obesity and sexual conflicts seemed probable to the therapist, and he introduced this interpretation to the patient with some success. Whereas she initially sought medication for her weight problem, she began to accept her responsibility for overeating and agreed with the therapist that her obesity provided her with protection against sexual advances from men, which confused and angered her when they did occur. Her obesity evidently allowed her to be a sexless person in a job situation that brought her into contact with many men.

While the therapist's interpretation in this case may have been absolutely correct and certainly seemed to have had beneficial results for the patient, comparison with the control group leads us to discount the possibility that obesity is very specifically

connected with conflicts about incest, since about 20 percent of
the control group women were also obese. A fairly high incidence of obesity therefore seems to characterize psychologically
disturbed women, and the small difference between the groups
may be due to a specific connection with incest or to chance.

Patients seen for an intake interview generally present
one or more problem areas that they consider to be responsible
for their current difficulties. These "presenting problems" or
"complaints" may or may not square with the therapist's perception of the origins of the patient's discomfort, but they do give
a rough impression of the patient's view of her current life situation. The intake reports of incestuous daughters and control patients were therefore read, and patient complaints were enumer-
ated in the categories shown in Table 6 without any regard for

Table 6. Presenting Problems, in Percentages

	Incest Group	Control Group
Conflict with (or fear of) husband or sex partner	64	40
Physical problems	52	30
Depression	48	48
Conflict with parents or in-laws	44	14
Anxiety	16	24
Hostility	24	18
Suicidal thoughts	20	18
Problems with children	16	16
Sexual problems	24	8
Phobias	8	10
Miscellaneous	20	26

the diagnosis given in the intake. The first and most obvious result of this count was that the patients reporting incest seemed
to have more complaints than the control patients: They aver-
aged about 3.4 presenting problems, whereas the other patients
typically presented about 2.5 problems. It appears that the
groups were very similar in the percentage of patients complaining of depression, anxiety, suicidal thoughts, hostility, phobias,
and problems with handling their children. The extra complaints presented by the incestuous daughters were in the categories of conflict with (or fear of) husband or sex partner, con-

flict with parents or in-laws, physical problems, and sexual problems (other than incest). Therefore, one emerges with the tentative impression that the incestuous daughter seen as a psychotherapy patient at least three years after incest is slightly more disturbed than other females in psychotherapy in that she presents more complaints; these complaints are especially likely to center on conflicts with her family of origin and past or present heterosexual relationships.

A crude measure of disturbance severity that required no subjective judgments on the part of the researcher was the fact of psychiatric hospitalization. When the number of patients who had ever been hospitalized for psychiatric reasons was counted, it was found that 23 percent of the incestuous daughters had required hospitalization, as compared to 14 percent of the control female patients. Again, the difference is not large enough to exclude the possibility that it is due to chance, but it is in the direction of greater disturbance in the incest group.

Another obvious aspect of the intake report is the diagnosis usually given at the conclusion. Table 7 summarizes the

Table 7. Diagnostic Categories, in Percentages

	Incest Group	Control Group
Depressive neurosis	35	23
Anxiety neurosis	12	18
Other neurosis	8	5
Personality disorder	12	14
Adjustment reaction	12	14
Schizophrenia	12	16
Alcohol addiction	0	2
Sexual deviation	4	0
No diagnosis	8	9

major diagnostic categories to which incestuous daughters and control patients were assigned on the basis of one or two interviews with an intake clinician, and the comparability of the two groups in this respect is quite evident. About half of each group was thought to be neurotic, and most of the remaining patients were categorized as adjustment reactions or personality disorders; a minority of each group initially presented as psychotic or borderline. None of the patients in either group received a primary diagnosis of character disorder (antisocial, sociopathic, or psychopathic personality), a notable fact in view of the findings of incest studies done in legal or social agency research settings, where such diagnoses are relatively common. However, the intake diagnoses were tentative and often based on a single fifty-minute interview at the end of which the clinician was required to select a diagnosis, and this process may have been a rather unreliable gauge of the "true" state of the patient.

Some previous clinical researchers have taken the stance that father-daughter incest seldom eventuates in a daughter who is frankly psychotic or neurotic but frequently is one of the background factors in development of a character disorder. Heims and Kaufman (1963) thought that daughters who had overt incest experiences later developed character disorders rather than neuroses or psychoses. A clinical study by Lukianowicz (1972) seemed to lend credence to this view in that only 15 percent of the daughters were neurotic, none was psychotic, and an impressive 42 percent were called "character disorders" because of a general pattern of antisocial behavior. However, because an unknown proportion of this sample was drawn from a home for delinquent girls, this finding may have been the result of sample bias. Since there were no primary diagnoses of character disorder (psychopathic or sociopathic personality) assigned to the daughters in the psychotherapy sample, the present findings therefore tend to contradict the notion that diagnoses of character disorder predominate in the clinical picture of women who have had experience with father-daughter incest in their early years.

Other clinical investigators have emphasized the role of incest in the development of psychoses, especially schizophrenia. This topic will be discussed more thoroughly in the context of mother-son incest in Chapter Eight. While no author has claimed that father-daughter incest is very frequently a background factor in schizophrenia, some (Fleck and others, 1959) have maintained that it is more frequently of etiological significance than has been recognized. Others (Kubo, 1959

Barry, 1965) have featured cases of schizophrenia so prominently in their reports of incest that one could easily get the impression that many postincest daughters become psychotic. Kubo specifically commented that he found daughters in father-daughter incest to be much more disturbed than sisters in brother-sister incest and that they often seemed "mentally confused," while Barry advanced the hypothesis that incest may frequently result in psychosis because incestuous families severely distort reality for the child during critical stages of her development. Peters (1976) has also given us some interesting insights with regard to the possibility of long-delayed effects of father-daughter incest. He reported a case history in which two daughters, aged three and six, were molested by their pedophiliac father and appeared to have been unharmed by the incest as children. Both girls became schizophrenic as adults, and the circumstances of their breakdowns strongly suggested a link with the unresolved incest trauma. The younger girl developed a postpartum psychosis with the delusion that her father was the father of her newborn child, and the elder sister suffered an acute psychosis during her first serious courtship by a man and remained hostile to men as a group while in remission.

It is my opinion that there is no association between father-daughter incest and the development of any particular kind of personality disorder or serious psychopathology in the daughter as an adult. Previous studies that have found the daughter to develop a character disorder or a psychosis as opposed to other diagnostic entities have been done in research settings that favored those outcomes and have relied on a very small sample of daughters or on a larger sample without the necessary control group. In the psychotherapy sample, for instance, 12 percent of the daughters were diagnosed schizophrenic as adults, and this finding might be regarded as impressive, since schizophrenia is relatively rare in the general population. The existence of a control group of female psychotherapy patients effectively squelches any such "impressive" finding, however, since it shows us that the daughters are no more likely to be diagnosed as schizophrenic than other women who seek psychotherapy. The same analysis would apply to character disorders and neuroses—but this is not to say that incest has no effect.

It seems that incest is a serious source of stress that usually occurs in association with many other unfavorable background factors. As such, it tends to predispose the daughter to become psychologically disturbed, but the precise nature of that disturbance—character disorder, neurosis, or psychosis—is not conditioned by the incest but by a host of other genetic and environmental factors that are only tangentially connected with incest. On the one hand, in the cases of psychosis presented by Peters (1976), for example, it is difficult to believe that incest played no role, in that the timing of the psychotic breakdowns and the delusional content seemed definitely linked to the incest trauma in childhood. On the other hand, it seems equally difficult to believe that the incest was sufficient cause for a psychosis to develop as opposed to a neurosis or a character disorder. It seems much more likely, in view of the evidence presented earlier, that the occurrence of incest does not create psychiatric conditions *de novo* but does predispose the individual to certain kinds of problems, such as difficult relationships with men or sexual maladjustment, which, in post-incest adult daughters, cuts across traditional diagnostic categories.

Psychological Disturbance

Before considering the specific problem areas reported by incestuous daughters, let us examine some previous notions about their level of psychological disturbance in light of the data obtained in the psychotherapy sample. In order to test these notions, a more sensitive measure of disturbance than intake diagnosis was sought. I therefore reviewed the entire clinical record, in addition to the intake report, of each patient in the incest and control groups and assigned her to one of three classifications: *mildly disturbed* (personality disorders and adjustment reactions), *moderately disturbed* (neuroses), and *severely disturbed* (psychoses, borderline conditions, and serious attempts at suicide). While still rather crude, this classifica tion revealed a trend toward greater disturbance in the incest group, since only 32 percent of the incest group were seen as mildly disturbed, compared with 43 percent of the control group; at the other end of the spectrum, 32 percent of the incest group were judged to be severely disturbed, while only 20 percent of the control group were thus classified.

An examination of levels of disturbance within the incest group was suggested by the common belief of therapists that the patient disclosing incestuous experience during the first interview betrays a deficiency in ego controls and is thus likely to be psychotic or borderline. Of the twenty-three cases in which a first-interview revelation was definitely known to have occurred or not, thirteen had disclosed incest almost immediately, while ten had waited until a subsequent interview and sometimes had not revealed the incest during several months of psychotherapy. When the disturbance ratings of these two groups were compared, it was found that 38 percent of the women who disclosed incest in the first interview were rated as severely disturbed, while 30 percent of the women who withheld the incest disclosure were similarly rated; this difference is in the expected direction, but it is so small that it could easily be the result of chance factors. Apparently, immediate disclosure of father-daughter incest is not the serious prognostic sign that many therapists have assumed it to be. While it is probably true that psychotic patients as a group are characterized by inappropriate self-disclosures, it is doubtful that nonpsychotics think of an initial therapy interview as an inappropriate time to disclose the intimate details of their lives. Many patients think of a psychotherapy interview as an appropriate time to enumerate the adverse life events they have suffered that could possibly account for the problems that they are presently experiencing, and their disclosure of incest at this time does not necessarily mean that they have poor social judgment in their relationships outside of psychotherapy. Many patients who told their therapists of incest immediately insisted that they had never told anyone else outside their immediate family.

Another analysis of the level of disturbance within the incest group was suggested by Sloane and Karpinsky's (1942) hypothesis that incest during adolescence causes more serious psychological disturbance than incest during childhood because adolescent girls would experience more conflict about feelings of sexual pleasure and about their own role in the initiation and maintenance of the incest affair. To test this hypothesis, I divided the psychotherapy sample into women who were twelve or younger at the time of incest and women who were over twelve, and these groups were compared with regard to their estimated level of disturbance. It is notable that 76 percent of this sample of psychologically disturbed women were under twelve at the time of incest, a fact that in itself argues against the hypothesis under consideration, since it is generally thought that the incidence of father-daughter incest is higher in the daughter's early teens than in the prepubertal period (see Maisch, 1972, for instance). The predominance of women who experienced incest in the prepubertal years in a sample of psychologically disturbed women suggests that disturbance is especially likely to result from incest in the early years. When the estimated levels of disturbance in these two groups were examined, it was similarly found that 37 percent of the prepubertal daughters appeared to be seriously disturbed as adults, while only 17 percent of the adolescent daughters seemed seriously disturbed. It therefore appears that the evidence provided by this sample clearly runs counter to the Sloane and Karpinsky hypothesis.

A reexamination of the Sloane and Karpinsky (1942) rationale for hypothesizing greater disturbance in women who had experienced incest during adolescence reveals that it was based on the clinical evidence then available but that this evidence was rather meager. Their own study of five postincest cases (three of which were father-daughter) had shown that female incest participants were quite disturbed in their early twenties, whereas an earlier study by Bender and Blau (1937) that included some prepubertal incest cases had emphasized that subjects had displayed much less disturbance than had been anticipated. Since an obvious difference between the studies was the age at which incest had occurred, it was natural for Sloane and Karpinsky to suppose that the "age at incest" vari able was responsible for the discrepant results. However, as we have already pointed out, Bender and Blau studied only two cases of father-daughter incest shortly after the discovery of incest, and they remarked at the time that these children seemed more disturbed than other children who had been sexually involved with nonrelated adults. Moreover, when Bender and Grugett (1952) followed up these two cases they found that one of the daughters appeared to be reasonably well adjusted as an adult, although she was still completely alienated from her father, and that the other daughter had become a chronic schizophrenic. It therefore appears that the early evidence for a lack of incest trauma in prepubertal children, as perceived by Sloane and Karpinsky, simply did not stand up to the test of time, and the evidence presented earlier suggests (but does not prove) the opposite hypothesis: The younger the daughter at the time of incest, the more likely that she will be psychologically disturbed as an adult.

A number of studies and literature reviews have contended that the effects of overt incest on adult personality are minimal, and a few have even suggested that father-daughter incest may have beneficial effects. Henderson, in the 1975 edition of the *Comprehensive Textbook of Psychiatry,* (p. 1537), tells us that "Incestuous relationships do not always seem to have a traumatic effect. The father-daughter liaison satisfies instinctual drives in a setting where mutual alliance with an omnipotent adult condones the transgression. Moreover, the act offers an opportunity to test in reality an infantile fantasy whose consequences are found to be gratifying and pleasurable. It has even been suggested that the ego's capacity for sublimation is favored by the pleasure afforded by incest and that such incestuous activity diminishes the subject's chance of psychosis and allows a better adjustment to the external world." The source of the suggestion that overt father-daughter incest may result in a better adjustment was probably a report by Rascovsky and Rascovsky (1950, pp. 45-46), who concluded that "The actual consummation of the incestuous relation . . . diminishes the subject's chance of psychosis and allows better adjustment to the external world. In some cases in which there is an incestuous situation of great intensity but in which consummation has not taken place, we have seen a similar constellation but with intense accentuation of manic-depressive psychotic traits." The evidence for their assertion that overt incest renders the patient less susceptible to psychosis is one case history of a woman in psychoanalysis who had had sexual relations with her father and brother. Comparing her to an unknown number of female patients who fantasized incest but never became overtly involved, Rascovsky and Rascovsky postulated that her disturbance would have been even more intense if overt incest had not occurred in a family context that strongly predisposed her to this behavior. Heims and Kaufman (1963) also reported more disturbance in adolescent girls whose father stimulated incest fantasies but never engaged in overt incestuous behavior, but they did not describe these cases or reveal how many such cases were studied.

The level of disturbance found in the psychotherapy sample suggests that the postincest adult daughter is at least as disturbed as other psychotherapy patients if not more so, even though she is seldom seen as psychotic. None of the patients or therapists thought that incest had improved the daughter's adjustment. Of course, to disprove the hypothesis that incest can be relatively beneficial one would have to study a group of women whose fathers stimulated them to have incest fantasies but never consummated the incest affair; however, even if such a group were available for study, there would be a conceptual problem, since the emergence of overt incestuous fantasies into consciousness is generally considered to be symptomatic of psychosis. If incest fantasies are considered psychotic, then a group of women with incest fantasies is going to be a psychotic group, and it is quite possible that this circular definition has led some clinicians to infer that incest fantasies are more destructive to adult personality than is overt incest.

It is my own view that clinicians should assume that overt incest is more damaging than unfulfilled incest fantasies, even though the absolute evidence for this supposition is not yet available. As has been pointed out, the evidence for the Rascovsky and Rascovsky (1950) thesis that incest helps to prevent psychosis is very meager indeed—in the psychotherapy sample, many of the postincest daughters were psychotic, and many more were very disturbed in ways that seemed to be connected to the overt incest. Moreover, acceptance of the Rascovsky and Rascovsky view would suggest that the consummation of father-daughter incest be urged in cases where the daughter is already plagued with incest fantasies, and it would certainly seem that the burden of proof should fall on those who imply such a course of action.

These considerations should not lead the reader to conclude that incest fantasies should be altogether discounted as serious sources of psychological disturbance. Perhaps this is the time to mention the phenomenon of "incest envy," recently described by Berry (1975). In incest envy, a daughter is aware that her father has been sexually involved with her sister, and this knowledge becomes a source of serious psychological disturbance many years after the occurrence of incest, since the unchosen daughter experiences fear of incest plus feelings of rejection by her father and guilt centering on her envy of the chosen daughter. In the two cases presented by Berry, these women were perceived as being even more disturbed than their sisters who had actually experienced incest.

Understandably, knowledge of incest can be disturbing to the other siblings, but incest envy is not necessarily more traumatic than being personally involved with incest. Although I made no attempt to find cases of incest envy, I accidentally discovered one in the course of the survey that may serve as a useful contrast to those described by Berry (1975). A twenty-year-old woman reported to her therapist that her identical twin sister had been frequently molested by their stepfather while in early adolescence; the patient admitted to having residual feelings of anger and guilt in relation to her sister's incest affair and did not reject her therapist's suggestion that she had felt some sense of rejection by the stepfather however much she may have hated him. She also attributed her disastrous early marriage to her desire to escape the conflictual situation in her home. However, in this particular case of incest envy, the "chosen" sister was described as being much more disturbed than her unchosen twin, having gone through a period of indiscriminate promiscuity in mid adolescence followed by marriage to an extremely abusive man. Thus, while this case affirms the existence of incest envy as a source of disturbance, it argues against premature acceptance of the idea that incest envy is even more pathogenic than overt incest.

Postincest Marital and Family History

Let us first examine the statistics pertaining to marital history in the adult postincest daughter. Of the twenty-three daughters who were eighteen or older when seen as patients and whose incest affairs had been over for at least three years, five (22 percent) had married prior to the age of eighteen. However, 29 percent of the control group had also married before eighteen, so this life event seems to be a relatively common one in female psychotherapy patients. A crude measure of marital stability is the number of marriages for each patient who ever married. The average "ever married" patient in the control group reported about 1.4 marriages, while her counterpart in the incest group had married 1.5 times. In the incest group, 39 percent of the women had never married, whereas only 20 percent of the control group patients had never married. The percentage of time that each patient had been married since the age of eighteen was also computed, and it was found that the postincest daughters had been married 39 percent of the time, while the female patients in the control group had been married 55 percent of the time since eighteen. None of these differences is large enough to exclude the possibility that the result was due to chance, but, with the exception of early marriage, the indicators point in the direction of greater marital instability and rejection of marriage as a life-style among the women in the incest group.

Looking now at the qualitative aspects of the daughter's marriages, let us take up the question of "neurotic exogamy," one of the few previous hypotheses about the marital behavior of postincest daughters. Abraham (1921) believed that sexual attraction or marriage to members of other races or nationalities was rooted in the neurotic individual's desire to flee from an actual or fantasized incest situation. A few case history reports have given illustrations of this kind of psychodynamic pattern; Berry's (1975) description of a woman with a family history of incest who married an African tribesman is a case in point. When the psychotherapy sample was examined in light of this hypothesis, however, no instances of neurotic exogamy were found. The daughters did not marry outside their major ethnic group, although we might have expected to find a few such marriages just by chance, since mixed marriages were not extremely uncommon in their cultural milieu. While this finding does not disprove the possibility of neurotic exogamy as an unconscious motive in some cases of mixed marriage, such as that presented by Berry, it does suggest that out-marriage is seldom attempted as a solution to the conflict engendered by incest in psychologically disturbed women.

Another hypothesis that has emerged over the years (Tompkins, 1940; Rascovsky and Rascovsky, 1950; Rhinehart, 1961; Herman and Hirschman, 1977) states that the incestuous daughter unconsciously seeks "father figures" in her adult heterosexual relationships, either to regain the positive aspects of the incest affair or to work through the conflicts created by it. What constitutes a father figure varies from woman to woman, but he is generally understood to be a man who is significantly older than the woman in question or who occupies some position of benign authority in her life, such as a physician, teacher, or religious counselor. In the psychotherapy group, however, daughters were very seldom perceived by their therapists as seeking father figures as sexual partners. One woman had married, and one been the mistress of, men who were more than twenty years their seniors, but their behavior could hardly be called a pattern, since they had generally been attracted to men in their own age group. A third woman was generally attracted to "safe, inaccessible father figures," in the view of her female therapist, but was afraid of sexuality and was only attracted to men who *remained* inaccessible. It therefore seems that a self-destructive search for a father figure in an adult sexual partner or husband is a relatively rare outcome even in a sample of psychologically disturbed women, and it was much more frequently observed that the adult daughter was trying to escape from men and sexuality rather than making unconscious attempts to recreate the incest situation.

Given that the daughter rarely engages in neurotic exogamy or the pursuit of fatherlike men, how does she bring about the high level of conflict and dissatisfaction that occurs in her adult heterosexual relationships? Some daughters had avoided having problems with men by becoming isolated from them, but the majority of daughters in the psychotherapy sample had engaged in a series of marriages or nonmarital love relationships that had given little satisfaction, sexually or personally. Although this kind of personal history has no doubt become more common as divorce has become more acceptable in American society, the postincest daughter seemed especially likely to present such a history, even when compared with other disturbed women in psychotherapy.

One answer to the question posed in the preceding paragraph is the existence of serious problems with sexual response, which will be discussed at length in the next section of this chapter. Another probable explanation lies in the fact that 42 percent of these women were described as "masochistic" by their therapists. Since this label is not especially uncommon in descriptions of disturbed women, its occurrence in the written records of the incest and control groups was noted, and it was found that 23 percent of the incest group and 10 percent of the control group were called masochistic in their written records. While this difference is not overwhelming, it justifies a closer examination of the concept of masochism and some speculation about the role of father-daughter incest in bringing about a masochistic orientation to sexual or "love" relationships.

The concept of masochism is a complex one. Since the term originated in the sexually tinged novels by von Sächer-Masoch, its first meaning implied that specifically sexual pleasure was derived from physical or mental abuse, and it is often associated by the layperson with bizarre, fetishistic rituals, such as those described in *The Story of O*. The term has acquired a more general meaning, however, in that it is used to describe people who seek out or passively tolerate relationships in which they are victimized. In some cases, an unconscious sexual motive for playing the victim role may be suspected, but the term *masochism* often is used with no sexual implications at all. What is nearly always implied, however, is that individuals described as masochistic actually like to be mistreated because they fail to avoid or escape situations in which they are abused. This implication is unfortunate, because it frequently causes us to overlook other possibilities for explanation of the behavior once the label has been applied. For instance, it is usually possible to interpret the nonsexual variety of masochistic behavior as a failure to perceive the alternatives to enduring abuse, and this interpretation has different treatment implications from those derived from an assumption that the patient positively enjoys being abused.

The kinds of masochism found in daughters in the psychotherapy sample were largely of the nonsexual variety. One true case of sexual masochism in which the woman could experience orgasm only while fantasizing being beaten was discovered. There were also two cases in which a connection between pain and sexual pleasure was suspected by the therapist. In the first, the woman's husband was potent only when the couple staged a make-believe sadistic scene, but the patient herself found the situation disturbing and denied that she derived any sexual pleasure from playing the victim role. In the second, the therapist suspected that the patient was provoking her boyfriends into beating her up, although the sexual significance of her behavior was unclear. But the majority of masochistic daughters were similar to those in the following illustrative cases:

> After many years of sexual abuse by her father, Edith married a high school boyfriend, and his physical abuse of her began immediately. He often came home drunk and beat her with his fists, whether or not she reproached him for his condition, and his alcoholic excesses and other personal problems made it so difficult for him to hold a job that Edith was obliged to work sixty hours a

week to support them. While she was working, he had numerous ill-concealed extramarital affairs and eventually contracted syphilis, which was promptly transmitted to Edith. When she advised him of her condition, however, he accused her of infidelity so insistently that she begin to wonder if she had been hypnotized and sexually abused by some other man without her knowledge. Nevertheless, she continued to be loyal to him until he left her for one of his girlfriends. Eventually, she settled into a long-term nonmarital relationship with a gentle, nonaggressive man who seemed to be at the opposite pole from her father and former husband. Some difficulties remained, however, in that she continually anticipated mistreatment from her lover, and she thus spent some of her time in therapy working on her inability to truly believe that a man could be kind to her without having ulterior motives.

Adele had a long history of being in the victim role with men and her parasitic relatives when she sought psychotherapy in her mid thirties for depression. She had been abused by both parents as a child and forced to take care of the house and her younger siblings. In her teens, she had obediently married an older man who had been selected by her parents, and she remained married to him for ten years for the sake for her four children despite his tyrannical domination and physical abuse. Her second marriage lasted only nine months, because her husband was alcoholic and violent. Her third marriage was to a man several years her junior, and at the time she entered therapy she proclaimed herself to be "helplessly" in love with this husband. Unfortunately, he saw her only as a source of income, since he chose to remain unemployed and expected her to furnish him with an expensive car and clothing. When he saw that she was willing to put up with the situation, he announced to her that his sixteen-year-old cousin from San Diego was coming to visit them. This "cousin" appeared to be a seductive looking twenty-one-year-old woman, who moved in with them for an indefinite stay, while Adele continued to support them. She told her therapist that she disliked the situation but could not live without her husband.

In these cases and in several other cases not described, the women seemed to have taken a generally masochistic stance in their relationships. They were not usually perceived as actively inviting abuse, but their willingness to tolerate mistreatment allowed them to endure relationships that a more mature, assertive woman would have ended or never begun at all. In most of these cases, there were no definite indications that the woman gained pleasure from the abuse itself, but the therapist used the term *masochistic* to describe the patient's inability to avoid or terminate such relationships. Informally, therapists also used such terms as "doormat," "punching bag," and "dish rag" to describe the passive, dependent woman who would suffer almost anything in order to be attached to a man.

What purpose did the masochistic stance serve for the women who assumed it? It is always sensible to look for the covert "payoffs" that may be sustaining behavior that appears to be self-defeating on the surface, and with the kind of masochism described earlier one is not required to look very far. In many cases, the complaints about being "used" by men were accompanied by a degree of self-righteousness that suggested that the woman obtained some satisfaction from her victim role. Again and again, her mistreatment by men demonstrated to her that men were "beasts" and that she was morally superior and justified in her increasing expressions of hostility to them. This cyclic pattern occasionally spiraled into a complete rejection of heterosexual relationships at the point where the woman felt she had proved conclusively that men were not worthy of relating to her. However, this kind of payoff was not always present in women described as masochistic, and when it was observed it did not necessarily explain how the pattern originated. Often the woman's therapist would make such statements as "It's all she's ever known" or "She just doesn't know any better" to account for the masochistic behavior and implied that the woman in question had simply failed to learn adequate interpersonal skills and had very limited expectations about what she could reasonably demand in a heterosexual relationship.

Assumption of a masochistic stance in heterosexual relationships may be directly related to the occurrence of father-daughter incest, or it may be somewhat coincidental. In the incest affair, most of the daughters felt that they had been victims of an all-powerful man who had "used" them sexually and betrayed them by failing to maintain his parental role. Possibly their early introduction to the victim role vis-à-vis men had set the tone for their later relationships and also kindled the hostility that some of them expressed toward men as a group. However, it is equally possible that some of the daughters became incest victims in the first place because they were already passive, dependent little girls at the time the incest began. We have observed that the preincest family frequently consisted of a passive, masochistic mother and an abusively dominant father, and it seems likely that the daughter in such a family would learn by observation and modeling at a very early age that women are helpless, suffering creatures at the mercy of the men in their families. The family constellation that often produces incest would therefore seem likely to produce masochistic behavior patterns in the daughter whether or not incest actually occurs, and thus we may be seeing a somewhat coincidental relationship between incest and masochism.

Another aftereffect of father-daughter incest that has been occasionally observed in the past is the occurrence of father-daughter incest between the adult daughter's husband and daughter. Weinberg (1955) mentioned that some daughters manifested open suspicion of the relationship between their husbands and daughters and became anxious at any open show of affection between them. Berry (1975) has discussed the possibility that incest is a "transmissible phenomenon," in that the incestuous daughter may reenact her mother's role and set her own daughter up for incest by encouraging her to play the "little-mother" role. If the daughter is passive and masochistic as an adult and if she has problems with sexual response that frustrate or deprive her husband, she may be unwittingly acting as an "incest carrier." This possibility was clearly present in one of the cases in the psychotherapy sample:

> Sabrina had repeatedly had incestuous relations with her father while her mother worked out of the home, and she eventually eloped with a high school boyfriend in order to escape from the situation. Within two years, she gave birth to a daughter. She found it necessary to work outside the home in order to be financially comfortable, but her working hours required that her husband take on most of the responsibility for their daughter's care, and she observed that husband and daughter developed a "special" relationship that seemed to exclude her. As time went on, the marriage slowly deteriorated. She had enjoyed sexual relations with her husband in the first months of marriage but became increasingly averse to sexual activity and finally denied him any physical contact with her. While not physically abusive, her husband was portrayed by her as a self-centered, hedonistic man who became involved with psychedelic drugs and joined a countercultural group that approved of casual sexual relationships. The daughter was still very much attached to her father and became openly hostile to Sabrina when the marriage was finally ended. While in therapy, Sabrina expressed the suspicion that sexual activity had been involved in the alliance between father and daughter, but her daughter refused to talk to her about the relationship, so the occurrence of incest could not be confirmed.

In this case, one wonders whether the suspicion of incest would have occurred in a woman who had not had personal experience with incest, and it is possible that the patient was misinterpreting her perception of the affection between husband and daughter. Still, there are some aspects of the case that suggest that the patient had "set up" her daughter for incest. She denied sex to her husband and left her daughter alone with him for long periods of time when she knew that he was taking drugs and interested in unconventional sexual experimentation, so perhaps her suspicions of incest were entirely appropriate.

Note that most of the daughters in psychotherapy did not seem to be incest carriers in the sense just described and seemed determined to prevent any such special relationship from developing within their own families. However, there was one very unusual case in which a psychotic daughter was tempted to recreate the incest situation in a rather bizarre way:

> Nadine had been hospitalized on three occasions for severe depression and attempts at suicide, and she was often preoccupied with feelings of being "perverse" because she experienced intense homosexual desires over which she felt she had no control. A few weeks after her latest discharge from the hospital, she seemed to be doing well and had begun to feel positively happy just before a dramatic relapse occurred. Over the dinner table one evening, she was watching her ten-year-old daughter and abruptly became aware of a desire to engage the child in sexual activity. Although she did not act on her desire, her feelings of self-depreciation for having experienced it were so strong that she became panicky and had to be readmitted to the hospital that evening and heavily sedated. The incestuous desire did not recur in the year following this incident.

In this case, it seemed that the patient's openly expressed feeling that she was a perverse person because of her homosexual desires may have made her fearful of experiencing other kinds of taboo sexual desires, and her own experience with incest may well have made this particular fear prominent for her. In her emotionally unstable condition, it is possible that she experienced sudden incestuous desire as a self-fulfilling prophecy.

In the previous chapter, we followed the incestuous daughter's relationship with her parents through the period immediately following the end of the incest affair and remarked that feelings of guilt and anger toward both parents, but especially toward the mother, were often intense and that sometimes family relationships were severed. Now we will examine the adult daughter's relationships with her parents many years after the incest affair, recalling that the daughters tended to present more "problems with parents" than the control female patients. Previous studies have presented conflicting findings, some emphasizing that adult daughters were bitter toward their father (Vestergaard, 1960) and others finding that anger and conflict with the mother were most prominent (Herman and Hirschman, 1977).

Most of the daughters in the psychotherapy sample discussed their feelings about their parents in the course of therapy, and it would appear that the results present some support for the hypothesis that anger at the mother is more often a serious problem in adult life. Of the daughters, 40 percent continued to experience strong negative feelings toward their fathers, while the other 60 percent could be described as forgiving, although there were often problems with past resentments cropping up in the present. The opposite result was found with regard to the mothers—60 percent were definitely disliked by their daughters, while 40 percent were positively regarded. While the trend is toward more negative relationships with the mother, the observed difference is not large, and it should be emphasized that outcomes were quite varied.

The daughter who continued to express hatred and contempt for her father usually had no contact with him as an adult, sometimes by her own choice and sometimes by virtue of the fact that he had deserted the family. Occasionally these daughters expressed feelings of sadness about the estrangement, and one of them risked sending her father a birthday card for the first time in several years, but she was still far from a reconciliation with him. The forgiving daughters maintained contact with their fathers and usually had fixed on an explanation for the father's incestuous behavior that allowed them to think that he was "not his normal self" at the time of incest. None of the daughters justified the incest as an acceptable form of behavior, but they found it to be understandable if they perceived that the father was drunk, psychotic, or under unusual stress at the time it occurred. Nevertheless, they continued to experience some conflicts in relation to the forgiven father. For instance, one daughter attempted to live with her father and new step-mother and within a month became so disturbed that she had to be admitted to a psychiatric hospital; it seemed that the situation revived feelings about the original incest situation that she still had not mastered. Another daughter invited her father, a reformed alcoholic, to stay at her apartment while on a visit from their home town. Since she wanted to have a closer relationship with him, she attempted to be affectionate in physical ways that were inappropriately sexy and caused him to withdraw from her; it seemed as if she had never learned the role of daughter adequately and was confused about the distinction between sex and affection. In yet another case, the daughter was subject to having "anniversary reactions" on the date of her father's death, having never adequately reconciled her love for him with her feeling that he had "used" her.

When the daughter continued to love her mother, the relationship was usually nonconflictual, because the mother was not perceived as being responsible for the incest situation. However, when the mother was disliked the relationship with her was a serious source of stress in adult life, because, in contrast with disliked fathers, very few daughters had cut off the relationship with their mother, despite high levels of anger and tension. The mothers were often seriously disturbed women who were extremely dependent on their daughters and kept them feeling sufficiently guilty to prevent an escape from the relationship. The following case is not atypical:

> Now in her forties, Sally was continually plagued by her elderly mother, whom her therapist perceived as being an extremely annoying and totally insensitive woman. The mother was an incessant talker who would, on occasions when she accompanied Sally to the clinic, direct nonstop, one-sided conversations at clinic secretaries or other patients in the waiting room, thus emptying

the room within minutes of her arrival as her victims found excuses to escape. Sally told of an occasion when her mother shared a semiprivate hospital room with a woman who was immobilized in a total body cast and talked continuously until the unfortunate woman's relatives rescued her. Although her mother had abandoned her as a child and left her in the care of an aunt and uncle, Sally had allowed her to follow her to California and take up residence within a mile of her own house. Despite frequent flare-ups, they saw each other often enough to renew their hostilities, and there appeared to be no prospects for ending or changing the relationship, since Sally refused to focus on it during her two years of psychotherapy.

In cases such as this, the mother hung like an albatross around the daughter's neck many years after the incest affair. Although she was overtly angry with her mother for her past and present failures to be nurturant, she continued to tolerate a conflictual relationship with her out of guilt or a vague hope of finally obtaining the mothering she had missed as a child. Some of these women related to their mothers in the pathetic, futile manner described by Kaufman, Peck, and Tagiuri (1954) in their composite picture of the mother's relationship to her own mother (the grandmother of the incestuous daughter).

Sexual Problems

The most striking finding in the psychotherapy sample of incest case histories was the frequency of sexual problems that had occurred some time after the incest experience. There were twenty-three cases of father-daughter incest in which at least three years had elapsed since the incest experience *and* in which the daughter was over eighteen at the time she was seen for psychotherapy. In twenty of these cases (87 percent), the patient reported that she had a current problem in the sexual area or had had a serious problem in sexual adjustment some time after the incest. Sometimes the sexual problem was one of the "presenting problems" that had motivated the woman to seek treatment; much more frequently, however, it was only one aspect of a constellation of personal difficulties, and sometimes the problem was not discovered for some time after the beginning of therapy. The specific types of sexual problems included frigidity, promiscuity, and confusion about sexual orientation, plus some unusual difficulties such as sexual masochism. Each of these major problem areas will be discussed at some length. These problems, of course, are not mutually exclusive; it was not unusual for a patient to report two or three of them.

The overwhelming number of sexual problems reported by these women requires careful examination, and one may well ask whether there was something in the research setting or case collection method described in Chapter Three that would have biased the sample in this direction. Obviously, if cases were collected in a clinic that specialized in the treatment of sexual problems, such problems would be found in association with incest histories. During the time period of the study, the clinic had formed a team of therapists who had studied the Masters and Johnson techniques for treating sexual dysfunction, and this team was beginning to receive referrals specifically for sexual problems. When the sample was reexamined, however, it was found that only one incest case (a brother-sister case history) was discovered after referral for sex therapy; more frequently, sex therapy was suggested to the patient after the therapist had discovered the sexual problem in the course of psychotherapy for other kinds of problems. It therefore appears that the finding of specifically sexual problems, as opposed to other kinds of disturbed behavior, was not determined by the research setting.

The next logical question is whether the high incidence of sexual problems is unique to incest case histories or is simply a reflection of the typical problems presented by women in psychotherapy. Perhaps sexual problems are simply very frequent in women referred for psychotherapy and have no special association with incestuous experience. To answer this question, the control group described in Chapter Three was examined, and it was found that only 20 percent of the treatment records of women over eighteen contained some mention of a sexual problem. The difference between 87 percent in the incest group and 20 percent in the control group is significant, and it seems that the high incidence of sexual problems in association with reports of father-daughter incest is not simply a reflection of the number of sexual problems in nonincestuous female psychotherapy patients.

Another possible source of bias was the data collection method itself. When therapists were interviewed, they were specifically asked whether the patient who had reported incest had also reported any sexual problems. In some instances, the therapist was unaware of any sexual problems at the time of the interview but subsequently asked the patient about her sexual adjustment and found that there were problem areas. Possibly the researcher stimulated some of the reports of sexual problems in the incest group simply by asking about their existence. This process could not have occurred in the control group, because all information on the control subjects was gathered by reading their charts. This potential source of bias was assessed by examining the intake reports on patients in the incest and control groups. These reports were almost always dictated prior to the therapist's interview with the researcher and often before the discovery of incest in the case history; they are based on information obtained in one or two initial interviews with the patient, and thus an examination of intake reports equalizes the amount of information per patient in the incest and control groups. When only the information contained in the intake report was utilized, the incest group patients reporting sexual problems dropped to 62 percent, while the analogous percentage for the control group remained at the 20 percent figure given earlier. This difference between the groups is still a significant one and indicates that the method of data collection cannot fully account for the large number of sexual problems reported in the incest group.

Apparently, there is a higher incidence of sexual problems of all types among patients reporting father-daughter incest than among randomly selected female patients who have not reported incestuous backgrounds. While this finding was even stronger than had been anticipated, the report of sexual problems as long-term aftereffects of incest is certainly not un-precedented in the incest literature. Several studies have reported one or two case histories in which a daughter was known to be promiscuous or frigid several years after incest (Sloane and Karpinsky, 1942; Howard, 1959; Rascovsky and Rascov-sky, 1950; Berry, 1975; Magal and Winnick, 1968; Masters and Johnson, 1970). Some large studies (Weinberg, 1955; Kubo, 1959) have reported that some of the daughter participants later experienced sexual problems—chiefly promiscuity—but very little information was given on the exact nature of the problems, the time of their occurrence, or the number of daughters thus involved. The most specific reports of sexual problems following incest have been given by Lukianowicz (1972) in Northern Ireland and Medlicott (1967) in New Zealand, both of whom reported on sexual problems divulged in psychotherapy an unspecified number of years after incest. Lukianowicz found that 62 percent of his sample were promiscuous or frigid; Medli-cott's data do not allow computation of an overall percentage of sexual problems, but his report that about one third of the sample was promiscuous, one third had "serious homosexual problems," and one third had "serious difficulties in hetero-sexual adjustment" probably indicates that the majority of daughters studied by him were sexually disturbed. And, finally, a very brief report by Molnar and Cameron (1975) on eight women reporting incestuous experience to their therapists described the symptom picture presented several years after incest as consisting of "sexual problems stemming from previous un-treated incest in otherwise varying clinical pictures."

Cases with No Sexual Problems

It would have been interesting to compare cases with sexual problems to those without them in order to develop hypotheses about which aspects of incest may be related to sexual disturbance. However, the fact that only two of the daughters seemed to have a satisfying sexual adjustment in the present and reported no acute problems in the past leaves us with too little information for a truly meaningful comparison. These two cases are briefly described:

Gabrielle's stepfather attempted to have sexual relations with her when she was twelve years old, but she struggled so furiously that he did not approach her again. She continued to live with him, although their relationship was strained. He later paid for her college education. She married in her late twenties and has had a good sexual relationship with her husband for several years. Contact with the clinic occurred because she was having gynecological problems that were thought to be psychological, but a later physical work-up revealed that there was an organic basis for her complaints.

Sally was raised by an aunt and uncle, since her mother was an extremely unstable woman. Between the ages of eight and twelve, she was molested by her stepfather on occasions when she visited her mother's house, but she finally became upset by his approaches and told him that she would not visit anymore if he continued them. He desisted. As an adult, Sally was a hard-working, responsible woman who had had some difficulty in marital relationships but seemed well adjusted in her third marriage at the age of forty-three. She contacted the clinic because of the behavior problems of two of her five children and appeared to be only mildly depressed when she was interviewed.

Although there are only two cases to consider, note that both of these women seem to have been competent and assertive both as children and adults. As children, they had insisted, without any help from their mothers, that the incest relationship be ended, and as adults they had refused to tolerate abuse from boyfriends or husbands. Both sought treatment for relatively mild conditions and were seen as being essentially normal by their therapists. Additionally, the patients in two other cases reported definite problems with sex in the past but seemed to have overcome them prior to seeking psychotherapy:

Ida had pretended to be asleep when her father got into her bed and fondled her sexually; she hoped that he would stop making sexual approaches, but she never had the courage to tell him to stop. At age twelve, she arranged to live with her mother in order to escape the incest relationship, but she continued to be disturbed about the incest and accused her stepfather of making a sexual approach. At nineteen, she had intercourse with a boyfriend for the first time and not only felt no sexual pleasure but went through a period of night terrors in which she awoke crying and screaming after dreaming of sex with her father. However, she continued to have sexual relations and gradually began to enjoy sex and to suppress thoughts of incest. Although she continued to enjoy the sexual aspects of her relationships with men, she was quite mistrustful of them and often placed herself in the victim role in her first marriage. At age twenty-six, she had been divorced and remarried to a man who proved to be impotent unless he played a sadistic role in their sexual relations, but her persistent efforts during nearly two years of psychotherapy to gain insight into her victim role with men apparently enabled her to deal with this problem in an adult manner.

Una had been raped by her psychotic father at ten years of age, and her mother had handled the situation well by being emotionally supportive and providing her with opportunities to talk about the experience. She often dreamed of the experience in later years but never felt that she was acutely disturbed by it. At age nineteen, she married and found that she was very fearful and nonresponsive with her husband until her mother told him about the incident with her father and urged him to be patient with her. She gradually began to enjoy sex with her husband, and sex seemed to be the least of her problems at age thirty when she became depressed and suicidal during a period of serious financial strain and difficulties with her husband of a nonsexual nature. Despite a somewhat schizoid social adjustment, she had managed to hold a responsible job and to function well in her

role as mother up to that time, and it seemed very
likely that she would regain her balance after treatment.

It appears that both of these women were less assertive and
competent than the two women who had reported no sexual
problems but that they were able to overcome the association
between incest and sexuality with persistence and support from
others, although they were still struggling with distrust of men
and a tendency to be masochistic in their relationships.

In the incest literature, most reports of "no effect" of incest in later life have not mentioned the woman's sexual adjustment. An exception is a case history reported by Lukianowicz
(1972, p. 303) in which a thirty-three-year-old woman was described as being "sexually well adjusted." Both she and her husband, who knew of the incest, minimized its effect by making
such philosophical statements as "Oh, I don't mind it. I think it
was quite natural for him [her father] to do so after his wife
had left him. Besides, I know that he loved me." Although there
may have been sexual problems at the beginning of their marriage not mentioned by Lukianowicz, the case sounds quite
similar to those reported earlier in that the knowledge of incest
was shared with a supportive person who evidently helped the
daughter to handle any residual feelings about the relationship
with her father by a process of intellectualization. As the husband put it, "Many fathers have intercourse with their daughters. You just have to accept it."

Promiscuity

Using the definition of promiscuity given in Chapter
Four, only 19 percent of the daughters now over eighteen had
gone through a period of promiscuity subsequent to incest. In
the most extreme cases, the problem had continued over a long
period of time and was still a source of stress when the woman
was seen in therapy many years after the incest:

After being repeatedly molested by her father, stepfather, two uncles, and various neighbors

before puberty, Adelaide began an active sex life with her age peers in junior high school and continued to have numerous sexual relationships before her marriage at age twenty. After a brief period of marital virtue, she began to seek sexual excitement outside the marriage in an extended series of brief affairs. While her husband did not condone her extramarital activity in the sense of having an "open marriage," he somehow managed to overlook the telephone numbers and notes to boyfriends that were left indiscreetly around the house and did not become extremely upset when she stayed out late at night without adequate explanations. This situation continued after almost two years of psychotherapy, during which she showed occasional insight into the motivations for her sexual behavior but seemed to be decompensating rather than improving as time went on. She seemed increasingly confused and bizarre and required major tranquilizers to maintain her tenuous grip on reality. Her therapist believed that her hostility toward men was central to the compulsive promiscuity, since she liked to tell about how much she enjoyed verbally abusing them at the end of an affair.

Tania had been sexually promiscuous since the age of sixteen. She had run away from home several times and been placed in facilities for sexually delinquent girls, and she gave birth to two illegitimate children while still in her teens. Four more children were born while she lived with a man in her early twenties, and she kept all of the children, despite the fact that several of them had behavior problems and the family had to live on public assistance most of the time. She continued to have numerous sexual relationships and seemed to enjoy sex only at the beginning of a new affair or in unusual "scenes," such as group sex situations. When first seen in therapy, she was being supported by a man thirty years her senior in exchange for sexual favors that even she considered to be perverse and repulsive, but she was tolerating the situation in order to provide a home for her children.

In both of these cases, the sexual acting out was chronic and had seriously affected the woman's adjustment to adult life. The compulsive, self-destructive quality of their relationships strongly suggested that they were motivated by nonsexual needs, at least in part. In both cases, also, whatever sexual pleasure was experienced occurred only at the beginning of a casual relationship and not in the context of a long-term love relationship. However, these cases were only the most extreme instances of promiscuity, and it was more usual to find that the woman had "outgrown" sexual acting out sometime in her twenties, as in the following case:

> Madeline went from one extreme to the other. She was not sexually active in high school, preferring to keep boyfriends at a distance and trying to maintain a sisterly role with them. In this manner, she remained a virgin until the age of twenty-one, when she moved to San Francisco and acquired a group of friends who were heavy LSD users. She began to have casual sex while under the influence of drugs and at first was only able to enjoy it when she was "stoned." After two years of heavy drug use and numerous sexual escapades, she became very frightened of the course that her life was taking and suddenly left San Francisco in order to escape the influence of her friends. In Los Angeles, she abstained from drug use and limited her sexual activity to serious relationships with boyfriends. While her childish expectations led to numerous difficulties, which caused her to seek therapy, she seemed to enjoy the sexual aspects of these relationships. She eventually married and was content to limit her sexual interests to her husband.

The relatively small number of women who had been labeled *promiscuous* in this sample contrasts with the impression

derived from previous studies. Several authors (Sloane and Karpinsky, 1942; Rascovsky and Rascovsky, 1950; Kubo, 1959;
Howard, 1959) have reported follow-ups of a few cases in which
the daughter had become very conspicuously promiscuous some
years after the incest. Lukianowicz (1972) reported on a sample
of twenty-six daughters and found that 42 percent of them had
become promiscuous and many also had criminal records. Medlicott (1967) found promiscuity in 35 percent of a sample of
seventeen daughters seen in psychotherapy. These findings are
at least partially attributable to sample bias, since many of the
cases, except in Medlicott's study, were located through public
agencies or homes for delinquent girls and thus could be expected to be antisocial or socially stigmatized persons. Another
ready explanation lies in the definition of promiscuous behavior. Most authors have not defined it at all, probably assuming
that their readers would know what it meant in that context. If
the definition of promiscuity employed in the psychotherapy
sample had included premarital sex with more than one partner
or any kind of extramarital sexual activity, many more of these
women would have been labeled promiscuous, but their behavior was not very deviant from the norms for female sexual behavior now prevalent. It seems more reasonable to apply the
promiscuity label to behavior that is truly extreme and not to
behavior that simply departs from an idealized social or religious standard that is, in fact, seldom achieved in reality.

The psychodynamic explanation of cases of promiscuous
behavior following incest is by no means clear, and it may be
that several interacting factors are involved. Kaufman, Peck, and
Tagiuri (1954, p. 275) have stated one of the few formulations
of the motivation of incest-related promiscuity: "The purpose
of the sexual promiscuity seemed to be to relive the experiences
with the father and hence, through the mechanism of the repetition compulsion, to work through their anxiety and at the same
time achieve a restitution of the lost parent." Other authors
(Gordon, 1955; Howard, 1959) have suggested that sexual acting out can be motivated by hostility toward the parents, which
can be especially intense in cases of father-daughter incest. Yet
another explanation was suggested by Maisch (1972) who ob-

served that promiscuous postincest adolescents were manifesting symptoms of a character disorder that had been developing as a result of extreme emotional deprivation and instability in the home long before incest had occurred. Thus, although promiscuity frequently seems to follow incest, there is no necessary connection between the two. Perhaps Lukianowicz (1972) found a high incidence of promiscuous daughters because his sample contained an unusually large number of psychopathic fathers, and, whether through their genes or through their callous behavior toward their families, such fathers would tend to have children with similar character disorders.

These factors did not figure prominently in the cases of postincest promiscuity in the psychotherapy sample, according to the therapists' descriptions. None of the promiscuous daughters over eighteen was thought to be a simple character disorder in the sense of displaying antisocial behavior in other areas of adult adjustment, and the motives of revenge and repetition compulsion were not obvious. Many of the therapists mentioned, however, that they thought that the patient had a tendency to sexualize all of her relationships and was unable to differentiate sex and affection because of the confusion of parental love and overt sexuality in her childhood. The patients also tended to be described as masochistic in their relationships with men and may have been using their frequent sexual adventures as further proof of their belief that men only want to "use" women and that they are helpless to prevent their being used. A final hypothesis derived from this sample relates to an interesting kind of orgasmic dysfunction. In the two extreme cases described earlier, the women were orgasmic only in situations where their sexual partner was new to them, and their ability to experience sexual excitement diminished rapidly as the relationship continued, thus motivating them to change partners frequently. In one case, the woman was orgasmic with her fiancé before marriage but experienced vaginismus on her wedding night and remained nonorgasmic with her husband, although she was sexually responsive in extramarital relationships. It seemed as if sex with a man who was close to the daughter in an emotional sense, in other words *related* to her, was so conflict laden that sexual response was suppressed, whereas sex with a new, emotionally unrelated lover evoked far less conflict and allowed her to be orgasmic, at least for a time.

Prostitution

Prostitutes are usually promiscuous before going into "the life" (Greenwald, 1958), but promiscuous women do not usually become prostitutes. If promiscuity is somewhat more common in women with incest histories, then one would expect prostitution to be found in a small minority of such cases. The psychotherapy sample was rather unlikely to include prostitutes, since all the patients had to have health care coverage through their place of employment. Nevertheless, one woman with a history including both father-daughter incest and two years of prostitution in her early twenties was found in the sample of daughters:

> Marcia had had several affairs with women during her adolescence and had never been attracted to men. At twenty, she fell in love with a woman whom she found intensely attractive but who treated her cruelly and insisted that she join her in prostitution. Although she had had a good job, she gave it up in order to comply with her lover's demands and win her favor. She found the heterosexual relationships that her new "job" required disgusting, but there was some pleasure for her in that she considered that her customers were more demeaned than she was because they were forced to pay for sex. In fact, her greatest pleasure was to service men who were "perverted" in some way because then she could feel very superior to them and be even more convinced that her hatred of men was warranted by their despicable behavior. After two years of prostitution and continued mistreatment by her lover, she felt increasingly desperate and alone. When a missionary from a fundamentalist religious sect knocked at her apartment door, she was so lonely that she invited her

in. Having undergone a sincere conversion to this
faith, she found that the companionship provided
by the sect gave her a "family," and she immediately gave up prostitution and sought therapy for
some of her other problems. When last seen in therapy, she was in her early thirties and had never
been tempted to resume her former profession.

In one of the earliest follow-up studies, Sloane and Karpinsky (1942) reported that one out of the three cases of
father-daughter incest that they studied involved a period of
prostitution some years after incest. Lukianowicz (1972) found
four cases of prostitution in a sample of twenty-six daughters.
Most other studies (for example, Weinberg, 1955; Kubo, 1959;
Peters, 1976) have mentioned finding prostitution as an aftereffect of incest in a minority of women who had become promiscuous in adolescence. Approaching the question from the
other side, Greenwald (1958) obtained case histories for twenty
upper-class prostitutes ("call girls") and was impressed with the
regularity of finding that adult males had rewarded these
women for sexual favors when they were little girls. In at least
two of Greenwald's cases, the adult male was a stepfather, and
in several other cases he was another relative or a close friend of
the family. Since almost all of the prostitutes came from chaotic family backgrounds and were emotionally deprived by both
parents, their sexual delinquency was conditioned by many
more factors than the early sexual experiences, but Greenwald
thought that the early connection between sex, affection, and
"goodies" was influential in determining what direction their
future personal disturbance would take.

Perhaps coincidentally, in the case of prostitution just described, the daughter was the only incestuous daughter in this
sample to have been given material rewards specifically for incest. As we have remarked, her prostitution was not primarily
motivated by financial need but by a need for personal self-
abasement and an expression of extreme hostility toward men
that she herself attributed to mistreatment, sexual and otherwise, at the hands of her father and the stepfather who followed

him. Her therapist was also of the opinion that her early sexual experiences had led to a confusion of sexuality, affection, and hostility. It should be reemphasized, however, that this case was an unusual one and that the other daughters who had gone through periods of promiscuity after incest had never turned to prostitution. In fact, in cases where an extreme hatred of men had developed, it was much more usual for the woman to avoid them altogether.

Orgasmic Dysfunction (Frigidity)

An impressive 74 percent of women in the psychotherapy sample who were over eighteen had had one or more hetero-sexual relationship in which orgasmic dysfunction was a major problem. The nature of the problem ranged from the "selective" frigidity already described to frigidity in all sexual relationships over a long period of time. Sometimes the problem was of brief duration and had been overcome before the woman presented in psychotherapy for other problems. Other cases revealed a primary nonorgasmic sexual adjustment with frigidity persisting despite a woman's efforts to overcome it, as in the following examples:

> Sabrina had had sexual intercourse with her father for two years prior to her elopement at age seventeen with a boy whom she had dated but with whom she had no sexual intimacy until their wedding night. She recalled having an orgasm with her husband on one or two occasions at the beginning of their marriage, but she soon became pregnant and was increasingly averse to sex following the birth of her child. Her lack of sexual response was one of several presenting problems when she sought therapy at the age of twenty-five. Since she had come from a family in which sex was considered sinful on religious grounds (even while incest was occurring), it seemed that part of her suppression of sexual feeling could be explained by the general attitude toward sex that had been con-

veyed to her in her home. However, she also felt that the incest was specifically connected with her sexual difficulties because she could not overcome her tendency to think of the incest when she had intercourse with her husband, and sometimes she became massively anxious, having "visions" of her father while her husband attempted to arouse her. After nearly six years of insight-oriented therapy, she was still nonorgasmic, although she was less averse to sex with her second husband and had made significant progress in resolving her hatred of men and her feelings of anger toward her parents.

Cassandra also had had sex with her father but not with her fiancé when she married at age twenty. Although the marriage seemed satisfactory in most respects, after six years she still was nonorgasmic despite the fact that she and her husband had gone through a sex therapy treatment program. During the last two years of her marriage, she had been having an affair with a former boyfriend and was able to enjoy sex more with him than with her husband, but she was still nonorgasmic. Although sex continued to be a problem for her, she presented in therapy with acute anxiety and depression centered around her fear of becoming alcoholic like her mother.

In both of these cases, the women attributed their sexual difficulties to their incest experience, and Cassandra also considered that incest had ruined her older and younger sisters' marital relationships. As always, it is possible that incest provided a convenient explanation for a dysfunction rooted in other kinds of conflictual experiences, especially in the lack of mothering that they had suffered during critical stages of personality development. Sabrina's mother was weak and neglectful of her; Cassandra's mother was psychotic and had to be hospitalized for long periods of time in her childhood. However, there seems little doubt that incest had created unresolved conflicts in these women that tended to be aroused in later sexual situations. If they had been repelled by the incestuous relations, they found it difficult to suppress the emotional association in later sexual experiences. Also, perhaps one can speculate that they suppressed or denied sexual feelings during incest and then continued to unconsciously suppress their sexuality lest they be overwhelmed by incest guilt.

Several other women were nonorgasmic most of the time but had found that they could experience orgasm under very specific circumstances. The selective frigidity for some of the promiscuous women was seen again and again in different guises among other women reporting sexual problems, as in the following cases:

> Nadine had had some sexual experience before her marriage at twenty. At the time of her divorce, after fourteen years of marriage and four children, she reported that she had never had an orgasm in any relationship. During the next three years, she remained in psychotherapy and had to be hospitalized from time to time because her sex-related conflicts led to suicidal thoughts and gestures. A black woman, she expressed increasing amounts of rage toward black men, whom she saw as predatory and untrustworthy. She had one boyfriend during this period and disliked him as a person but managed to have her first orgasm with him while she had vivid fantasies of being beaten and hurt by him. When she realized how sexually exciting pain was to her, she asked her therapist, "Am I a sadist?" She also found that her sexual pleasure was increased when her partner was physically repulsive to her.

> Deanna was only twenty when seen in therapy for marital problems that were partially related to her lack of orgasmic response with her husband of two years. She reported no sexual interest in boys during her adolescence, although her future husband had insisted on having premarital relations with her. She described these relations with distaste and conveyed the impression that she had

endured them only to "prove her love" for him.
Her aversion to sex continued throughout her marriage, although she had found herself capable of
achieving orgasm on a few occasions when her
husband induced her to drink too much. Despite
these experiences, she made no serious attempt to
improve her sexual functioning, possibly because
she felt tremendous hostility toward her husband
for numerous perceived shortcomings. Her therapist concluded that she was not motivated to
change her extremely prudish attitudes toward sexuality and that her brief attempt at psychotherapy
was a pretext for ending the marriage while being
able to tell friends and relatives that she had made
a respectable effort to preserve it.

For many nonorgasmic women, the experience of orgasm
is a significant breakthrough and enables them to reexperience
it quite easily, given a cooperative sexual partner (Masters and
Johnson, 1970). In the cases just described, it seemed that sexuality was so anxiety provoking under "normal" circumstances
that the achievement of orgasm under unusual conditions that
enabled a temporary escape from conflict and inhibition did not
enable the woman to generalize her orgasmic response. Deeply
ingrained guilt feelings associated with sexual response could
not be erased by a few orgasmic experiences, although these experiences did serve to show them that they were physically
capable of responding.

In some of the remaining cases, the woman was nonorgasmic and was completely isolated from men at an age when most
women are married or dating:

Beatrice was a socially isolated person at the
age of twenty-three. She had maintained a tenuous
adjustment in a home for disturbed girls during her
late adolescent period and had finally been forced
to attempt an independent life-style. Living by herself in a small apartment, she had some contact
with girls she had known in the home, but she had
no male friends, had never been on a date, and was

afraid of the men she occasionally encountered on her job. She cited "fear of men" as her principal problem when she sought treatment at the clinic and asked to be referred to an all-female psychotherapy group. In the group, she revealed that she had occasionally experienced sexual desire for men, but she was always attracted to men who were completely inaccessible to her, such as religious advisers and psychotherapists. She also interpreted her obesity as a defense against men and sexuality, although it was possible that she was simply reciting the interpretation given by her former therapists in this regard.

Jane had been married at sixteen because of an unwanted pregnancy, but her husband had deserted her within three years. For the next seven years, she lived on welfare or with her mother when she was especially desperate, and she became an isolated, reclusive person. She was hateful and physically abusive toward her son, who reminded her of her husband and father. At twenty-six, she was hospitalized in an acute schizophrenic state. Shortly before her breakdown, she had discovered that her own daughter had been molested by an unknown man in a movie theater, and a well-meaning friend of her mother had insisted that she go out with a "blind date," who had rejected her rudely.

In both of these illustrative cases, we see a social isolation that went far beyond the common "wallflower" state that results from unattractiveness or lack of social skills in adolescence or early adulthood. These women were probably lacking in social skills, but they were also avoiding men and the possibility of having sexual relationships with them. There can be little doubt that they would have been orgasmically dysfunctional had they not successfully avoided all sources of sexual stimulation, and thus they have been counted in the frigidity category.

A variation of this avoidance behavior was found in the cases of three women who expressed a preference for associating with men whom they perceived as homosexual, and these women readily agreed that the attraction was grounded in their chronic fears of sexual exploitation. Two of them had fantasies that their male therapists were homosexuals and reported experiencing a sense of relief when they felt that they were sexually "safe" with a man who was in a position of authority. A third woman actually made use of this feeling of security to attain some degree of sexual responsiveness:

> Edith had attained a marginal sexual adjustment; she often enjoyed sexual intercourse and was occasionally orgasmic. However, she blamed her sexual relationship with her father for the frequent occasions when she failed to experience any sexual feelings during intercourse. She was still extremely hostile to her father, describing him as "nothing but a sex maniac" and telling her therapist with disgust that he had recently married a seventeen-year-old prostitute from Nevada. She had married a man who was just as exploitive as her father had been, and her negative feelings about sexuality were only increased by this relationship. After her divorce, she met a pleasant young man who appeared to be rather effeminate and had no heterosexual experience but wished to establish a relationship with her. They dated for several months, and he made no sexual demands of her, so she eventually initiated sexual activity with him and was able to proceed at her own pace as her own sexual feelings developed. Their sexual functioning was aided somewhat by "sensate focus" exercises suggested by her therapist, but it seemed that her feeling of security with a "safe" man who seemed very different from her father and her former husband was the crucial factor that allowed her to experience some pleasure in sexuality.

Orgasmic dysfunction was not even mentioned as a possible consequence of father-daughter incest by most early researchers (Bender and Blau, 1937; Sloane and Karpinsky, 1942;

Bender and Grugett, 1952), and even as late as the 1950s Weinberg (1955) mentioned the possibility of sexual delinquency or becoming "very shy of men" but said nothing about problems with sexual response. This neglect of what now seems an obvious possibility for long-term effects of incest can be attributed to the lack of knowledge about female sexuality that prevailed until very recently. In the mid 1970s, it is difficult to imagine the fact that the very existence of a female orgasm was seriously questioned prior to the 1960s and that the controversy about physiological differences between clitoral and vaginal orgasms continued to be an issue even after Masters and Johnson's definitive research was published in 1966. Outside of scientific circles, there was surely less expectation of sexual responsiveness and orgasm in women twenty or thirty years ago. Husbands may have been more content with a nonresponsive wife as long as she did not deny sexual access or act overtly rejecting, and wives, having lower expectations of sexual relationships to begin with, probably did not see orgasmic dysfunction as such a serious difficulty. Only when sexual response began to be expected of women was the lack of it seen as a definite problem.

In older studies, promiscuity was often the major focus of concern with the aftereffects of incest, no doubt because sexual acting out was considered to be the most serious personal and social problem in women. Studies of promiscuous women done more recently (for example, Malmquist, Kiresuk, and Spano, 1966) have shown that they are seldom orgasmic in their multiple sexual relationships and often seem to be tolerating sexual activities as the price to be paid for masculine attention. The coincidence of frigidity and promiscuity was neglected in the incest literature until quite recently. In 1950, Rascovsky and Rascovsky described the adult sexual adjustment of a woman undergoing psychoanalysis, who reported a history of incest with her father and brother. Their patient was frigid with her husband and "nymphomaniacal" with a long series of "father-figure" men. Somewhat later, Howard (1959) and Hersko and others (1961) presented cases of sexual delinquency in women who had experienced father-daughter incest and commented on the lack of sexual response with boyfriends and husbands. As late as 1972, however, Lukianowicz described promiscuity as an aftereffect of incest, as if it were separate from his "frigidity" outcome category.

It would appear that the promiscuity focused on in earlier studies was, in many cases, only one consequence of the generally poor relationships with men and lack of satisfaction in sexual activity that are now thought to result from father-daughter incest in many cases. Most women who are sexually nonresponsive present no problem to the community and can easily appear to be well adjusted if their sexual functioning is not considered to be important, and this lack of conspicuously antisocial behavior may have misled some early researchers (for example, Rasmussen, 1934) who concluded that incest seldom had unfortunate aftereffects. Also, many other incest studies (Weinberg, 1955; Gligor, 1966; Maisch, 1972) have assessed effects on daughters shortly after incest or have not followed them up beyond mid adolescence. Since many incestuous daughters are not sexually active during adolescence, there is no way of determining whether they are sexually responsive; even when the daughter is promiscuous, a lack of sexual response may not seem unusual, because many women are nonorgasmic as adolescents and become more sexually responsive as the years go by. Therefore, a sample of adolescent girls will generally reveal only the sexual delinquency outcome of father-daughter incest, and in order to fully assess the effects of incest one must look to a sample of women who have reached the age when mature sexual responsiveness can be expected. In American culture today, that age roughly coincides with the age at which marriage is socially approved—the late teens and early twenties.

In the psychotherapy sample, about three quarters of the women seen in therapy after the age of eighteen had had serious problems with orgasmic dysfunction or had remained isolated from sexual relationships. The average adult daughter was about twenty-eight years old when she sought psychotherapy; orgasmic dysfunction had often been apparent for some time prior to therapy, but the problem had usually not become obvious to the daughter until early adulthood, often several years after the incest had ended. While some previous studies (Berry, 1975;

Magal and Winnick, 1968; Masters and Johnson, 1970; Lukianowicz, 1972) have presented one or more case histories of frigidity associated with father-daughter incest, the frequency of this
association has not been previously demonstrated. The lack of
evidence for incest-related frigidity in prior studies can be ac-
counted for by a failure to ask about sexual functioning in cases
where the woman was socially conforming and nonpromiscuous
and by studying adolescent girls only for a short time after the
incest affair has ended, long before orgasmic dysfunction would
become evident.

As with other findings reported in this study, one must
always recall that use of a clinical research setting for case collection biases the outcome in the direction of finding psychological disturbance of all types. It is theoretically possible that
daughter participants in father-daughter incest who never seek
psychotherapy are fully functional in a sexual sense and that in
the population there are a very large number of these women
whom we will never be able to study. However, the finding that
the incestuous daughters had more sexual problems than other
women seeking psychotherapy strongly suggests that the sexual
difficulties are specifically connected to the incest background
and are not simply the result of being disturbed enough to seek
psychotherapy.

No elaborate explanation is required to account for the
frigidity described by postincest psychotherapy patients. Sexual
activities had been associated with conflict and psychic pain
either during the incest affair or on its termination. In later sexual situations, these negative feelings and thoughts were re-
aroused and resulted in the suppression of sexual feelings. Masters and Johnson (1970) indicated that sexual dysfunction in
both males and females resulted from preoccupation with non-
erotic thoughts during a sexual situation, a point that has also
been stressed by Ellis (1962). Their patients reported a variety
of fears (for example, religious guilt, pregnancy, failure as a sexual partner, and a belief that age brings impotence), which were
associated with their sexual activity and served to render it non-
erotic. It seems that an incest association is a relatively rare
source of orgasmic dysfunction in women, since Masters and

Johnson mentioned only one case of orgasmic dysfunction out of their sample of 342 in which incestuous experience with a father was a crucial factor in the failure of sexual function. Nevertheless, when incest has occurred it seems to predispose the woman to a particular kind of fear and anxiety in the sexual situation.

Judging from the women in the psychotherapy sample, incest-related conflicts are somewhat different in each case, but some common forms seemed to emerge. In some women, the conflict took on the most obvious form—imagining the father during nonincestuous sexual activity. At least two women reported that they experienced "visions" of their father during their initial sexual activities with a fiancé or husband. By "visions," they evidently did not mean that visual hallucinations occurred but that they had very clear, compelling memories of incestuous experience accompanied by mental imagery of the father. Others were disturbed by thoughts about being "used" by their sexual partners, which they associated with the feeling that their fathers had used and betrayed them in the incest affair. Still others seemed to become very anxious when they experienced the slightest hint of sexual pleasure, and their therapists hypothesized that they had felt some sexual pleasure in the incest relationship and that their resultant guilt was so great that they suppressed erotic feelings in future relationships in order to avoid being overwhelmed with guilt. In several cases, the daughters were not aware of thinking about the incest situation during intercourse but reported having recurrent nightmares about incest that strongly suggested to their therapists that incest-related anxiety was still very much alive in their psychic functioning.

Some daughters, as we have already noted, had surmounted their incest-related sexual difficulties prior to the time that they sought therapy, usually by persistent sexual activity with a partner who was patient and understanding of their conflicts. A few somehow managed to dissociate incest from sexual pleasure in unusual situations or during brief affairs where their sexual partner seemed quite "unrelated" to them; this adjustment was maladaptive, however, and tended to make their close personal relationships chaotic, to say the least. In several cases, the women were still struggling with their lack of orgasmic function when last seen in therapy. One patient had achieved a great deal of insight and was judged to be much more mature after six years of therapy but still had never succeeded in reaching orgasmic levels of sexual excitement. Two other patients found the sensate focus exercises suggested by their therapists helpful but still were only intermittently orgasmic. And still others did not seriously attempt to work on their sexual response problems in therapy, either dropping out after the initial assessment or electing to concentrate on their serious difficulties of a nonsexual nature.

The sexual dysfunction associated with incest was apparently persistent and not easily overcome, even when it was the specific focus of psychotherapy. Similarly, in Masters and Johnson's (1970) research the one case history that involved overt father-daughter incest was reported in their "failure" section, and two cases of relatively overt mother-son incest were in their group of primarily impotent men, who proved especially difficult to treat. However, to recognize that it is a difficult problem is not to abandon efforts to ameliorate the dysfunction. It would seem that a "learning-by-doing" approach utilizing sensate focus exercises or other strategies for allowing the woman to relax and develop sexual feeling is important in overcoming negative feelings that prevent sexual response, and it is possible that the women who had overcome their dysfunction prior to therapy were employing these methods spontaneously. This approach should be carefully distinguished from indiscriminate sexual activity, which only served to increase the conflicts associated with sexuality and to harden the woman's stereotype of men as predatory and callous.

In addition to experience with a loving and patient partner, however, it should be recognized that the sex-related conflicts in some of these women are very deeply ingrained and thus cannot be expected to simply melt away during direct, experiential attempts to achieve orgasmic response. A direct attack on the conflicts themselves, involving a careful restructuring of attitudes toward men in general and the father in particular, should be attempted, utilizing whatever therapeutic techniques seem appropriate to the individual woman. Particular attention should be paid to the problem of masochistic orientation in this restructuring effort. Many women will not be able to acquire a patient and loving sexual partner until their attitudes are sufficiently rational to permit them to choose a nonabusive sexual partner and to insist on their right to be treated kindly by men. At all costs, a male therapist must resist any temptation to seduce the patient even if he genuinely feels that he could provide the relationship that would allow her latent sexual feelings to blossom. Even if orgasm were achieved, this situation would be fraught with dangers because the patient would construe it immediately or eventually as another betrayal by a father figure and as additional proof that men are "beasts."

The Lesbian Solution

It will be recalled that only one of the adolescent girls who were seen in therapy during or shortly after incest was homosexual,* and in her case the homosexual orientation had preceded incest with her stepfather, so that there was no reason to suppose that incest played a causal role in establishing her orientation, although it may well have reinforced it. It may come as some surprise, then, to learn that seven of the twenty-three daughters who were seen in therapy over three years after incest had become gay or had significant experiences or conflicts centered on homosexual feelings. This finding was unexpected, since most previous studies have not even mentioned this kind of outcome. It should be reemphasized that a sample collected in a clinical setting is biased toward finding more kinds of behavior in conflict with conventional social norms. However, the fact that homosexual behavior was rare in the control group of females in psychotherapy lends credence to the belief that the report of incest is specifically associated with

---

*The terms *homosexual* and *lesbian* will be used interchangeably to denote sexual activity with, or strong attraction to, other females. The term *gay* will also be used when I wish to imply that the woman shared the attitudes of the organized gay community.

a later report of homosexuality in a significant minority of the
cases. It should also be emphasized that the clinic did not attract any unusual number of gay patients, male or female, probably because counseling services were readily available within
the Los Angeles gay community.

Some of the women had recognized their lesbian feelings
during or after the incest affair, long before attaining adulthood. In the following case, already partially described, overt
homosexual behavior had begun in early childhood and persisted until the woman presented in therapy at the age of
twenty-four:

> According to Marcia, her father's sexual ac-
> tivities with her when she was less than eight years
> old stimulated her to try out his sexual techniques
> with her grade school girlfriends as a part of her
> childhood sex play experiences. After her parents'
> divorce, her mother married a man who was also
> alcoholic and physically abusive, and while he did
> not make sexual advances to her, he was so an-
> tagonistic that she ran away on numerous occa-
> sions and finally was placed in a juvenile facility
> for several months. While there, she participated in
> homosexual activity with other girls quite willing-
> ly. During adolescence, she attempted to fit into
> the heterosexual high school scene by dating a
> series of boys but had no difficulty remaining vir-
> ginal, since she could not tolerate being touched by
> any of her boyfriends. With her girlfriends, how-
> ever, she developed very intense and exclusive rela-
> tionships that sometimes involved pleasurable sex-
> ual activities and often broke up when her
> irrational jealousy of their other friendships mani-
> fested itself. This series of lesbian affairs continued
> into late adolescence, when she formed a semi-
> stable attachment to a girlfriend and continued the
> relationship for nearly five years. In her early twen-
> ties, she fell in love with a woman who mistreated
> her and induced her to work as a prostitute to sup-
> port them. Her infatuation with this woman was so

strong that she masochistically submitted to her every whim, gave her the small amount of money she had been able to accumulate, and quit her job in order to devote herself to prostitution full time. Eventually she became depressed and desperate in this life situation and made a sincere conversion to a fundamentalist religious faith that seemed to provide the moral structure and sense of purpose that she herself lacked. Her fellow believers, however, stressed the sinfulness of homosexuality, therefore creating a new conflict for her that she sought to resolve by establishing a sexual relationship with a man. After a few weeks of tolerating sexual relations with him, it was apparent to her that she enjoyed the feeling of physical closeness and affection with a man but still reacted to heterosexual activity with revulsion.

At this point, she presented herself as a patient in the clinic, requesting that the therapist help her to "go straight" in order to bring her sexual life into line with her religious convictions. The therapist was quite skeptical of the depth of her expressed desire to become heterosexual and pointed out that her whole life history seemed to show a deep commitment to a homosexual orientation, that her change of heart had been very recent, and that the destructive effects of her last homosexual affair might begin to recede soon. She agreed with this assessment but asked to continue in therapy anyway in order to work on her many other problems. Although the therapist continued to maintain a studiously neutral stance with regard to her sexual orientation, Marcia began to take an interest in the men at her new place of employment. When she allowed herself to become involved with one of them, she still experienced hostility and fear, which she ventilated in therapy, and in this way she apparently worked toward feeling more relaxed and in control of her heterosexual relationships. Less than a year after therapy had begun, she had established a sexually gratifying relationship with a man whom she later married, and she announced to her therapist that she no longer felt attracted to women. About six years later, she returned to therapy because she was experiencing acute neurotic symptoms brought on by some conflicts with her husband about her religious beliefs. She still seemed to have a basically good marriage, continued to enjoy sexual relations, and found herself attracted to other men but was able to resist the temptation to act on her desires. It was revealed that her two older sisters, who had also been involved in father-daughter incest, had also become lesbians, but it is not known whether they underwent similar conversions to heterosexuality.

In three additional cases, the lesbian involvement began in adolescence some time after incest had occurred.

Carl was being seen in therapy because of numerous problems with his second wife. After three interviews, his wife called the therapist in a very distressed state and reported that she had just received a call from Carl's younger daughter from his first marriage, who had insisted on telling her the family history. According to her, Carl had begun to have intercourse with his older daughter when she was twelve years old and continued incest with her until she left home in her late adolescence and joined the armed forces. While serving out her enlistment, she became involved with a group of lesbians and later joined the gay community on her return to civilian life. She had refused to talk to her father for several years. Meanwhile, the younger sister was approached for incestuous relations, but she vehemently refused him and managed to persuade her mother to seek a divorce. This daughter also left home as soon as possible and now lives near her gay sister. It was unclear whether she had also become gay, but she expressed an extreme hatred for men, and she was still very hostile toward her father, as her phone call to his second wife demonstrated.

Yvonne was the oldest child in a large family that remained intact until she was ten years old. Her mother, perceived by Yvonne as a very strong but unloving person, kept the children together and eventually married a man who was still in his twenties when Yvonne was in early adolescence. Her stepfather very quickly began to express a sexual interest in her. She noticed that he repeatedly tried to get her alone and flirted with her as if he were one of her schoolmates. On one occasion, he managed to get into bed with her in the middle of the night and fondled her genitals, while she pretended to remain asleep since she was afraid of her mother's reaction. She admired her mother for her strength and desperately wanted her love but had met with hostile rejection on numerous occasions when her mother kicked her out of the house for seemingly minor infractions of the rules. She began dating when she was fourteen and found that her mother loudly disapproved of all of her boyfriends. At sixteen, she became pregnant and went through with a frightening illegal abortion in order to avoid her mother's wrath. At seventeen, she finished high school and immediately left home in order to escape her mother and the continued amorous approaches of her stepfather. About this time, she acquired her first lesbian lover and experienced such relief in having a nonexploitive sexual relationship that she quickly identified as a gay person and very much enjoyed the sisterhood of gay women who attended a university near her home. On a visit home, she purposefully left her diary in a place where she knew her mother would find it in order to tell her of her conversion and was surprised to find that her mother was relatively accepting of it, disapproving far less than she had of her heterosexual activity. When she sought psychotherapy at the age of twenty-one, her sexual orientation was not an issue, and her female therapist did not attempt to make it one. While her problems with heavy alcohol consumption certainly indicated that she had more than her share of adjustment difficulties, she was reasonably happy with her lover of two years and did not envision a return to a heterosexual life-style.

Pauline had had an incestuous relationship with her father prior to her parents' divorce when she was ten years old, and she continued to see him frequently afterward, since he lived close to her. She never told her mother of the incest, because she loved her father and did not want to betray him. When she was fourteen, she had a regular babysitting job with a family that had a six-year-old daughter, and she initiated homosexual activity with this girl on numerous occasions, eventually being caught by the girl's mother. Her mother brought her to the clinic, but she refused to talk to anyone about the incident at that time. When she was sixteen, she asked to return to the therapist and finally told her of her incestuous involvement and complained that her new stepfather was making sexual advances. She had also begun to have sexual relationships with her boyfriends in high school and evidently had not repeated her lesbian experience as of that time.

In the four cases just described, the lesbian involvement definitely began after incest and seemed to allow the daughters to experience sexual feelings in a less conflictual atmosphere than was possible for them in a heterosexual relationship. In two cases, the conversion to a lesbian life-style did not occur until the late teens or early twenties, and in the last case the daughter was still in mid adolescence when seen in therapy, so it was not possible to determine whether the lesbian activity was an isolated incident or the precursor of a later turn to a gay life-style. Perhaps the quality of her heterosexual experience in high school will determine whether or not she will seek lesbian relationships as an adult.

Yet another pattern of lesbian conversion was found in two women who changed their sexual orientation in their early or mid thirties after many years of thoroughly unsatisfactory heterosexual experience:

Nadine's experience with incest occurred in her eleventh year, when she was fondled several times by her stepfather, who sought to prevent her telling about it by making threats. When she summoned up the courage to ask for her mother's help, her mother scolded her and told her not to mention the subject again, thus increasing the hostility felt toward both parents. She had some heterosexual experience in her late teens and married at age twenty when she became pregnant. Four children were born to the marriage before she began to have abortions instead. After eleven years of semisatisfactory marriage, her husband decided to accept a job offering in another state, and she refused to move her children to join him, so the decision to separate was finally made. During the first several months of being on her own, Nadine worked as a teacher's aide and appeared to be coping quite well with the situation, but internal pressures were accumulating. One day she called the school principal and told her that she was too depressed to come to work and might never come again, since she wanted to die as soon as possible. The principal insisted on her being seen as a psychiatric emergency at the clinic.

Because of her insistent suicidal threats, she was hospitalized immediately, and on intake she revealed that she had been increasingly obsessed with fears of becoming homosexual since the marital separation. She had never enjoyed heterosexual activity and now found herself looking at other women and having sexual fantasies about their bodies in which she imagined herself taking an active role in love making. Especially attracted to very feminine women, she was also beginning to think of little girls in sexual terms and found these thoughts very frightening in view of the fact that she was in daily contact with her daughters at home and her students at school. In her state of agitated depression, she talked about these temptations very frequently in group and individual therapy and associated the homosexual desires with her feeling that her mother had deprived her of affection as a child. She related that an essential element of the pleasure she felt during a fantasy was to imagine the feelings of the younger, feminine woman or girl being caressed and loved by the older woman (herself). These insights notwithstanding, she thought of her desires as "perverse" and often used them as justification for attempting suicide. Although her homosexual desires became less intense and disturbing as her depression responded to treatment, they were definitely still present when she left the hospital, and she had become very withdrawn and frightened that other people might also see her as perverse. During the next two years, Nadine was seen almost continuously as an out-patient, was hospitalized once more in a suicidal state, and was frequently given emergency consultations. She continued to carry out her job and family responsibilities, despite her personal upheavals. Attempting to resolve her sexual orientation crisis, she began to associate with gay women, going to gay bars and social gatherings; while she found that she was nonorgasmic in lesbian activities, she felt very comfortable with her gay friends on a social level. She also acquired a boyfriend for several months and occasionally was able to experience orgasm with him but only in imagined sadomasochistic scenes. From time to time, she experienced dreams about sex with her stepfather and was anxious and conflicted when she felt affection for him. A black herself, Nadine expressed increasing amounts of hostility toward men, especially black men (her stepfather was black), and she joined an all-black therapy group in order to work on these feelings; however, she found her hostility too intense to work with in this group and dropped out almost immediately.

At the conclusion of this study, she was still in therapy, being maintained on antidepressant medications and major tranquilizers. Her interest in gay companionship had continued, and she was trying to be more accepting of her lesbian feelings, although she continued to experience conflicts about whether or not to "come out" and tell her children and heterosexual friends about her identification with the gay community.

Tania was far less disturbed than Nadine, despite an even more tumultuous life history. Adopted shortly after birth by an unstable couple, she was raised by a cold, rejecting mother and a father who had insisted on having intercourse with her when she became adolescent. She ran away from home frequently and became sexually involved with many different men, giving birth to six illegitimate children and refusing to give any of them up for adoption. Four of the children were sired by a common-law husband with whom she suffered a long, chaotic relationship and by whom she had felt chronically "used." Since she only enjoyed sex in very short-term relationships, she was open to suggestions to participate in "swinging" activities and met many men in this way. Although she never became a prostitute, she allowed herself to be supported by a man in his sixties in exchange for providing sexual services that she considered disgusting. Despite her long-term unhappiness in relationships with men, her children's antisocial behavior was the major presenting problem when she began psychotherapy in her mid thirties. In the course of many individual interviews, she focused on her feelings of hatred and conflict in heterosexual relationships and on her self-disgust in regard to her economic dependency and general inability to live an orderly life.

After several months of therapy, she allowed

herself to be introduced to lesbian activities by the
bisexual wife of a male acquaintance and continued to seek out lesbian relationships on a regular
basis after that. Her therapist did not attempt to
oppose her conversion, observing that Tania
seemed more in control in these relationships and
far less conflicted and hostile than she had been.
Finding herself attracted to very feminine women,
she tended to play the "butch" role and began to
dress and groom herself in a slightly masculine, but
not exaggerated, manner. She went to an organized
center for the gay community in Los Angeles and
volunteered her time to help with community education projects, and here she met a woman with
whom she was involved as a lover for several
months. She soon found out that there could be
difficulties for her in relating to women also, since
her lover played on her affections and became heterosexual at the end of their relationship. Despite
these difficulties, it appeared that she would continue to identify as gay and her new self-image had
already paid off for her in terms of increased assertiveness. At last contact, she had been hired for a
traditionally male job and seemed to have good
prospects for remaining economically independent.

In the case histories just presented, the conversion to a
gay life-style occurred long after adolescence, and the existence
of such lesbian conversions serves to emphasize the fact that
sexual orientation is not necessarily fixed by heterosexual experience as a young adult. The two women just described had
had very different life histories and presented divergent symptom pictures, but they had in common a long and very stressful
history of heterosexual activity that had not been rewarding
from either a sexual or a personal standpoint. It seemed that
their willingness to experiment with lesbian affairs (despite considerable guilt in Nadine's case) was an effort to find a mode of
sexuality that would be less conflict arousing than heterosexuality and to escape the chronically masochistic lives they had
been living. In both cases, the women also experienced difficul-

ties in their gay relationships but seemed to have achieved a modicum of happiness in their new orientation. While a return to heterosexuality may have been in the offing, it was not being urged by their therapists.

In one final case, no homosexual behavior had occurred, but the patient was often preoccupied and disturbed by fears of becoming homosexual.

>At the age of twenty-three, Adelaide requested psychotherapy because of increasing depression about her inability to enjoy sexual intercourse with her husband and her compulsive acting out of sexual desires outside the marriage. During the intake interview, she revealed so much information about her incestuous past in such a rambling fashion that her therapist entertained the hypothesis that she was in a borderline psychotic state. She was also initially hostile toward her male therapist, making an immediate statement about how liberated and independent she was and how much she resented the traditional mistreatment of women by men. Just prior to seeking therapy, she had participated in a "consciousness-raising" group, where she had learned the rhetoric of radical feminism and had acquired some friends who were lesbians, although she reported no sexual interest in them. Paradoxically, her therapist saw her as a dependent, masochistic woman who was unable to act on her feminist ideas and seemed to be continually setting herself up with "chauvinistic" men in order to be abused again and again. As therapy continued, Adelaide became extremely dependent on the therapist and struggled with fantasies that he would rape her; when no sexual advances from him were forthcoming, she began to imagine that he was a homosexual and that she was therefore safe in the relationship. At first she seemed to be making progress in therapy, and the therapist began to discount his initial impression of a possible thought disorder.

After about one year of therapy, however, she became increasingly disorganized and bizarre. On one occasion, she was seen on an emergency basis and was prescribed antipsychotic medication after reporting an extreme feeling of depersonalization and confusion. Her therapist became concerned that she was on the verge of decompensation and might "accidentally" commit suicide with her car. A second emergency consultation was precipitated by a vivid nightmare in which she was involved in homosexual activity, and she began to discuss her homosexual desires in therapy, stating that she feared that her hatred of men and her increasing feelings of affection and sexual desire with women meant that she would become a lesbian. As of the end of the study, she had not acted on her homosexual feelings but continued her compulsive heterosexual acting out, which became even more overtly masochistic.

In the case just described, the patient may have been experiencing a breakthrough of homosexual thoughts and feelings as part of a broader picture of a developing psychotic state in which ego controls were disintegrating. However, it was quite possible that her awareness of lesbian feelings would eventually lead to overt homosexual relationships and a conversion to a gay lifestyle, just as a similar awareness did in the case of Nadine who had also been extremely disturbed by her first consciousness of homosexual desires.

Viewed as a whole, the cases presented provide evidence that a significant minority of psychologically disturbed women with histories of father-daughter incest later experience homosexual feelings that are sufficiently intense to motivate experimentation with lesbian relationships. Although the number of cases is too small to allow a conclusion on this point, it seemed that the women who were relatively accepting of their lesbian feelings were far less disturbed than those who saw themselves as perverse and who attempted to suppress their desires. As we have seen, these nonaccepting women went through very painful, self-destructive disturbances of psychotic proportions in which they were reported to be preoccupied with sexual thoughts. A second point that seems obvious is that the conscious awareness of lesbian feelings may occur after many years of heterosexual "adjustment," and therefore the number of lesbian outcomes discovered in this sample should be viewed as an underestimate because many of the daughters were still in their early twenties when seen in therapy. If some of the women presenting with problems in heterosexual response were to be followed up in their thirties and forties, there might well be even more lesbian conversions to report.

There is very little mention in previous studies of female homosexuality in association with father-daughter incest, so there are few prior hypotheses to consider when discussing possible explanations for this phenomenon. There were no findings of lesbian experience in early follow-up studies (Rasmussen, 1934; Bender and Grugett, 1952; Sloane and Karpinsky, 1942), in which researchers interviewed small samples of postincest daughters in their twenties or thirties. In Weinberg's (1955) large study, homosexuality was completely omitted from his discussion of the aftereffects of incest. Other large studies (Gligor, 1966; Maisch, 1972) have similarly omitted mention of such outcomes, and we do not even know whether the researchers inquired about homosexuality. Kubo (1959) specifically stated that he found no postincest homosexuality in his combined brother-sister and father-daughter sample. Since Weinberg and later large-sample studies gathered information on most of their cases soon after discovery of incest and only occasionally obtained additional information on some of the cases after a few years had elapsed, we may speculate that the samples were too young to show instances of lesbian conversions. However, even in adolescence female homosexuality is not rare, so we would expect that at least some instances would have been found had the researchers specifically looked for them and had the daughters been sufficiently cooperative to reveal lesbian feelings or behaviors to them. That many of the daughters would have sought to keep a homosexual orientation from public view is a proposition that seems very obvious indeed.

In clinical studies of incest, there have been more findings of homosexuality as an aftereffect of father-daughter incest, probably because therapists gain the confidence of their patients in a way that a researcher conducting one or two isolated interviews with an incest participant can seldom hope to achieve. Kaufman, Peck, and Tagiuri (1954) specifically mention homosexuality, along with promiscuity and "asceticism," as an aftereffect of incest in some of the eleven incestuous daughters that they treated for psychological disturbance shortly after incest had occurred. They speculated that the homosexuality might be motivated by the daughters' wish to be loved by older women to make up for the rejection they had experienced with their mothers and also acknowledged that the daughters' heterosexual involvement in incest had been traumatic and that the resultant anxiety associated with heterosexuality motivated their turn to homosexuality. However, there was no mention of how many of the eleven girls studied sought homosexual experience or what the experience, if any, consisted of. Medlicott (1967) is the only clinical researcher to have given a precise figure, having found that five out of seventeen (29 percent) daughters who were seen in psychotherapy some years after incest manifested "serious homosexual problems." Again, however, the nature of the problems was not revealed.

Even in clinical studies, lesbian outcomes have often not been mentioned. Lukianowicz (1972) recently catalogued the subsequent problems of twenty-six daughters and found promiscuity, prostitution, and frigidity but evidently no homosexual behavior. A number of other smaller studies (for example, Magal and Winnick, 1968; Hersko and others, 1961; Molnar and Cameron, 1975) focused on postincest adjustment of daughters and reported the existence of sexual problems without any mention of lesbian outcomes. In many cases, the daughters were not evaluated long enough after the incest incident for lesbian tendencies or behavior to have been manifested. Also, most of these studies were carried out in other countries, so we may well ask whether differences in societal norms pertaining to homosexuality could have biased the results. Surely the degree of censure or acceptance that a patient expects to receive on admitting lesbian feelings or behavior would influence her willingness to disclose them to a therapist and might in some cases determine whether the feeling would be repressed or expressed openly.

The psychotherapy sample reported on in this study was gathered at a time when the gay community in Los Angeles was campaigning for wider public acceptance of gay behavior as an alternative life-style, and media coverage of gay churches, gay counseling centers, and other kinds of community activities may have served to inform many women who were "closeted" with their lesbian feelings that there was a community of women like themselves from whom they could seek social support. In three of the cases reported earlier, the women did turn to the organized gay community and felt more comfortable and less lonely after doing so. Their therapists, especially female therapists, also seemed more accepting of the possibility of a gay life-style than would have been the case ten years before or in another, less tolerant cultural setting.

Although the increased acceptance and public visibility of the gay life-style may have induced more patients to disclose lesbian feelings and behavior to their therapists, it should be emphasized that there was no evidence that knowledge about the gay community had played a major role in "converting" these women. Their feelings of sexual desire for other women had always preceded any contact they had with the gay community, sometimes by many years. There were no reports of being seduced by lesbian friends; on the contrary, they actively sought lesbian relations with women whom they already perceived as being gay. It appeared that their knowledge of the gay community simply had given them a feeling that they could reach out for social support after they had recognized and begun to accept their lesbian orientation.

Apparently, father-daughter incest as a traumatic, conflict-inducing heterosexual experience in early life is associated with an increased incidence of lesbian feelings and behavior in maturity, although the majority of postincest daughters remain heterosexual. An absolute causal connection between these life events has not, of course, been demonstrated by this finding;

however, it is difficult to imagine how such a connection *could* be demonstrated within the framework of ethical research with human subjects. It seems plausible that overt incest may sometimes cause female homosexuality, but this hypothesis should not be read as implying that overt incest is a *frequent* causal factor in female homosexuality. There is some information in the literature on life history factors in self-identified lesbian women that bears on this point. Gundlach and Riess (1967), for instance, have reported on a nationwide survey of 217 middle-class lesbians and 231 comparable nonlesbians, and they found that more of the lesbians had experienced heterosexual trauma in the form of rape or attempted rape at age fifteen or earlier. It is not known how many of these trauma were incestuous in nature. However, the vast majority of the lesbian sample (82 percent) had reported no such traumatic experience. In a much more thorough report on the family backgrounds of twenty-six lesbians recruited for interviews through a homophile organization, Rosen (1974) found that two women had had sexual experiences with violent, abusive stepfathers in childhood and early adolescence. This incidence is probably higher than the number of such cases that would be found in the general population, but they still constituted a small minority (8 percent) of this lesbian sample. My own reading of Rosen's case history reports would seem to indicate that the women who had reported incest seemed psychologically disturbed as adults. The appropriate conclusion would therefore be that, while father-daughter incest frequently results in a lesbian orientation in women who are psychologically disturbed, incestuous experience is not a background factor for the great majority of self-identified lesbians.

As was the case with women who became promiscuous, the life histories of the lesbian women in the psychotherapy sample were replete with factors other than incest that may have played a role in the development of their adult sexual orientations. For example, difficulties in relating to their mothers may have fostered conflicts about assuming the culturally accepted female role in life; however, many of the nonlesbian women also had poor relationships with their mothers. Although the number of cases was too small to permit conclusions, the women showing lesbian outcomes were compared with the women who were nonresponsive in heterosexual relationships but had not sought homosexual relationships in an effort to generate hypotheses about the different outcomes. An important difference between these groups of women was the quality of the nonsexual aspects of their heterosexual relationships. The women who became lesbians expressed a great deal of hatred toward men as a group, whereas the others were more willing to relate to men in an affectionate way, even though their relationships were often stormy. The hatred of men had often been the culmination of a long series of relationships in which they either tolerated abuse or actively sought it. When their heterosexual relationships began to seem futile in both the sexual and nonsexual aspects, they turned to women for the affection and sexuality they had missed with men.

Finally, it should be stressed again that the psychotherapy sample studied here was by its very nature psychologically disturbed. Therefore, the lesbians whose backgrounds we have considered were not typical of lesbians in general, and the fact that their sexual orientation had been adopted for essentially negative reactions—hatred of men, frigidity in heterosexual intercourse—should not lead the reader to assume that lesbianism is simply a failure of heterosexuality. In his study of the life histories of twenty-six lesbians, Rosen (1974, p. 70), concluded that "One factor stands out as having more etiological weight than the others. This is the importance of the first sexual experience and whether it is pleasurable and positive with a woman or discomforting and negative with a man." In cases of father-daughter incest, we are seeing the effects of an early heterosexual experience that proved to be discomforting and negative; we should not lose sight of the fact that a lesbian orientation might also be positively motivated by early pleasurable experiences with women.

⊞ ⊞ ⊞ ⊞ ⊞ ⊞ ⊞ 7

Females in Heterosexual Incest: Sisters, Nieces, and Granddaughters

⊞ ⊞ ⊞ ⊞ ⊞ ⊞ ⊞ ⊞ ⊞ ⊞ ⊞ ⊞ ⊞ ⊞ ⊞ ⊞ ⊞

In the last three chapters, father-daughter incest has been extensively discussed, and we have focused on the incest affair as experienced by the daughter and its perceived role in personality development and adult sexual adjustment. In doing so, we have already highlighted many of the causal factors and aftereffects found in the other forms of heterosexual incest in which young females are involved. In contrast with the thirty-six cases of father-daughter or father-step-daughter incest found in the psychotherapy sample, only eight female patients reported incest with brothers, five with uncles, and five with grandfathers (either by blood or by marriage, in each case). In this chapter, the emphasis on effects on the fe-

262

male participant continues, and each of these other forms of heterosexual incest is described and discussed in comparison with father-daughter incest.

Brother-Sister Incest

As a theme in mythology and literature, sibling incest has been treated more frequently, and with much more sympathy, than parent-child incest; the interested reader is referred to Fox (1962) and Santiago (1973) for detailed reviews of this subject. As a theme in theories of psychopathology, however, brother-sister incest has received far less attention than the two parent-child forms. Although some recent evidence (Arndt and Ladd, 1976) suggests that repression of impulses to engage in sibling incest plays some role in adult personality structure, the usual absence of a dependency relationship between brother and sister and the less intense taboo against their sexual contact have led to fewer predictions of severe disturbance as a result of sibling incest. As discussed in Chapter Three, it has generally been assumed that sibling incest is more common than father-daughter incest in the "real," but unknowable population of incest cases, even though father-daughter incest is much more common in most research settings. In the psychotherapy sample, there were almost four cases of father-daughter incest for every brother-sister case, so it is quite possible that women involved in brother-sister incest are less frequently disturbed as adults and tend not to seek psychotherapy. The extent of this sample bias cannot be estimated but should be borne in mind. Still, it is instructive to compare the kinds of disturbance found in daughters and sisters who did seek psychotherapy at least three years after the incest affair.

Family Background Factors. The most consistent finding with regard to the family setting of brother-sister incest is that the children have lacked adult supervision, particularly with regard to their sex play activities. The youngest sister in a larger family with several older brothers seems to be particularly vulnerable to incestuous advances; probably the temptation exists in many such families, but the lack of effective restraining agents may allow tentative, playful approaches to develop into full-blown sexual relationships.

The key role of the father as a restraining agent in cases where the brother is in late adolescence or early adulthood has been emphasized by some researchers. Weinberg (1955) stressed that the father was often absent from the family when the incestuous situation developed; when he was present, he was sometimes incapacitated by disease or old age or was such a weak personality that he could not wield sufficient power within the family to restrain a son inclined to incest. Kubo (1959) found that the majority of his thirteen cases of brother-sister incest occurred in fatherless families where the older brother involved in incest had been elevated to a fatherly role and thus exercised considerable power within the family.

In about half of the brother-sister cases in the psycho-therapy sample, the father was dead or weakened by alcoholism or psychosis at the time of incest. The following case is representative:

> Leila's mother died when she was born, the youngest daughter in a large, impoverished family in the South. Her father, already an irresponsible, alcoholic man, could not contend with the chaotic family and had the children adopted out in groups. Leila went to an adoptive family with two older brothers and a sister when she was three years old, and after only three years with her new parents her adoptive father died. When she was eight, her brothers, now in their teens, began to have intercourse with her and her older sister on occasions when the adoptive mother was not at home. All of the siblings disliked the adoptive mother and defiantly rejected her rigid, puritanical ideas about sex. When she became aware of the incest, the adoptive mother rejected the three older siblings and arranged for them to be placed in a children's home. She kept Leila with her, however, since she believed that she was too young to have been involved in the sexual activities.

Most of the sibling incest cases in the psychotherapy sample emphasized the key role of the mother in defining appropriate behavior for the children. In contrast with the Weinberg (1955) and Kubo (1959) samples, most of the sisters and brothers were in childhood or early adolescence at the time of incest, so perhaps we can speculate that the mother plays a more important part than does the father in the supervision of young children's activities and in provision of early sex education. In three of the eight sibling incest cases, the children's natural mother had died of cancer prior to the occurrence of incest. In two of these cases, she was replaced by a stepmother or adoptive mother, but the siblings never regained the strong maternal attachment they had had previously. In another instance, the mother was so passive and ineffectual that the children actually felt that they had no mother:

Karen's father left her mother for another woman when she and her brother were in kindergarten. Although he provided generous financial support to his children, he could only manage to see them two or three times per year and thus played an insignificant role in their development. The mother was remembered as an extremely anxious and neurotic woman who was incompetent in managing the household and spent most of her time listening to soap operas on the radio. From the earliest time in her childhood, Karen had felt that her mother was dependent on herself and her brother, and she recalled hearing her mother admit that she relied on her children to "take care of her." It seemed as if Karen and her brother were pushed into the role of mother and father in their family triad, and they gradually established a quasi-marital sexual relationship that lasted for many years, although they concealed their activity from their mother and playmates.

Even more prevalent than the mother's absence or dependency was the mention of her very rigid, puritanical attitudes toward sexuality and the resultant lack of real sex education in the home. In five of the eight brother-sister cases in the psychotherapy sample, the sister specifically mentioned this background factor. Unlike the daughters in father-daughter incest, they had not received the impression that their mothers disliked sexual activity, only that sex was a *bad* thing that was not to be discussed at home except for occasional lectures on its supposed evils. It is possible that this maternal attitude had stimulated the siblings' curiosity about the delights that they were forbidden so frequently. Certainly, it distanced the mother and daughter and practically guaranteed that no sharing of information and sexual concerns would take place in the home. Quite unknown to the mother, her total prohibition of sexuality backfired on her, since it interfered with supervision of her children's play activities. If the children failed to internalize her total prohibition, they often became rebelliously experimental in their sexual behavior.

Weinberg (1955) mentioned a "loose sex culture" as one of the background factors in sibling incest. In such families, sex was talked about openly in obscene words, and the parents did not supervise their children's sexual activity, because they were unconcerned about it. The parents also made little effort to prevent the children from seeing them engage in marital or extramarital sexual activity in the home. Marcuse (1923) had also noted that siblings who witnessed parental intercourse were often sexually stimulated and attempted to imitate adult sexual activity with each other. In the psychotherapy sample, however, none of the sisters could recall witnessing open sexual activity in the home, and their families were anything but open in their communications about sex. One somewhat bizarre exception was a family that combined condemnation of sexuality with sexual acting out.

Daphne had been adopted by a fundamentalist minister and his wife along with two older adoptive brothers and one sister. The mother preached constantly to the children about the evils of sexuality, especially heterosexuality. The children were

aware, however, that the father was a closeted
homosexual who was risking very serious earthly
consequences by having affairs with young men in
his congregation. Eventually the mother also began
to have homosexual affairs so openly that gossip
among the neighbors got back to the children. In
this atmosphere of hypocrisy and sexual stimulation, the children openly experimented with both
heterosexual and homosexual incest.

A factor related to the sexually promiscuous family background is the prior occurrence of father-daughter incest. In the
five cases of combined father-daughter and sibling incest described by Weinberg (1955), father-daughter incest generally
occurred first and was known to other members of the family.
When the daughter was adolescent, she was very promiscuous
and tempted the brother into sexual activity at a time when the
father had lost his authority over the brother and no longer had
the intrafamilial power to restrain sibling incest. There are many
variations of this theme, however. In case histories reported by
Eist and Mandel (1968) and Magal and Winnick (1968), incest
with the father occurred first, but the brothers apparently had
no knowledge of it, and the sisters were not promiscuous outside of the family. Raphling, Carpenter, and Davis (1967) describe a father who had sex with his daughters and then urged
his son to have sex with them as well, evidently attempting to
recreate the sexual milieu of his family of origin, in which he
himself had witnessed father-daughter incest prior to engaging
in brother-sister incest. In the psychotherapy sample, the father-
daughter prior to brother-sister scenario occurred in one of the
eight cases reported by sisters:

> Laura was one of the youngest children in a
> family of thirteen siblings living on a farm in the
> Midwest. Their parents were sickly and approach-
> ing old age when Laura was a little girl, so the older
> siblings partially assumed a parenting role with her.
> The mother was puritanical and emotionally reject-
> ing of Laura; the father was a kindly man whose

attempts to be physically affectionate with her
aroused her anxiety because she and the other children knew that he had made sexual approaches to
an older sister. Throughout her childhood, two of
the adolescent brothers would engage her in
mutual genital stimulation whenever both parents
were absent from the home.

In addition to a lack of parental supervision or the provision of faulty sexual models by the parents, there are personality characteristics of the brother and sister that can increase
the likelihood of incest. With regard to the sister, Weinberg
(1955) found that adolescent sisters involved in incest were
more apt to have been sexually promiscuous prior to incest and
to have been of lower intelligence than adolescent daughters in
father-daughter incest. In the psychotherapy sample, two of the
eight sisters were thought to be of limited intelligence by their
therapists, a higher proportion than was found in the group of
daughters. Lest this finding create a stereotype of the sister as
consistently dull, note that one of the remaining sisters had
graduated from a prestigious law school, an accomplishment
that none of the daughters had come close to matching. With
regard to preexisting promiscuity, however, none was found
because the sisters in the psychotherapy sample were generally
under twelve years of age when the incest began. The one exception was a sister of thirteen who had had intercourse with a
little boy in a foster home prior to being adopted, but this was
evidently her only previous sexual contact.

Weinberg (1955) found that incestuous brothers were of
normal intelligence as a group and seemed to have a better
social and personal adjustment than incestuous fathers, although some of them were involved in juvenile delinquent subcultures. Imprisoned older brothers are frequently of low intelligence (Gebhard and others, 1965), but this finding is probably
the result of sample bias, since men of normal or superior intelligence are unlikely to be apprehended, much less imprisoned,
for sibling incest. In the psychotherapy sample, no brother was
described by his sister as being dull, but one brother was called

"emotionally disturbed," since his sister attributed his unwanted sexual approaches to her to his general proclivity to
experiment with animals and people. He was already well
known in the neighborhood for his bizarre sexual practices. Of
the other brothers in the sample, none was described by his sister as having any unusual characteristics.

Although no such cases were found in the psychotherapy
sample, other researchers (Schachter and Cotte, 1960; Weinberg, 1955) have reported cases of brother-sister incest in which
the siblings had been separated as children and reared in different homes. When the brother and sister met each other in adolescence or adulthood, they had only the intellectual knowledge
of their close genetic relationship, for the emotional component
of the brother-sister tie had never been established. An intense
love relationship sometimes developed in addition to the incestuous sexual contact, and these brothers and sisters occasionally
succeeded in marrying each other. Such cases reemphasize the
importance of the emotional reality of familial relationships:
Incest with a stepfather or stepbrother can seem intensely incestuous to a girl who has related to him as a daughter or sister
over a long period of time, while incest with a natural father or
brother seems less incestuous in its emotional character if there
is little feeling of relatedness present.

The Incest Affair. The dynamics of the brother-sister incest relationship have received far less attention than the father-
daughter affair. There seem to be no theories about family con-
spiracies, role reversals, or unconscious motives for the
occurrence of incest, probably because sexual contact between
brother and sister is seen as an understandable, completely natural consequence of a lack of parental guidance. Because brothers
and sisters are closer in age than parents and children, the incest
affair less often carries the additional stigma of "child molestation" and can be seen as akin to the heterosexual experimentation in which many children and adolescents engage. One would
therefore expect the sibling incest affair to be a less traumatic
life event than the father-daughter affair.

Sisters are more likely to describe incest with a brother as
beginning with mutual interest and participation than are

daughters reporting on father-daughter incest. Weinberg (1955) attributed the "aggressor" role to several sisters who were sexually promiscuous prior to the incest affair, but, as with most adolescent sexual relationships, it was still more frequent for the male to initiate sexual contact. In the psychotherapy sample, three of the eight sisters freely admitted that the sexual activity had developed out of a mutual curiosity about sex; none of the women thought that she had been the aggressor, but perhaps the strong cultural prescription that males take the initiative in sexual activity prevented their perception or admission of being aggressive. In the other five cases, the brother was said to have made the approach, almost always on an occasion when the parents were absent from the home. Two sisters described the sexual approach as a "rape," but one of these women seemed so blasé about it that her therapist doubted that serious violence or threat had occurred. More usually, the brother seemed to have persuaded his sister to cooperate with some combination of bribes and threats not unlike the ones that most siblings use in their power struggles with each other. In one case, the brothers would play "hide and seek" with the sister and then tie her to a bed when they found her, but she considered the "game" to be merely annoying and did not think of it as a rape even though some physical force had been employed.

Sibling incest is somewhat more likely to eventuate in genital intercourse and less likely to involve oral-genital activity than father-daughter incest. Because the siblings are closer in age and physical size and because the sister is often cooperative in the activity, it is easier for brothers and sisters to effect genital contact. It is also possible that some mild forms of mutual exhibition or fondling are unlikely to be labeled *incest* in the brother-sister context but seem more inappropriate between parents and children and thus receive the incest label. Since oral-genital relations tend to be "discovered" somewhat later in a person's sexual career, young brothers and sisters would be unlikely to use this method of stimulation. In line with these expectations, it was found that half of the brother-sister cases in the psychotherapy sample involved genital intercourse while there were no reports of oral-genital activity; in the father-daughter group, 44 percent of the cases involved genital intercourse, and 22 percent involved oral-genital techniques. The remainder of the sibling cases were instances of specifically sexual genital manipulation without attempts at intercourse.

Sisters are more likely than daughters to experience conscious sexual pleasure in the incestuous act. Although Weinberg (1955) did not discuss sexual response, his conclusion that many sisters were willing partners or even initiated the sexual activity seems to imply that they were sexually attracted to their brothers. Santiago (1973) reports an in-depth case history in which the brother and sister had sexual intercourse from early childhood through their twenties, and the sister was fully orgasmic in the relationship. As we might expect, in the psychotherapy sample there were fewer reports of disgust and repulsion during the incest affair for sisters than for daughters, although there was a wide range of reactions. In one case, a sister who had had relations with her younger brother for several years in childhood and early adolescence remembered the incestuous activity as intensely pleasurable and told her therapist that incest had been the best sexual experience in her life. In another, the patient experienced such intense guilt feelings when asked whether sex with her brother was pleasurable that her therapist inferred that it had been. The majority of the sisters could be described as slightly negative in their expressed reaction to the incestuous activity; they usually described the incest as having been annoying and bothersome to them and expressed resentment to the brother for having initiated it but did not generally feel the profound sense of betrayal that was so commonly found in incestuous daughters. However, one sister expressed revulsion that was equivalent to that of any of the daughters; in her case the sexual activity took place when two of her older brothers issued serious threats and made it clear that they intended the sexual contact to be humiliating to her.

Although the number of cases is small, there seemed to be a close relationship between the experience of incest pleasure and the voluntary participation of the sister. When brother and sister were close in age and incestuous activity evolved naturally from their mutual curiosity and playful interactions, the sister

was quite likely to experience sexual pleasure; however, when
the brother was several years older the sexual activity tended to
be motivated by his need for a sexual outlet, and the sister perceived the relationship as exploitive and thus unpleasant in both
a sexual and an interpersonal sense. An older brother would also
introduce sexual activity too abruptly for the sister to develop
feelings of pleasure, and a much older brother might be perceived as playing a nurturant role with the sister, thus injecting
a sense of "father-daughter" incest into the sibling incest situation.

   After sibling incest has occurred, the sister is in a less difficult choice situation than the daughter. Sisters do not seem to
foresee a family breakup as a possible consequence of the disclosure of incest, although they often anticipate being punished
by their parents. In fact, brothers in the psychotherapy sample
seldom issued threats to their sisters and seemed to correctly
assume that the sister would not tell any adult authority about
the incest for fear of being punished herself. In father-daughter
incest, the daughter's motive for telling her mother is usually
her hope of enlisting her mother's aid in terminating the incest
relationship. In sibling incest, the "relationship" usually consisted of only a few incidents in cases where the sister was uncooperative, and thus there was less reason for her to take any
perceived risk by telling the mother. Remember that many of
the mothers were perceived as puritanical, so it is easy to imagine that the sister would dread her mother's horrified reaction
to a revelation of incest. Seven out of the eight sisters in the
psychotherapy sample did not reveal the incest to their mothers. The following case was the one exception:

   Therese was one of several children in a very
   disturbed family. Her father, an unemployed
   assembly-line worker, had been hospitalized for
   psychosis, and his outbursts of anger and sexual
   jealousy kept the family in a constant state of tension. Not surprisingly, several of the children developed behavior problems. A brother four years
   older than Therese had been unusually interested
   in sex since early childhood and also displayed a

sadistic bent in his relationships with pets and younger children. When Therese was eight years old, the disturbed brother enlisted the help of a younger brother to tie her to a bed and experiment with inserting objects in her vagina. At the instigation of the older brother, these incidents were repeated many times over a period of about four months on occasions when the children were left alone together. After the first incident, Therese tried to avoid her brothers because she found the activity annoying and felt humiliated by it, but they were usually able to catch her. She finally resorted to telling her mother about the activity, and her mother immediately punished the boys and ensured that the incidents would not continue.

The brother-sister incest affair is quite variable in its duration. Weinberg (1955) emphasized that sibling incest was more often very transient in nature than father-daughter incest but that an occasional brother-sister pair would manifest "incest love" and even attempt to be legally married. Of the eight sibling incest cases described by sisters in the psychotherapy sample, two consisted of a single incident, five involved several incidents over a period of several months, and only one incest affair endured for several years. This is in contrast with the 53 percent of father-daughter affairs that lasted over one year and probably reflects the fact that brother-sister affairs are usually not continued beyond a few incidents unless the sister is genuinely cooperative, while unwilling daughters were often prevented from leaving the relationship by their fathers' authoritarian stance.

In Weinberg's (1955) study, many of the brother-sister relationships terminated with the pregnancy of the sister, and it was noted that sisters became pregnant more frequently than daughters, evidently because fathers were more cautious than brothers. In the psychotherapy sample, none of the eight sisters became pregnant as a result of incestuous contact, possibly because all of them were under fourteen years of age at the time of incest and thus relatively unlikely to conceive. Incest affairs that went beyond a single incident generally terminated when the siblings lost interest in the activity and directed their sexual attention outside the nuclear family. There were two exceptions. In one case, already described, the mother enforced the termination of incest after the sister enlisted her aid. In the second, the brother and sister were still very much attracted to each other but decided to abstain from intercourse when the sister was fourteen because they knew that her chances of becoming pregnant were increasing.

Long-Term Aftereffects. In three previous studies, some of the sisters in sibling incest samples were evaluated an unknown length of time after the termination of incest, and the author commented on their adult adjustment in comparison with daughters in father-daughter incest. Weinberg (1955) found that daughters were better adjusted as adults than sisters, who engaged in more promiscuous sexual relationships and were more likely to become prostitutes. However, Kubo (1959) thought that adult daughters experienced more mental confusion than sisters, although he gave examples of some sisters who were psychotic and experienced vivid hallucinations centering on their guilt about participation in incest. Lukianowicz (1972) implied that sisters were less disturbed than daughters since he attributed no "ill effects" to the sibling incest affairs, even though the sisters in his study must have been psychologically disturbed because they were all in psychotherapy or residential treatment.

In the psychotherapy sample, there appeared to be little difference in level of overall disturbance between the daughters and sisters when they entered treatment at least three years after the incest affair. About 38 percent of the sisters were judged to be severely disturbed, as compared with 32 percent of the daughters; 25 percent of the sisters and 23 percent of the daughters had been hospitalized for psychiatric reasons. Thus there were very small differences in overall psychological disturbance, although it must be remembered that the percentages given for sisters are based on only eight cases. There were, however, some interesting differences in the kinds of problems presented by postincest daughters and sisters.

Almost 31 percent of the daughters were described as obese when they sought psychotherapy or as having been obese at some time subsequent to the incest experience, while none of the eight sisters was obese. If obesity is sometimes an unconscious effort to avoid sexual relationships, then these sisters were manifesting less avoidance behavior.

The marital history of sisters over eighteen also suggests that they were less likely to avoid sexual involvement than the daughters. All of the sisters over eighteen had been married at least once, whereas nearly 40 percent of the daughters over eighteen had never married. The sisters had slightly fewer marriages (1.4, on the average) than the daughters (1.5), and were married for longer periods of time. The average daughter had spent about 39 percent of her years since age eighteen in a marital state, as compared with a figure of 72 percent for the sisters. It would appear, then, that the adult sisters tended to have a more stable marital history than the adult daughters, and one might be tempted to infer from these figures that the sisters were happier in their marriages than the daughters. However, this was definitely not the case.

Although the typical sister was not afraid of men and seemed less conflicted about entering heterosexual relationships, she often suffered passively in extremely unsatisfactory relationships over long periods of time. The daughters were described as being masochistic in 42 percent of the cases, but nearly 71 percent of the sisters were thus described. Usually the therapist assigned the "masochistic" label on the basis of the quality of the sister's "love" relationships, as in the following case:

> Nancy was the youngest child in a middle-class family that stressed very strict adherence to a traditional religious faith and set up rigid standards of behavior for the children. From her earliest childhood, she felt that she had been scapegoated by her parents and older siblings, and she vividly recalled being beaten with straps by both of her parents and being forced to apologize and atone for very minor infractions of the family rules. She

viewed the incestuous incidents with her brothers as merely another manifestation of her helplessness within the family and did not dare to tell her mother about the incidents because she believed that she would receive more punishment than her brothers.

After graduating from high school, she left her family to marry a boy she had known for a few months, and they remained married for nearly nineteen years. Since her religion forbade birth control, she gave birth to a child every year or two for the first ten years of marriage. In addition to a large family, she endured increasing amounts of physical abuse from her husband, who enjoyed the creation of sadistic scenarios during sexual intercourse with her. He evidently went far beyond playful "pretend rape" scenes and inflicted injuries that left permanent scars on her body. Nevertheless, she continued to take the advice of her religious counselor, who forbade her to use birth control and advised her that divorce was an immoral alternative to her miserable marriage. After several more years of patient endurance, she separated from her husband and endured severe criticism from her family of origin, who let it be known on frequent occasions that they thought she was a "fallen woman" because she was seeking a divorce. Soon after the divorce, she met a man who expressed an interest in her and indicated that he would like to marry her but was not yet in a financial position to do so; however, he planned to purchase a franchise for a "fast food" outlet that would supposedly provide him with a steady income, and he swiftly prevailed on Nancy to sell her house in order to provide him with the required capital for this venture. At this time, she sought therapy at the clinic for depression, and it seemed to her therapist that she suspected that she was about to become a victim again but felt utterly at the mercy of her life situation.

As with daughters, it appeared that the incest was only one factor in a background of family abuse that trained the sisters to play the victim role repeatedly as adolescents and adults. As in the case just presented, the sisters frequently came from strictly religious backgrounds, which may have reinforced the masochistic orientation as the proper role of women in life, so perhaps this aspect is responsible for finding more masochism in the group of sisters. Again, it should be remembered that there were only eight sisters in the psychotherapy sample, so the formulations given here should be treated as speculations rather than conclusions.

The daughters had continued to have stressful relationships with their parents, particularly the mother, during their adult lives. In the group of sisters, problems with the family of origin were less common. In three cases, the mother had been dead for many years; in two cases, the sister continued to have a stressful relationship with her, and in the remaining three cases their relationship continued on a satisfactory basis. In two cases, the adult sister's relationship with her father was a source of stress, and in three other cases the father had had so little contact with the sister since childhood that she considered herself fatherless. As an adult, the sister generally was not alienated from her incestuous brother, although the sisters who had considered themselves victimized by their brothers continued to distrust them. In the one case where the sister had described a long-lasting incest affair with sexual pleasure for both siblings, there was an uncomfortable sense of estrangement between brother and sister as adults. The sister reported that her brother had moved to a distant city and corresponded with her but resisted her attempts to visit him in person. She suspected that he was fearful that she might reveal the incest affair to his wife, and she felt saddened that their enjoyment had created such an uneasy separation between them.

The daughters in the psychotherapy sample seldom were attracted to men who seemed to be "father figures," despite findings from previous studies that suggested that they would be. No such prediction was made for the sisters, but it appeared on the basis of this small sample that they were more inclined to pursue father figures than the daughters had been. Of the seven sisters who were over eighteen at the time they were seen

in therapy, two had married men who were over ten years older
than they were during their twenties, and another two had
fallen in love with their older male therapists. In one case, the
relationship with a private practice therapist was so intense and
sexually tinged that the patient suddenly fled from it and
sought therapy at the clinic with a female therapist. In another,
the patient sent her therapist a steady stream of love letters and
threatened to commit suicide when he continued to insist on
seeing her in conjoint sessions with her husband rather than
individually. It is especially interesting that both of these
women had lost their fathers through death or desertion between five and ten years of age; from the evidence in this small
sample it seems that such an early loss is more likely to produce
"father-seeking" behavior in later life than are the conflicts engendered by father-daughter incest.

An unexpected finding with regard to later family relationships of the sisters was extreme difficulty in relating to their
sons, and the nature of the difficulty suggests that the sisters
were displacing onto their sons their feelings about their brothers. In four of the six cases in which the sister was currently
over eighteen and had at least one son, there were serious problems in the mother-son relationship. The correlation between
the nature of the mother's incest experience and the problem
with her son can be readily observed in the following case descriptions:

> Laura felt that she had been a victim of her
> older brothers and that they had treated her as an
> object in order to gratify their sexual curiosity. She
> attributed her hatred of men in general to her
> childhood experiences and freely told her therapist
> that she had cried bitterly when she discovered
> that her first baby was a boy. When her son was
> eight, she beat him on the slightest excuse and
> regularly threatened to kill him by pushing him out
> of her car on the freeway.

> Nancy's brothers had bullied her into mutual
> masturbation as a child, and she had always felt
> afraid of them while she was growing up. At the

time of therapy, her nineteen-year-old son lived out of the home and belonged to an antisocial subculture. When he returned for visits, he threatened her until she gave him whatever money she had left over from her monthly welfare check.

Therese had been molested by an older brother who was psychologically disturbed and given to bizarre behaviors that frightened and disgusted her. Her ten-year-old son was so disturbed that he already had a long juvenile record for such bizarre activities as torturing cats and stealing underwear in coin-operated laundries. She was both terrified and angered by his behavior.

Karen had loved having sexual relations with her younger brother and freely admitted that she had initiated the activity. When seen in therapy with her eighteen-year-old son, she was overtly seductive toward him, and he became so uncomfortable with her behavior that he withdrew from her and refused to spend his college vacations at home.

These cases suggest the hypothesis that having a young son reactivates the conflicts originally associated with sibling incest and that the sister's manner of relating to her son tends to recapitulate some aspects of her relationship with her brother, possibly even molding her son in her brother's image.

Nearly 90 percent of the daughters who were eighteen or over when seen in therapy had at least one problem in the sexual area; all of the seven sisters over eighteen had some difficulty with sex, although the problems were minimal in two of the cases. Although the incidence of such problems was about the same for daughters and sisters, the pattern was different and suggested that sisters were more inclined to be experimental and promiscuous and less likely to withdraw from heterosexual relationships than were daughters.

First, let us briefly examine the two cases in which the sister presented some mild sexual problems in the context of a generally good adjustment:

Karen's long, mutually enjoyable incestuous relationship with her brother had ended in early adolescence. An extremely intelligent, ambitious young woman, she worked full time to support herself in college, and at age twenty married a classmate whom she knew to be bisexual. Their marital relationship was good for many years, and she was nearly always orgasmic in intercourse. However, her husband eventually lost interest in her, began to have homosexual affairs, and urged her to become involved in "swinging" activities during the final months of their marriage in order to assuage his guilt about leaving her and their children and adopting a gay life-style. For several months, she participated in group sex and enjoyed both hetero- and homosexual activities in this context with minimal guilt, but she gradually lost interest in the "swinging scene." Her tendency to sexualize relationships also led to some problems in interactions with her son and her male therapist.

Ingrid and her brother had gone through a period of mutual manipulation that stopped short of intercourse when she was eleven years old. She was also the victim of a rape while in high school, but she did not believe that either the rape or the incestuous incidents had seriously affected her later sexual relationships. While in college, she had sexual relationships with two boyfriends and was orgasmic with them. In her mid twenties, she married an older man who had children from a previous marriage and soon began to experience difficulty with sexual response in relations with her husband. She requested sex therapy, and an initial evaluation indicated that her problem was more related to the deterioration of her marital relationship than any deep-rooted conflicts about sexuality in general.

Like the daughters who were minimally affected by incest, these sisters had been well-adjusted children from relatively healthy, nonabusive families. Even more significantly, their incestuous involvement had arisen from their own sexual curiosity and had not been imposed on them by the brother. In the first case, it seemed that whatever "problems" the woman manifested with sex as an adult could be viewed as a continuation of her willingness to experiment with sexual activity as a child. Both women were extremely competent in their occupational roles as adults, and they were also the only sisters who were not labeled *masochistic* by their therapists.

Like the daughters, about 85 percent of the sisters had had serious problems with orgasmic response as adults, either failing to achieve orgasm at all or achieving it only in very unusual circumstances. The nature of the unusual circumstances described by the sisters suggested that they were masochistic in the strict sexual sense in addition to suffering nonsexual kinds of abuse in their interpersonal relationships. One woman had had only one orgasm in her life, and this occurred during a paid sexual incident with an older man when she was in early adolescence. Another had had her only orgasm while being raped by a stranger who wore satin gloves and a bizarre mask. And a third woman could experience orgasm with her husband only when they acted out an elaborate "rape" scenario. All three of the selectively orgasmic women were ambivalent about their incestuous experience, having experienced some pleasure in the sexual activity but also feeling that their brothers had victimized them.

Despite these difficulties with orgasmic response, none of the sisters had isolated herself from heterosexual contact. On the contrary, 71 percent of the sisters over eighteen had gone through periods of sexual promiscuity, compared with only 22 percent of the daughters, and this finding fits well with the higher incidence of masochistic orientation in the group of sisters. In two instances, the promiscuity consisted of numerous extramarital affairs condoned by the woman's husband. In the other three instances, indiscriminate sexual acting out had begun in early adolescence and continued until the sister married, as in the following case:

Laura had been molested by two of her brothers throughout childhood and was raped by a neighbor when she was fourteen. She began to date in junior high school and became known as an easy sexual conquest in her rural community. Between the ages of fourteen and eighteen, she had one illegal abortion and gave birth to two illegitimate children, whom she put up for adoption. To get away from her reputation, she moved to Los Angeles after the second birth, but she soon began her pattern again. She continued to have sexual relations on a casual basis until she met a bartender who married her after three weeks of courtship. After two children were born to them, her husband lost sexual interest in her and began to have numerous, ill-concealed affairs with women who frequented his bar. When her husband finally ran off with one of his girlfriends, Laura became depressed and began psychotherapy, complaining bitterly about the mistreatment she had had to endure from men all of her life. She attributed part of her hatred of men to her experience with sibling incest, saying that it had "got her off on the wrong foot" in her sexual relationships and that she had very seldom been orgasmic in any of her sexual contacts. However, despite her expressed dislike of men and sexual experience, she repeatedly went to bars, picked up strangers, and brought them home to sleep with her. Her therapist gained the impression that she experienced no feelings, sexual or otherwise, in these fleeting relationships but was actually seeking drinking companions as she became increasingly alcoholic.

An unexpected finding in the sexual histories of the sisters was that they had often been rape victims, usually in adolescence. Four of the eight sisters described being raped by unrelated men, and one of them had been raped by three different men on separate occasions. None of the thirty-six daughters was known to have been raped. For the sisters, then, the effects of incest are confounded with the effects of rape in half of the cases, but the sequence of incest and rape suggests that rape was indirectly a result of the incest experience. Usually, the incest had been the girl's first sexual contact, and the rape(s) occurred after she began to have sexual experiences outside the family. It seems likely that some of the sisters were perceived as "bad girls" deserving to be raped after they began to have casual sexual relationships. Another possible causal link was their rebelliousness and willingness to take risks such as hitchhiking and leaving bars with strangers in the course of their promiscuous sexual behavior. Since some of the sisters later appeared to be sexually masochistic, it is possible that they unconsciously wanted to be raped and actively invited it; however, it seems just as plausible that their sexual behavior as adolescents simply increased their vulnerability to rape for the reasons suggested earlier.

   None of the sisters had adopted a gay orientation, although two of the seven sisters now over eighteen years of age had experimented with lesbian relationships. Unlike the 30 percent of daughters who had been homosexually involved, the sisters were not especially attracted to other women but were willing to try out unusual kinds of sexual activity in order to please their sexual partners. One sister's lesbian activity took place only when she attended "swinging" parties at which she was encouraged to have sexual relations with women in order to excite the men who were present. A similar pattern was involved in the following case.

> Daphne was an adopted child in an extremely disorganized family where the brothers and sisters freely had sex with each other while the parents both had extramarital homosexual affairs that were known to the children. In early adolescence, Daphne's behavior was so disturbed that she was placed in a home for delinquent girls for six months, and she passively participated in homosexual behavior with older girls during her stay. At eighteen, she married one of her cousins and found that her interest in having sexual relations with him dwindled until she was only able to experience orgasm every several weeks by pretending to be

raped by her husband. About this time, a female neighbor began to act seductively toward both of them, and the husband arranged situations in which the two women would have sexual relations with each other and then with him. After several of these "three-way" scenes, Daphne consented to see her neighbor alone and played a passive feminine role in homosexual relations. She seemed to have little guilt about any of her past or present sexual activity when seen in therapy but did ask her therapist repeatedly if he thought it was "normal" for her to enjoy sex with her neighbor as much as sex with her husband.

Although one previous study (Lukianowicz, 1972) reported that there were no ill effects of incest observed in sisters in psychotherapy, most other evidence (Sloane and Karpinsky, 1942; Weinberg, 1955; Kubo, 1959) has pointed to promiscuity as a prominent characteristic of the postincest sister. Some scattered reports (Greenland, 1958; Magal and Winnick, 1968) have also indicated that an aversion to sexual activity may be an aftereffect of brother-sister incest. The small sample of brother-sister incest cases reported on here lends some support to the earlier findings of promiscuity and frigidity in association with sibling incest and further suggests that the sister's sexual history is conditioned by her masochism or her willingness to experiment with unusual kinds of sexual activity.

In general, sisters seemed less traumatized than daughters by the incest itself and were less inclined to attribute their later sexual difficulties to unresolved conflicts about incest. In cases where the brother had clearly initiated the sexual activity, the sister often viewed the incest as one of a number of ways in which her family of origin had mistreated her, and she went on to a promiscuity based on masochism and feelings of personal helplessness during her adolescent years. These families were often large and chaotic, living in poverty in isolated rural areas, and they seemed to fit the "subcultural variety" of incest families better than any of those described by daughters in father-daughter incest. If one could compare these sisters with an appropriate control group—psychologically disturbed women from chaotic but nonincestuous families—one might well find a similar incidence of masochism and promiscuity. Yet some of the problems described by these sisters, such as specifically sexual masochism and conflicts with sons, seemed on their face to be related to the sibling incest experience.

In brother-sister incest cases where the sister admitted that her own sexual curiosity had led her into incest, she was not characteristically masochistic in her later relationships, and whatever "promiscuity" she engaged in seemed to be motivated by her own sexual desire and her willingness to experiment with unusual sexual relationships. Possibly these characteristics had preceded the occurrence of sibling incest and paved the way for brother-sister sexual experimentation that went beyond the bounds of "playing doctor."

Uncle-Niece Incest

The Kinsey study of female sexual behavior (Kinsey and others, 1953) found that uncle-niece sexual relationships were the most common kind of incest in the sexual histories of women who were not selected on the basis of being psychologically disturbed. In contrast, there were only five women in the psychotherapy sample who reported sexual involvement with uncles, as compared with thirty-six cases of father-daughter incest. Therefore, we must give especially serious consideration to the possibility that only the most disturbing kinds of sexual contacts with uncles are eventually reported to psychotherapists and that there are a large number of women in the general population who were not particularly unsettled by such experiences. With this caveat in mind, let us briefly examine three cases of uncle-niece incest (two nieces, Adelaide and Deanna, were also involved with their fathers and have been described previously):

> Ada was twelve years old when she was brought to the clinic by her older brother, with whom she was currently living. The brother ex-

plained that Ada's father had disappeared before
she was born, her mother had died when she was
an infant, and she had lived with a great-aunt and
great-uncle until she was eleven. Beginning when
she was four years old, the great-uncle insisted on
fondling her genitals and simulating intercourse
once or twice per month while the great-aunt was
out of the home working, and whenever she ob-
jected to the activity he would use a combination
of bribes and threats to ensure her continued cooperation. When she asked her great-aunt for help,
her great-aunt laughed and seemed not to believe
her, but Ada eventually became more insistent
about getting away from the great-uncle and persuaded her family to allow her to live with her
older brother and his wife. In her new home, she
immediately began to have difficulty with her
brother and interpreted any show of affection
from him as a possible sexual advance. She also
became extremely wary of a male teacher, whom
she accused of persecuting her. When seen in
therapy, she was an extremely attractive, prematurely developed girl who wore a low-cut dress
that made her look like a sexually provocative
seventeen-year-old. Paradoxically, whenever she
was asked about her sexual experiences she appeared frightened and spoke of them only with
great difficulty; in fact, her brother was able to
scare her by warning that sex with boys her age
would be "like that" (referring to her great-uncle).
She had recently become involved with a gang of
delinquent girls and had been arrested for shoplifting. All in all, her therapist felt that her adolescent years would be very difficult ones.

Barbara had been the victim of an attempted
rape by an uncle when she was three years old, and
she vividly remembered that he had injured her
vaginal area so seriously that she had to be treated
in a hospital. After the incident, she repeatedly
tried to talk to her mother and aunt about her fear
of the uncle, but they both refused to acknowledge

the seriousness of the event and insisted that she not talk about it anymore. Now in her forties, Barbara still expresses anger toward her mother for not protecting her as a child. Since she was seen in therapy for her problem with a delinquent teen-age son, little was known about her early heterosexual relationships. She had had a long, stormy marriage with several separations during which she lived with other men. One of these boyfriends was ten years younger than herself, and she eventually discovered that he was sexually involved with her thirteen-year-old daughter. During the argument that followed this discovery, she hit him on the head with a heavy lamp base, and he died within a few hours. She served eighteen months in prison for second-degree murder and attributed her violent outburst to her own experience with sexual molestation as a child.

Jacqueline had been approached by her twenty-one-year-old uncle when she was twelve, and he had persuaded her to have intercourse with him in a friendly manner. She allowed him to repeat this experience on several occasions when her mother was out of the home and recalled no sexual pleasure on her part but did recall a feeling of happiness that her uncle felt such intense pleasure during intercourse. Two years later, she was similarly approached by her uncle's forty-five-year-old father (her stepgrandfather) and had intercourse with him several times. As an adult, she experienced guilt about these early relationships and had some difficulty in experiencing sexual pleasure with her husband, being passive and vaguely anxious during intercourse. Now forty, she has had numerous marital difficulties, but sex has been the least of her problems, and her overall adjustment is very good.

In these three cases, we can glimpse the variety of uncle-niece incest situations. In the last case presented, the incest was not an especially disturbing incident because the uncle obtained his niece's cooperation in a gentle, persuasive way and because she felt no sense of strong relationship with the uncle, who was not involved in her day-to-day care. A number of researchers (Bender and Blau, 1937; Landis, 1956; Peters, 1976) have found that nonviolent sexual approaches to children by non-related adults are less disturbing than incest because they are less likely to disrupt the child's relationship with her family. Possibly the "typical" uncle-niece incest incident involves an uncle who is quite distant from the niece's nuclear family and has no important role in her upbringing, and we would there-fore expect much less psychological disturbance to result from this kind of incest, because the conflicts that characterize the father-daughter incest situation are usually absent.

Uncle-niece incest has the potential for being extremely disturbing if it is violent or if its occurrence disrupts the child's relationships within the nuclear family. Especially in cases where the uncle is serving as a father surrogate, the relationship becomes father-daughter incest in all but name, as it did in the first case presented above. In one of the very few uncle-niece cases reported in some detail in the incest literature (Greenland, 1958), the niece, as an adult, experienced extreme psychological disturbance centering around a long-standing incest affair with an uncle who had served as the girl's father for many years. Pos-sibly, the "tip of the iceberg" of uncle-niece incest cases that are found in a sample of psychologically disturbed women are those which most resemble father-daughter incest.

Grandfather-Granddaughter Incest

As with uncle-niece incest, there are very few reports of grandfather-granddaughter incest in the literature, but neither is there any reason for strong suspicion that these relationships are especially common. Our cultural stereotype dictates that an older man would be less tempted to engage in illicit sexual ac-tivities because of a diminished sex drive, and those who do become involved with young girls are pictured as being senile degenerates. In the psychotherapy sample, there were five women who reported incest with grandfathers; in two cases (Adelaide and Jacqueline) the woman had also been involved with a father and with an uncle, respectively, and these cases have been reported elsewhere. Let us now examine the remaining three cases of grandfather-granddaughter incest and ascertain the extent to which they fit the stereotype we have mentioned:

> Caroline's parents took her to see her grandparents once a week throughout her early childhood. When she was about four, her grandfather took her into his bedroom in the afternoon on the pretext of having a nap and then removed some of her clothing and fondled her genitals. These incidents were repeated frequently for more than a year, and she later learned that her older sister had had similar experiences with him. She loved her grandfather and, like the rest of her family, looked up to him as a beneficent patriarch, so she was pleased that he paid so much attention to her and enjoyed the presents that he often gave her after the sexual incidents. However, as an adult she felt intensely guilty about this relationship and thought that she must have been to blame for it. Her family reported that she had become extremely religious and was fanatical in her desire to practice her religion down to the most minute detail of her life. Her husband was a sexually inadequate man who could never satisfy her in intercourse because of premature ejaculation, and since her religion prohibited masturbation she was often severely frustrated. Although she never had an extramarital affair, she dressed so seductively that men sometimes mistook her for a prostitute. She entered therapy to obtain help for her eight-year-old son, who was so intensely interested in sex that his classmates and teachers were rejecting him, and she remained in therapy for two years, obtaining a divorce during that time but still remaining without an adequate outlet for her pent-up sexual desires.

> Felicia's mother was an alcoholic who was legally declared incompetent to care for her children, and her grandmother was awarded custody of

her when she was five years old. The grandmother was a very strong, successful woman who was independently wealthy and the unquestioned head of her household. For three years after she came to live with the grandmother, Felicia was regularly subjected to genital manipulation by her passive, devalued grandfather, in whose care she was frequently left. As a child, she felt anger at her grandmother for not protecting her and confusion about her proper role in the family structure; as an adult, she felt intense guilt about the relationship, believing that it must have been her fault, yet she continued to be very attached to the strong, arrogant grandmother and professed a mixture of hatred and admiration in her regard. She married a weak man whom she despised and disliked their two sons so much that she insisted they remain with their father after the divorce. She was a defiantly independent woman whose generalized contempt for males was so extreme that rapport with her male therapist proved impossible.

Helen came from a very poor family in which she and her mother lived with her grandparents out of economic necessity. Between the ages of five and ten, her grandfather engaged in genital manipulation with her on numerous occasions, and she vaguely felt that the sexual activity was wrong at the time. In later years, she experienced strong guilt feelings about the incest affair. During her adolescence, she had numerous boyfriends and enjoyed having intercourse with them, although she often got into difficulties as a result. She had given up one child for adoption and also had an illegal abortion. She was seen in psychotherapy while in her late twenties because of dyspareunia in her sexual relationship with her husband of several years. She expressed intense feelings of guilt about her previous promiscuous behavior as well as about the childhood incest experiences.

It seems obvious that the incestuous grandfathers described in these cases did not fit the "dirty old man" cultural stereotype—none was reported to have been senile, psychotic, mentally defective, or drunk. All of the grandfathers were gentle in their sexual approaches, and none of them attempted to have intercourse with a prepubertal granddaughter. They did not threaten or intimidate their incest partners, and because of their quality of gentleness the granddaughter was cooperative during the incest affair itself, although she later developed very serious misgivings about it. These women tended to blame themselves, rather than their grandfathers, for the affair. As adults, they often enjoyed sexual intercourse but still manifested a number of conflicts in heterosexual relationships that they themselves attributed to incest.

Unexpectedly, the granddaughters were the most middle-class and most well-educated group of women in the psychotherapy sample. Four out of five of them came from middle-class backgrounds. All five were described by their therapists as being above average in intelligence, and four of them were thought to be unusually creative and artistic; all had attended college, and two had graduated. There seems to be no ready explanation for this finding, and it may well be due to chance in such a small sample.

Males in Heterosexual Incest: Brothers and Sons

■ ■ ■ ■ ■ ■ ■ ■ ■ ■ ■ ■ ■ ■ ■ ■

The most common form of heterosexual incest of which we have substantial knowledge is father-daughter incest, and we have already focused on the incestuous father in Chapters Four and Five. Incestuous uncles were briefly described in Chapter Seven. There is widespread agreement in the literature that mother-son incest is the rarest and most strongly taboo form of heterosexual incest. Even rarer, but somewhat less taboo, are reported cases of males incestuously involved with older female relatives outside the nuclear family, such as aunts and grandmothers. Lukianowicz (1972) mentions finding two cases in which nephews were seduced by aunts, one of whom was hypomanic and the other "slightly elated"; the nephews were not described. Kubo (1959) has given us a case history of grandmother-grandson incest in which a sixteen-year-old grandson, who was both psychotic and feeble-minded, attempted to rape his sixty-six-year-old grand-mother on two occasions before he was institutionalized. The sparse literature on males involved in these kinds of incest comes as no surprise; what is somewhat puzzling is that a similar situation exists with regard to what many believe to be the most common form of incest—brother-sister.

Brother-Sister Incest

Although characteristics of brothers are sometimes mentioned in studies of recently occurring incest, such as Weinberg (1955), Lukianowicz (1972), and Kubo (1959), they have almost totally eluded follow-up study. Both Weinberg and Kubo reported that brothers seemed less personally disturbed than fathers and usually did not fit into the seclusive "endogamic" category so frequently observed in the case of fathers. Although Santiago (1973) has presented a detailed case history of a brother who was very seclusive and unable to approach females outside of his nuclear family, the most typical brother has no outstanding neurotic or psychotic symptoms and is not alcoholic or mentally defective. He is often the oldest brother in a large family with weak or absent parents and thus has the intra-familial power to effect incestuous relationships with his sisters. In a minority of cases, he is psychopathic and has no scruples about using other family members as objects for his gratification; more usually, he seems to be a reasonably well-adjusted individual who may be involved in a delinquent subculture and have had minor brushes with the law that fall into the category of "crimes against property."

The fact that fathers are occasionally imprisoned for incest has given researchers a method of collecting data about their life histories, however biased these prison samples may be. But incestuous brothers are rarely found in prison, and the sample of eight such brothers obtained by the Kinsey Institute researchers (Gebhard and others, 1965) is the largest in the literature. These eight men had approached much younger sisters when they themselves were in their late teens or early twenties, so that the incest offense had the character of child molestation, which was no doubt responsible for the fact that charges were brought against them. It was remarked that none of these brothers blamed their incest offenses on the use of alcohol, quite unlike the imprisoned fathers but that five of the eight brothers had definite mental handicaps that may have played a part in the incest offense. The Kinsey Institute group (1965, p. 401) emphasized that the brothers' subnormal intelligence had allowed them to "blunder into conflict with society in the sexual as well as other aspects of their lives." The bias in this sample seems obvious: Sibling incest is much more likely to be treated lightly by authorities than is father-daughter incest, so it would seem to require a certain naiveté (not to say, stupidity) of a brother to be caught, charged, and imprisoned for such an offense.

The Kinsey Institute study (Gebhard and others, 1965) also asked sex offenders, men imprisoned for nonsexual offenses, and a noncriminal control group about previous incestuous involvements. Only .2 percent of the control group and 1.7 percent of the other prisoners admitted to having incest experiences with sisters, but sibling incest was noticeably more common in the histories of some of the large categories of sex offenders. About 3 percent of the homosexual offenders had had heterosexual incest experience with sisters, 3.5 percent of the incestuous fathers and stepfathers reported histories of sibling incest, and rapists reported such experiences in 4.5 percent of the cases. Since these groups also tended to have higher incidences of other unusual kinds of sexual outlet, such as animal contact, the Kinsey Institute group inferred that they were more generally willing to breach all sorts of taboos on sexual conduct. A causal relationship between sibling incest and later sex offenses is possible but, of course, not proven by the correlation observed by the Kinsey Institute group.

The psychotherapy sample contained eight cases of brother-sister incest described by sisters and three described by brothers. This differential incidence of postincest brothers and sisters in psychotherapy is probably the explanation for the almost total lack of clinical literature on aftereffects of sibling incest for the male participants. Males are less likely to seek psychotherapy than females in general, and this is especially true in the case of rural or urban working-class populations. Also, perhaps brothers, who tend to be the dominant partners in sibling incest affairs, are less disturbed by the experience than are sisters and thus are uncommon in clinical research settings.

The ten brothers who were described by eight sisters in psychotherapy were generally unremarkable. Unlike the fathers, the teen-age or adult brothers were not heavy drinkers, and no sister blamed the offense on alcohol. To the extent that the brothers were described at all, the sisters pictured them as "bullies" who teased them and liked to demonstrate their superior strength. Only one brother was definitely psychologically disturbed at the time of the incest and remained disturbed as an adult.

In the three cases where the brother himself was in psychotherapy, there was only one case of "pure" sibling incest. One brother was also sexually involved with his mother and will be described in the next section of this chapter; a second was involved with a brother and a stepfather as well as with a sister, and his case history will be examined in Chapter Nine. In the following case, incestuous activity was limited to the sister:

> Jack and his wife initially sought psychotherapy for their two sons, who manifested learning problems in school and behavior problems at home. After several months of conjoint therapy, Jack asked to see their female therapist individually and related, with great difficulty, a complex sexual history which he felt might be responsible for some of his marital problems as an adult. Describing his childhood in a border town in Arizona, he told the therapist that he was the oldest son in an intact family of ten children. When he was seven years old, a group of older boys involved him in mutual masturbation on several occasions, and he became known in their neighborhood as a boy who was receptive to homosexual approaches. When word of this activity got back to his family, he was severely beaten, and the family moved to another

neighborhood, where he again became involved in homosexual activities. In the new neighborhood, one of his sisters would join the sex play group, and Jack began sexual experimentation with her that progressed to genital intercourse when he was about twelve. As he later described it, the incest relationship allowed him to feel acceptably masculine in the face of being stigmatized as a "queer" by his family and neighbors. The relationship was concealed from their parents, and both brother and sister enjoyed the sexual activity without great anxiety since they were ignorant of the connection between intercourse and conception until late adolescence.

Their relations continued until Jack was nearly nineteen, at which time his sister became engaged and complained to her fiancé that her brother continued to insist on sexual relations after she had lost interest in him. The fiancé, a very large man, confronted Jack, who then affably agreed to end the incest affair. A few months later, Jack married a girl he had met in high school and joined the Navy. While in the service, he began to be overwhelmed with guilt about his childhood sexual experiences and with fear that he was becoming a homosexual because he began to experience conscious sexual desire for men. Up until that time, he had always played the passive role and had engaged in homosexual activity without guilt, since he attributed the homosexuality to his partner. Throughout adolescence, he had accepted money from older men for homosexual activity and rationalized that he himself was not really interested in it, but his experience of desire for other sailors called his heterosexual self-image into serious question. When he returned to his wife, he began to exhibit hypersexual behavior, insisting on having sex several times per day and usually feeling dissatisfied only minutes after intercourse. Since he was a premature ejaculator, his wife found this pattern of relations extremely frustrating and became less and less responsive over the years, until it became obvious to him that she submitted to his advances only out of a sense of family obligation. He began to accuse her of having extramarital affairs and refused to let her leave their house alone. Meanwhile, he had extramarital affairs of his own. When seen in therapy, he appeared to be very disturbed, exhibiting a level of hostility and suspicion that caused him to be labeled *paranoid*. He expressed intense guilt about the incest relationship and deeply regretted that it had caused him to become estranged from his sister as an adult. Although he never agreed to discuss his sexual history with his wife, he wanted to continue their marriage and requested sex therapy for his problem with premature ejaculation.

In this case of sibling incest, heterosexual involvement with the sister was, by the brother's own account, an attempt to defend himself against his anxieties about being "queer" in an environment that emphasized "machismo" as the ultimate goal of a man's life. The fact that he chose a sister while attempting to prove his masculinity may be explained by his paranoid defense structure and his ineptness in extrafamilial relationships. In fact, he may have been very similar to the "endogamic" father in his unwillingness to leave the family for sexual gratification. Ironically, the explanation of incest as a defense against unconscious feelings of homosexuality has been proposed in the case of father-daughter incest (Weiner, 1962), but no evidence for conscious or unconscious homosexual feelings was found in any of the incestuous fathers in the psychotherapy sample. The finding of conscious homosexual feelings and fear of homosexuality in this one case of brother-sister incest suggests that this motivational pattern does occur occasionally in cases of heterosexual incest, even though it may not be as frequent as has been thought.

It should be strongly emphasized that the "defense against homosexuality" pattern discovered in the brother just described is not believed to be typical of brother-sister incest cases. As with father-daughter incest, there are probably several personality types and family constellations that predispose brothers to incest. If a large enough sample could be obtained, one would probably find brothers who were mentally defective (Gebhard and others, 1965), endogamic (Santiago, 1973), psychopathic (Weinberg, 1955; Lukianowicz, 1972), psychotic, and even quite normal. The case presented here is an interesting example of the role that brother-sister incest can play in the life of a psychologically disturbed man. Surely there are many brothers who are far less disturbed or who manifest very different patterns of preincest motivation and postincest emotional repercussions.

Mother-Son Incest

Incest between mother and son is regarded as being the least common and most intensely taboo form of heterosexual incest. As we have discussed in Chapter Three, the unique dependency relationship that usually exists between a mother and her child seems to be antithetical to overt sexual behavior between them. Larger case samples (say, over thirty cases) usually contain one or two instances of mother-son relations, fewer if the research criterion for incest is genital intercourse as opposed to other kinds of overt sexual stimulation. In Weinberg's (1955) sample of 203 cases of nuclear family incest, only two were mother-son. Most of the literature on mother-son relationships consists of isolated clinical reports on one or two cases (for example, Wahl, 1960). It may seem somewhat surprising, in view of its acknowledged rarity, to learn that there is a much more substantial literature relating to mother-son incest than is the case with sibling incest, which is widely regarded as the most common form. Perceived rarity can stimulate the interest of researchers and cause them to write up and publish cases that would otherwise be lost in the file drawers of a clinic or court, but factors other than rarity also seem to be involved.

Much has been written about the role of repressed incestuous feelings for the mother in personality development. The central role of the oedipal situation in psychoanalytic theory need hardly be emphasized, and more recent theorists (for in-

stance, Parsons, 1954; Schwartzman, 1974) have also under-
scored the importance of the child's erotic attachment to the
mother in motivating successive stages of personality development and the consequent necessity of keeping oedipal feelings
repressed. Contributions to the meager knowledge of the aftereffects of mother-son incest are therefore seen as important on
a theoretical basis.

Perhaps because of the central role of the oedipal situation in personality development, theorists and researchers alike
have made clear-cut pronouncements about the relationship between mother-son incest and serious psychopathology. For
instance, Barry (1965) asserted that the son subsequently became psychotic in almost all cases of mother-son incest; Parsons
(1954) believed that an obvious corollary of his theory of personality development was that mother-son incest would constitute a severe regression and would thus be associated with serious psychopathology, especially in the son; and Frances and
Frances (1976, p. 242) concluded that "In those rare families
where mother-son incest is actually consummated, either or
both partners are almost always psychotic, with clear evidence
of lack of psychic differentiation." No such dire predictions are
made for father-daughter or sibling incest. Cases of mother-son
relationships have therefore been published by clinicians attempting to confirm or contradict the connection between
psychosis and the consummation of mother-son incest.

Among the clinical reports on mother-son incest, there is
only one (Barry and Johnson, 1958) that found a consensual,
marriagelike relationship between a mother and son, neither of
whom was mentally defective or suffering obvious psychopathology. The family lived in an isolated area of Kentucky,
and the father was a heavy drinker who deserted his family
when the son was twenty-three years old. The family physician
advised the son that it was his duty to remain with his sickly
mother and take his father's place in the household. The son
evidently interpreted this advice literally and manifested no
feelings of guilt about the incest at the time of discovery, because an unquestioned authority had, he thought, told him to
do it.

In the great majority of reported cases in which the son

initiates incest with his mother, the son is schizophrenic or severely disturbed in some other way prior to incest. Sometimes the incest or incest attempt occurs in the context of an acute psychotic breakdown. Medlicott (1967), for instance, gives an account of a young man in the early stages of a paranoid schizophrenic episode who attempted to have intercourse with his widowed mother. His voices had told him that he must have intercourse with someone, and he thought that intercourse with another woman would mean that he was an unfaithful son. Shelton (1975) also described a young man who suffered a schizophrenic breakdown at age twenty-one, shortly after his father's death. He had entered his mother's bedroom in the middle of the night and had intercourse with her on just one occasion. The mother was extremely disturbed by this incident and remorsefully admitted to a court psychiatrist that she had not resisted her son's advances because she thought he was "sick." The son remained schizophrenic, manifesting a hebephrenic symptom picture. Wahl (1960) similarly outlined a case in which the son initiated incest shortly after a schizophrenic breakdown in early adulthood on an evening when he returned home to find his mother nude and extremely drunk.

In some of the other son-initiated incest cases, the son had not been diagnosed as schizophrenic, but he was obviously severely disturbed. Kubo (1959) gives a case history in which the son was brain damaged by meningitis at age three, resulting in mental retardation and violent and hypersexual behavior. At the age of ten, he was observed making sexual advances to neighborhood girls, dogs, cats, and pigs, and he also began to threaten women with a knife. His widowed mother submitted to his sexual advances on several occasions because she thought sexual release might prevent his delinquent acts. After her death, he engaged in rape and exhibitionism and also sexually assaulted the daughter that a mentally retarded woman bore him. A similarly extreme case is described by Brown (1963). A son who had been adopted in infancy seduced his widowed mother on several occasions during his adolescence. He was a borderline mental defective who was homosexually oriented except for the mother-son incest. A hairbrush fetishist, he murdered his mother when she discovered his collection of stolen brushes.

In still other son-initiated cases, the son seemed far less disturbed. In a case described by Weinberg (1955), the adolescent son raped his mother, who reported the attack to police and had him successfully prosecuted. The mother had been a prostitute and had an arrest record for drunk and disorderly conduct. She was indifferent or actively abusive to her children, and they often witnessed her sexual activities with men. The son had been involved in some delinquent activities but did not seem grossly disturbed at the time of the attack, which occurred when he returned to live with his mother after several years of living with other relatives. He complained that she had teased him because he had had no girlfriends, and the rape seemed motivated by both revenge and sexual desire. Bender and Blau (1937) reported a case that was later followed up by Bender and Grugett (1952) in which a six-year-old boy was hospitalized after repeated attempts to have intercourse with his mother, who allowed him to sleep with her. He had been separated from his mother for the first four years of his life and had taken a precocious interest in sexual activity after being sexually stimulated by an uncle. Although he had behavior problems such as lying and stealing, he was not psychotic and appeared to be making a reasonably good adjustment as an adolescent after several years in various institutions.

In summary, the literature on son-initiated cases of mother-son incest suggests that the son is typically very disturbed at the time of the incest attempt; psychopathology observed in these sons after incest is merely a continuation of the disturbance that allowed oedipal fantasies to be acted out. It is interesting that, in the two cases where the son did not appear to be psychotic, retarded, or brain damaged, long separations had occurred between mother and son prior to incest, and these separations may have enabled the sons to act incestuously by destroying the nurturant mother-child relationship that militates against the expression of incestuous impulses. The mothers in son-initiated cases usually were not grossly disturbed, although they were sometimes promiscuous in such a blatant way that the sons were both antagonized and sexually tempted by them. In none of these published cases was the father present in the home at the time of mother-son incest.

Mother-initiated incest presents a slightly different picture, in that there seems to be somewhat less psychopathology in the son and more in the mother. Also, the son's disturbance tends to occur after the incest and can often be interpreted as a consequence of it. These kinds of cases, then, are the acid test of whether incest that is more or less imposed on a male child by his mother can severely disrupt personality development. The prominence of grossly seductive maternal behavior has been noted in some cases of young schizophrenic males (Fleck and others, 1959; Wahl, 1960), and there seems little doubt that severely deviant parental behavior can contribute to the development of severe forms of psychopathology. Whether mother-son incest inevitably leads to schizophrenia and how its effects differ from other kinds of childhood stress are the questions that will now be posed.

In some cases of mother-son incest, the sexual activity never proceeds to intercourse, and the mother may cloak it with pretenses of personal hygiene or make stealthy attempts at genital manipulation. Berry (1975) describes the case of a seventeen-year-old boy in psychotherapy because of anxiety about his homosexuality. Not only had his mother slept with him during childhood and early adolescence but she had also insisted on regular inspections of his penis "to see if it's growing properly" and had also insisted that he inspect her genitals on at least one occasion. When he began to perceive the inappropriateness of her behavior, he bluntly asked her whether she was thinking about having sex with him, and, following a long pause, she replied, "Well . . . not seriously." This patient withdrew from psychotherapy, so his subsequent history is unknown. Masters and Johnson (1970) have reported three cases of adult males in therapy for primary impotence who gave histories of sleeping with their mothers well into their adolescent years. One of them remembered awaking one night to discover that his mother was manipulating his genitals; another had frequently experienced orgasm while his mother scrubbed his genitals in the bathtub. Since Masters and Johnson screened out cases of severe psychopathology before treatment for sexual inadequacy, it would seem that these men were not schizophrenic as adults. Finally, Medlicott (1967) gives a very brief account of a man who had shared his mother's bed since early childhood and later married but proved to be impotent. After his mother's death, he became an "eccentric recluse," a phrase often used to describe schizophrenia in an upper-class individual.

In a slightly different sort of case, the son clearly perceives the activity as sexual at the time it takes place, but full sexual intercourse does not occur. Raphling, Carpenter, and Davis (1967) give a detailed case history of multiple incest in which the son witnessed intercourse between his father and sister at age eleven and then became sexually involved with the sister himself. At age fourteen, his mother became overtly seductive toward him and induced him to manipulate her genitals on one occasion, after which he felt extremely depressed and guilty. As an adult, he had no scruples about approaching three of his daughters for sexual activity. He also urged his son to make sexual advances to his mother, which seems surprising in view of his expressed negative feelings about sex with his own mother. His wife repelled the vague sexual approach made by their son. In his psychiatric evaluation, it was concluded that this man was not psychotic and functioned well in his job and as a church-going member of his community. He was, however, sadistic in his sexual relations with his wife and displayed a generally paranoid defensive structure.

One of the two cases of mother-son incest in the psychotherapy sample was also of this sort—the mother initiated activities that were perceived as sexual by the son but that stopped short of intercourse:

> Earl was born into an isolated, poverty-stricken family in a depressed rural area of the Midwest. His father, a locally notorious alcoholic, died of cancer when his was two years old, leaving his mother to devote herself full time to prostitution. The mother was psychotic and alcoholic. She

would bring home her customers, have intercourse in front of her two sons, and then beat them with a strap if she felt angry at the customer. When Earl was about four, she took him into her bed one night and rubbed her genital organs against his in order to masturbate; after obtaining sexual gratification, she found some excuse to beat him. These incidents recurred many times in the next two or three years and seem to have been the only occasions on which Earl received any warmth or emotional involvement from his mother. He and his brother were later placed in a foster home after hitchhiking to Los Angeles to escape her abuse. As an adolescent, he became a voyeur and was caught several times peeking through bedroom windows at unsuspecting women and attempting to steal lingerie from clotheslines. While in a forestry camp for juvenile delinquents, he met a counselor who took an interest in him and helped him get a scholarship at a state college.

He married at age twenty-one, and his wife worked while he finished a B.A. program, which enabled him to get a job at a detention facility for juvenile delinquents. For the next fifteen years, he did quite well occupationally and was able to maintain a facade of competence with regard to his job and his family while slowly becoming an alcoholic in his thirties. At the time he presented for psychotherapy, he was very anxious lest his "Jekyll and Hyde" life-style be discovered. He related that whenever he felt tense he had several drinks and then went looking for a prostitute. After finding a woman, he would order her to undress, tell her that he had no intention of paying her, and then laugh at her sadistically. Ironically, he also had visited his mother once a week since she had moved to Los Angeles about ten years prior to that time. She had become senile at an early age and was living on welfare in a convalescent home. His visits to her continued despite the fact that she cursed and spat when he entered her room, and his therapist thought that his hatred of women was intensified by his futile attempts to relate to his mother.

Mother-initiated incest that involves intercourse usually occurs when the son is between the ages of ten and eighteen. An exception is given by Weinberg (1955) in the case of a son who was mentally retarded. His mother was an unstable, neurotic woman whose inability to relate to adult men had propelled her through three stormy marriages. She had few friends and centered all of her attention on her son, who was allowed to sleep with her and who was bathed by her well past adolescence. He was entirely dependent on her and did not resist her incestuous approaches when he was twenty-eight years old.

Lukianowicz (1972) reported three cases of fully consummated mother-son incest in his large sample, but very few details were given about them. One mother was a chronic schizophrenic who approached her mentally retarded son when he was eleven years old. The other two mothers were women who had become very dependent on their sons in the absence of their husbands and had begun to see the sons in idealized romantic terms when they were in their teens. One of these women was definitely neurotic and evidently developed no feelings of guilt after incest was revealed, rationalizing that her husband was really to blame for it because he had never supplied her with the kind of emotional relationship that she desired. The other was not known to have been neurotic at the time of incest but did develop an involutional depression with feelings of guilt centered on incest. In these two cases, one of the sons was schizophrenic, but it is unclear whether the schizophrenia occurred before or after incest; the other son was described as normal a few years after the incest, having left home and married his girlfriend. Wahl (1960) gives a thorough case description of a schizophrenic patient in his twenties who was having a continuing sexual affair with his mother at her insistence. When he was first hospitalized for an acute schizophrenic breakdown, he frequently referred to sexual stimulation by his mother but was not taken seriously by the staff. Subsequently it was noticed that each time he improved sufficiently to be released in the care of his mother he was returned to the hospital in a catatonic stupor. When hospital authorities sought to curtail the home visits, the patient's mother wrote letters to her congressional representative and the American Legion, complaining of interference with "mother love." Finally, the patient was able to tell his therapist of his history in a coherent manner. His mother, although not psychotic, was an extremely unstable woman who had been married five times. When she was married, she cruelly rejected her son, but when she did not have a sexual partner she became grossly overprotective and solicitous of him. On many occasions, she initiated sexual activity with him, threatening him with the possibility that he would become homosexual if he did not submit to the "special training" that she offered him. The incest experiences set up a severe conflict between sexual desire for his mother and incest guilt, complicated by fears of homosexuality, and there seemed to be little doubt that mother-son incest was one of a number of severe life stresses that had precipitated his schizophrenic breakdown.

A case of mother-initiated incest in which the son (at least in early adolescence) gave no specific signs of schizophrenia has been described in some detail by Yorukoglu and Kemph (1966). When the son was ten, his divorced mother would come home drunk and initiate sexual activity with him and also with his sister on a few occasions. Their sex play led to intercourse, although the young son could not achieve orgasm in the incestuous relationship. After two years, the incestuous relationship became known to authorities, the mother was imprisoned, and the son and daughter placed in institutions. The son was a behavior problem at first, setting fires and making sexual advances to both boys and girls. After transfer to a psychiatric hospital, he experienced guilt and shame in regard to the incest and became phobic, fearing that some catastrophe would surely befall him. He wished to return to his mother if she could give up drinking, because he said she had been a good mother to him between her drinking bouts; he thought of her as a "Jekyll and Hyde" personality. The mother, who was diagnosed as an "hysterical personality disorder," had grown up in a small town where her father was a fundamentalist minister. As a child, she had had a quasi-incestuous experience, having been raped by an older brother-in-law when she was twelve years old. The rape had been doubly traumatic for her because her family had been concerned only with covering up the incident in order to preserve their standing in the community. After two unsuccessful marriages, she had begun heavy drinking and promiscuous sexual acting out with both men and women. At the end of her prison sentence, she appeared to be well organized and very concerned about her children.

In the psychotherapy sample, there was one case of mother-initiated mother-son incest in which the son was very seriously disturbed but not definitely schizophrenic. Unlike the case just described, this son was assessed nearly twenty-five years after the incest had occurred, so that the effects of incest in his marital and sexual history could be evaluated:

> Dale is now in his mid forties and, to all external appearances, enjoys a comfortable, middle-class life-style in suburban Los Angeles. He is married, has three young sons, and has worked for fifteen years as the supervisor of a laboratory performing medical tests for physicians. He describes himself as introverted and impresses strangers as a polite, intelligent man, albeit rather colorless. When he first appeared at the clinic and requested psychotherapy, his major complaints were heavy drinking, suicidal ideation, and an obsession with thinking about incest while having sexual relations with his wife. On intake, the therapist assumed that the thoughts about incest were merely fantasies, and Dale did not contradict this interpretation. After several months of regular psychotherapy, however, he told his therapist with great emotion that the "fantasies" were actually memories, and he was believed. He related that he had grown up in an intact, working-class family in a small city in New England. His father was usually drunk and ignored his wife and children much of the time. His mother came from a family in which

many members had been mentally ill, and she herself was a highly "nervous" person who was hospitalized once during Dale's childhood "for her
nerves." When she was with the children, she
alternated between very loving but overprotective
behavior and physical abuse during episodes of un-
explained rage. When Dale was three years old, she
began to regularly manipulate his genitals while
bathing him, and this behavior continued throughout his childhood. She would explain from time to
time that their family doctor had told her to play
with his penis so that it would not become dis-
eased. He also recalled many instances of seeing his
mother nude and becoming sexually excited by the
sight of her body. Sometimes his mother would
notice his excitement and comment on how "cute"
she thought it was.

At puberty, he became involved in a sex play
group along with a sister one year his junior. His
first experience with intercourse was with an eight-
year-old girl who was a member of the play
group. He continued to enjoy sex play with his sister, and they began to have intercourse on a very
irregular basis during middle and late adolescence.
When he was sixteen, his mother became even
more overtly seductive and began to sleep with him
whenever the slightest excuse presented itself. She
often complained to him about the unsatisfactory
nature of her sexual relationship with his father,
and on one occasion she confided that she had had
a very enjoyable sexual relationship with her twin
brother when they were sixteen. She presented
Dale with many opportunities to have sexual intercourse with her, but the incest affair was not fully
consummated for three more years because he
would become impotent at the last minute. Finally, his mother took him out to dinner on the occasion of his nineteenth birthday, he became intoxicated, and she suggested that he try to think of her
as a girl his age "just for this evening." He then succeeded in having intercourse with her and repeated

the experience on several occasions until he left home at the age of twenty-three.

He recalled these experiences as intensely exciting but always felt very guilty "the morning after" and came to hate his mother as an adult. After leaving home, he found himself very desirous of sexual relations but unable to achieve full potency with "nice" women. He spent several years visiting prostitutes and a psychoanalyst before he married at age thirty-three. He was also intermittently depressed, drank heavily, and had made several attempts at suicide, which seemed to dramatize his unhappiness to his quiet, patient, but undemonstrative wife. In addition to being obsessed with thoughts of incest, he felt himself powerfully attracted to prepubescent girls and was constantly fighting against his pedophiliac tendencies. He found some relief from these sexual tensions by dressing in his wife's lingerie from time to time, but he could not explain why this transvestite behavior was appealing to him. He had no history of homosexual behavior. Although he functioned well in his occupation and presented a good façade to his community, his therapist thought he was a borderline psychotic who had to make a constant effort to cling to reality.

The two cases of mother-son incest in the psychotherapy sample have been described in detail because the literature is so sparse in this area that it is unlikely that any researcher in the foreseeable future will be able to assemble a large sample of these cases, to say nothing of obtaining an appropriate control group. Even so, reading through the mother-son case histories that are currently available leads to some definite impressions about the aftereffects of mother-son incest that can now be stated as hypotheses for future researchers to test.

First, it appears that mother-son incest is seldom an important causal factor in schizophrenia. In many instances, the son is schizophrenic at the time of incest and also afterward, but it seems that the son's gross personality disturbance and lack of ego controls allowed an incestuous approach to the mother to occur. In other words, the son's schizophrenia "causes" incest, not vice versa. There are also cases of mother-initiated incest in which the son does not appear to be schizophrenic on follow-up, although he may be very disturbed in other ways. In the few cases (for instance, Wahl, 1960) in which a schizophrenic breakdown appeared to follow mother-initiated incest, the incest could be seen as a major life stress that may have precipitated a schizophrenic breakdown in a predisposed individual. In these cases, it seems more accurate to say that the long-term pathological relationship between mother and son that preceded the consummation of incest, plus other genetic and environmental factors, was the major cause of schizophrenia and that overt incest was only "the last straw."

Mother-son incest is seldom associated with a homosexual orientation as an adult. Previous research on neurotic homosexuals (Bieber and others, 1962) has stressed the importance of sexually seductive maternal behavior in producing a homosexual orientation as a defense against unconscious fears of incest. It would seem to follow that actual sexual approaches by the mother would also eventuate in a conscious or unconscious flight from heterosexuality and thus a neurotic homosexuality, but this can seldom be the case because the majority of post-incest sons seem to be heterosexually oriented as adults. Personality theorists and future researchers should address themselves to resolving this apparent conflict: If covert maternal seduction produces a change in sexual orientation, why does *overt* maternal seduction seldom seem to have this effect?

Finally, it appears that sons in mother-son incest, like daughters in father-daughter incest, tend to have specifically sexual problems as adults. Researchers who have reported no serious aftereffects of mother-son incest (Lukianowicz, 1972; Yorukoglu and Kemph, 1966) have not reported on adult sexual functioning in their subjects, and this is the crucial area to be examined in assessing the effects of incest. Lukianowicz (1972), for instance, reported that one of the sons was "normal" after incest and stated that the young man left home and got married. If marriage and outward appearances of occupational and social adjustment were adequate criteria for normality, we would have to conclude that the two sons in the psychotherapy sample were as "normal" as the case reported by Lukianowicz. However, we have seen that these adult postincest sons manifested a warped kind of heterosexual expression that they themselves attributed in part to the incestuous relationship. Future reports of "no effect" of incest for either males or females should be viewed with skepticism unless adult sexual functioning has been adequately assessed.

Homosexual Incest

▦ ▦ ▦ ▦ ▦ ▦ ▦ ▦ ▦ ▦ ▦ ▦ ▦ ▦ ▦

Several major incest studies (for instance, Weinberg, 1955) have not included homosexual relationships in their definitions of incest. When homosexual incest is included, a few cases are found in large clinical samples, and the preponderance of these involve male relationships, as in the psychotherapy sample, where three of the four cases of homosexual incest were male. Males are very rarely imprisoned for homosexual incest—Gebhard and others (1965) found too few cases to analyze in their large prison sample. Most of the literature therefore consists of individual case reports of patients seen in hospital or clinic settings.

Male Relationships

The most commonly reported kind of homosexual incest is the father-son combination. The clinical literature in this area is almost as extensive as the case reports of mother-son incest, although there have been far fewer theories and predictions about the consequences of father-son incest. Personality theorists have largely neglected the possibility of repressed erotic

312

tensions between father and son or mother and daughter, so there are no prominent hypotheses about the aftereffects of such relationships. As with mother-son incest, the scattered case reports indicate a wide range of outcomes.

Bender and Blau (1937) reported a case of father-son incest that was followed up by Bender and Grugett (1952). The father was a mentally retarded man who married his own niece after an incestuous affair with her produced a child. He made sexual advances to all of his children, male and female, and although he was resisted by his ten-year-old son he succeeded in engaging in sex play with a six-year-old son. This son and a younger daughter then engaged in sex play with each other, which caused their mother to seek psychiatric help for them. The son, who was of normal intelligence, expressed fear and resentment of the father and seemed quite bewildered about the role relationships in his family. He adjusted well to hospital treatment and was able to reestablish a relationship with his father during his teen-age years. His marriage at age eighteen suggested to the researchers that he had attained a moderately successful adult adjustment.

Rhinehart (1961) gives a brief account of an eighteen-year-old psychotherapy patient who had made several suicide attempts and who expressed a desire to become a woman. He was extremely effeminate in manner but did not appear to be psychotic. His history revealed that his alcoholic father had had homosexual relations with the patient and his brother when the patient was twelve and that brother-brother incest had followed these experiences.

A father who molested his son and daughter when they were under twelve years of age was described by Weiner (1962). The patient's family of origin had broken up when he was five years old because his father was charged with sexually molesting his daughter (the patient's sister); he had grown up in a series of foster homes but nevertheless succeeded in getting a college education. As an adult, he had difficulty with pedophiliac tendencies that caused him to lose several jobs as a schoolteacher prior to sexually approaching his own children, but he had become a successful door-to-door salesman and seemed quite well adjusted in his nonsexual functioning. Weiner gave no description of the son in this case.

Medlicott (1967) described three cases of father-son incest. Little was known about the fathers except that they were occupationally successful and evidently not psychotic; one father was terminally ill at the time he approached his son. The sons reacted to the homosexual activities with a combination of fascination and repulsion. As adults, two of the sons were chronically neurotic with conflicts centering on fear of homosexuality, and the third son was so disturbed by his fears of homosexuality that he suffered a psychotic breakdown and eventually committed suicide. So far as was known, none of these men had engaged in actual homosexual behavior as adults.

An extensive case history of homosexual incest in two generations of a family has been reported by Langsley, Schwartz, and Fairbairn (1968). A twenty-year-old college student was admitted to a psychiatric facility in an acute psychotic state that began when the patient experienced, under the influence of LSD, the feeling that he was becoming homosexual. He reported that at age twelve he had had numerous homosexual experiences with his father when he and his father routinely lifted weights together in the basement of the family home. The hospital staff initially believed his revelation to be a psychotic fantasy, but the father corroborated his account of the incest and expressed the fear that his behavior had brought about his son's severe disturbance. This father related a case history of growing up in a religious family in a small town where the evils of sexuality were constantly stressed. He had had homosexual experiences with a young uncle at age twelve and with a cousin at age twenty-five, and during adolescence he had fallen in love with an eight-year-old boy. At thirty-six, he married, established a satisfactory sexual relationship with his wife, and named his first son after the eight-year-old boy he had loved in his youth. He was occupationally successful and was perceived as a "good family man." Nonetheless, his desire for homosexual fulfillment persisted. He made only one attempt at an extramarital homosexual affair prior to his introducing mutual masturbation to his twelve-year-old son during their weight-lifting sessions. When his son became emotionally distant from him in late adolescence, he began to fear that he had harmed his son and suffered a severe depression that caused him to retire early from his job. Langsley and his colleagues studied the family dynamics in this case carefully and concluded that incest was largely attributable to the father's unresolved feelings about his sexual orientation and his inability to express his homosexual desires outside of his family.

Raybin (1969) reported another case of homosexual incest in two generations of a family, and there were many striking similarities to the case just described. The son had a psychotic breakdown at age twenty, precipitated by an LSD experience, whereupon the father became so depressed that he was admitted to a psychiatric hospital, where he revealed the incest and his fears that he had harmed his son. He described his own father as a family patriarch who was a successful businessman and who had never been known to act out homosexually in their small community. However, the father would frequently steal into his bed at night and manipulate his genitals. Stimulated by this activity, the son initiated an incest affair with a younger brother that continued into adolescence. In addition, he had an affair with a male cousin for several years and continued to be involved in extrafamilial homosexual activities throughout his adult life. He was also interested in heterosexual expression and was married twice but eventually lost all sexual interest in his second wife. For many years, he was very physically affectionate with his son, but it was not until the son confessed to being involved in homosexual relationships himself that the father openly suggested that they have sexual relations with each other. The son's psychotic break followed the incest.

Berry (1975) described the case of a twenty-four-year-old nonpsychotic male who sought psychotherapy because of concern about his limited ability to enjoy heterosexual activity. In early childhood, his father had begun to stimulate him anally when they took showers together, and he had later developed a fascination with anal stimulation, although his sexual fantasies were heterosexual. During psychotherapy, he worked through his sexual conflicts and began to enjoy his heterosexual relationships.

Finally, Awad (1976) has described an unusual case in

which a drunken father homosexually assaulted his fourteen-year-old son after the son, a lifelong behavior problem, had been arrested for breaking and entering. The father had no history of homosexual behavior, and he claimed that he was so drunk during the incest that he could not remember what he had done or why he had done it. Since the father had frequently been dominant and overbearing with his wife and children in the past, it was thought that the homosexual incest was a primitive attempt to punish his son and reassert control over him.

The psychotherapy sample contained two cases of father-son incest. In one case, there was very little information on the incest and its effects, since the patient was seen only once; in the other, father-son incest occurred along with homo- and heterosexual sibling incest. Nevertheless, these two cases further illustrate the diversity of father-son incest backgrounds:

Adrian was briefly evaluated at the clinic for his continuing problems with alcoholism while in his mid thirties. He listed, without further description, father-son incest as one of a number of severe stresses in his family of origin. His mother had been repeatedly hospitalized for psychosis when he was a child. At age nineteen, he was convicted for burglary and assault, and he spent several years in prison. On his release, he married and attempted a number of jobs but failed to adequately support his wife and children and began to have episodes of severe depression during which he went on alcoholic binges. He also experienced sexual problems of an unknown nature for which he was intermittently treated at psychiatric facilities. After his marriage disintegrated, he spent several years as a "Skid Row bum" and was seeking treatment for alcoholism when seen at the clinic.

Gary was born when his mother was a college freshman, and his parents were divorced almost immediately. His mother remarried after graduation from college and had two more children, a girl and a boy. The mother and stepfather shared very liberal opinions about nudity in the home, and Gary remembered feeling sexually stimulated by the sight of his mother's body. He was also breast fed by her on request when he was nearly five years old and his younger sister was being nursed. When he was ten, he began sex play with his six-year-old sister, and their play progressed to intercourse over a period of about three years. Sometimes the younger brother would also be included, and mutual oral stimulation would occur between the boys. When Gary was about thirteen, his sister began to object to his sexual demands and terminated the relationship by threatening to tell his friends about it. So far as he knew, neither of his parents was aware of the sibling incest situation in their home.

At age fourteen, Gary was approached on several occasions by his stepfather on arriving home from school in the afternoon. His mother, now a university professor, was working full time, while the stepfather was at home during the day because he was unable to find work in the legal profession. After several sessions of mutual masturbation with the stepfather, Gary felt very confused and was able to express hostility to the stepfather and demand that he discontinue the relationship. Nevertheless, although the incest relationship ceased, Gary felt insecure in the home and ambivalent about the man, who had been his father since early childhood. He continued to experiment with homosexual activity with boys his own age and also became very attached to a male teacher whom he described as effeminate; although he was soon labeled a "fag" at school, he did not self-identify as gay, since he continued to be attracted to girls, including his sister. At fifteen, he took LSD and experienced a sexual panic that culminated in a brief psychotic episode, after which his family insisted that he seek treatment at the clinic. During his year of psychotherapy, he made con-

siderable progress and no longer seemed in danger
of psychosis. He was seen as an extremely intelligent and talented young man who was struggling
with his bisexual identity and with the extremely
confusing role structure within his family of origin.
His stepfather, who felt intense guilt about the incest, was understanding and helpful to Gary, and it
appeared that they would succeed in reestablishing
a nonsexual father-son relationship.

Summarizing what is known about father-son incest on
the basis of the sparse literature just presented, it would seem
that sexual activity is nearly always initiated by the father. In
cases where the father's history has been obtained, it has generally been found that he has had strong homosexual desires since
early childhood but has married and presented a heterosexual
façade to the community. Often he has experienced or witnessed incest within his family of origin. He is usually an intelligent man with a good occupational adjustment and has no history of severe psychological disturbance prior to the incestuous
relationship. Not a psychopath, he often feels a strong attachment to the son whom he choses for incest, and he experiences
guilt and depression after it becomes apparent to him that incest has alienated his son and possibly caused him psychological
harm.

The son in father-son incest generally does not resist sexual activity with his father—he is curious about sexuality and
wants to please his father. In most cases, the affair is not long-
lived because the son develops misgivings about it, and the
father agrees to stop the activity without the need for intervention by the mother or any outside agency. In late adolescence
or early adulthood, the son often becomes extremely disturbed
and experiences panicky feelings about becoming homosexual
against his will. In most cases, however, he is heterosexual or
bisexual as an adult, although he may develop some problems in
heterosexual functioning because of his fears of homosexuality.

There is far less literature on brother-brother incest.
Raybin (1969) and Rhinehart (1961) have given clinical reports

of brother-brother incest occurring in the same family as father-son, and we may speculate that sexual stimulation by the father resulted in sexual interest in other males in the family as well as in a knowledge of homosexual techniques. Cory (1963) mentioned that he knew several "confirmed homosexuals" who had a history of brother-brother incest, but he gave no details of the incest or of the brothers' adult psychological adjustment. One case of brother-brother incest was found in the psychotherapy sample, and it illustrates one variety of psychological disturbance that may follow such experiences:

> Barry had been in treatment for about two months when he came for an early evening session after stopping at a local bar. Half intoxicated, he began to weep and told his therapist about a childhood experience that still upset him as an adult. During his early years, he and his many brothers and sisters were neglected by their parents for long periods of time while the parents worked or pursued extramarital affairs. One day when he was about ten years old, he was alone in their house with his fifteen-year-old stepbrother and was subjected to an anal rape by the stepbrother despite strong resistance on his part. He felt mortified by this experience but never expressed any anger toward the stepbrother, with whom he maintained a superficially friendly relationship as an adult. Despite his impoverished family background, Barry had managed to finish college and obtain a master's degree in teaching. He had married in his early twenties, and the threatened breakup of his marriage was the reason for his entering therapy eight years later, giving "sexual problems" as one of his presenting complaints. Since the first few months of marriage, he had felt an irresistible urge to have brief extramarital encounters in which he would pursue a woman whom he met on a casual basis and then lose all interest in her once sexual intercourse had occurred. These "affairs" happened as frequently as once per week and appeared to be a

compulsive kind of activity that gave him little real
sexual satisfaction. His therapist described him as a
handsome young man who tended to "sexualize"
all of his relationships, with both males and females. He expressed loathing for male homosexuals, who often misjudged his seemingly seductive behavior and made sexual overtures to him.

In this case, it would seem that the traumatic experience with
homosexual incest created a need for the patient to "prove his
masculinity" again and again in adult life. He was not conscious
of fears of homosexuality, but his overall behavior pattern
strongly suggested that they were present. If he had ingested
LSD, as occurred in some of the father-son cases discussed earlier, perhaps these fears would have surfaced quite dramatically.

Even less is known about the other possibilities for male
homosexual incest. No reports of grandfather-grandson incest
have appeared in the clinical literature. Machotka, Pittman, and
Flomenhaft (1967) have described a case of uncle-nephew incest in two generations of a family. The patient had been seduced by his uncle as a child, and many years later his sons were
seduced by the same uncle. Because of the patient's guilt about
his own incest experience and his fear that others would find
out about his past, he denied the occurrence of uncle-nephew
incest involving his sons for several years, until a direct con-
frontation occurred.

Female Relationships

The most unstudied area in incest research is the occurrence of female homosexual relationships within the nuclear
family. For two of the relationship possibilities—sister-sister and
aunt-niece—there have been no reports in the clinical literature.
Such incest experiences must therefore be either very rare or
very unlikely to produce psychological disturbance. It is also
possible that females can engage in a higher level of physical
contact with each other without the activity being labeled "sex
play," and therefore "incest," by the participants if the participants happen to be related to each other.

Barry and Johnson (1958) described a patient in her early twenties who had slept with her father for several years prior to leaving home at age eighteen. She had also engaged in incest with her paternal grandmother, who when ill would ask the patient to sleep with her and then initiated mutual genital stimulation while they were in bed together. The granddaughter was at first anxious about these activities and later felt repelled and successfully terminated the relationship at age fifteen. In her mid twenties, she was employed as a nurse and had problems with intense feelings of hostility toward elderly female patients.

Weiner (1964) described a case in which mother-daughter incest occurred in a technical sense. Since the daughter had been placed in a foster home in her infancy and had had no contact with her mother until she was twenty-six years old, there was no feeling of emotional relationship between them when they engaged in a brief homosexual affair on being reunited. Neither of them was psychotic but both had had severe problems with marital and sexual adjustment, and the daughter was later hospitalized for depression following the breakup of another homosexual affair.

Medlicott (1967) has reported a case in which mother-daughter incest was "psychologically real." The mother insisted on sleeping with her daughter during early adolescence in order to avoid sleeping with the father, who had become severely alcoholic. The mother initiated sexual play with her daughter on these occasions, which the daughter remembered with disgust. As a young adult, the daughter was seen in psychotherapy for chronic tension, headaches, and "morbid sexual fears." Occasionally, she was bothered by sexually tinged fantasies of receiving enemas from her mother as if she were a child again.

In the psychotherapy sample, there was one, somewhat marginal case of mother-daughter incest:

> Carol described a relationship with her mother that seemed pathologically close from the beginning. Her mother was extremely religious and also so suspicious of persons outside her immediate family that she had no friends and concentrated all of her social attention on Carol and her older sister. When Carol was about eight, her mother went

through a period of extreme suspiciousness about
the possibility that her husband was sexually molesting the children and insisted on conducting frequent "pelvic examinations," inspecting Carol's
vagina for any signs of irritation. Carol experienced
these physical intrusions by her mother as strange
and bothersome but did not resist them. Through
the years, she remained very close to her mother
and was still living with her in her mid twenties.
Beginning at age eighteen, she had sexual intercourse with numerous boyfriends, and her mother
insisted on being told about these experiences.
Carol never succeeded in establishing a satisfactory
relationship with a man, and in her early twenties
she was having sex with as many as five different
men per week, experimenting with "unusual
scenes" and allowing herself to be physically mistreated by her sexual partners. Her mother called
her a tramp but continued to insist on being told
all the details of these escapades. In her late twenties, Carol sought psychotherapy with multiple
complaints of boredom, depression, and a vague
feeling of aimlessness in life. She expressed curiosity about homosexuality, and her therapist suspected that she was experiencing desire for other
women, although she reported having had no lesbian experience up to that time.

From the cases that have been reported, nothing can be
concluded about the aftereffects of female homosexual incest,
but one is left with the impression that difficulties in adjustment during early adulthood were partially related to the incest
situations that these women had experienced.

10

Multiple Incest

Having considered all of the incestuous relationships, heterosexual and homosexual, that may occur within the nuclear family and with aunts, uncles and grandparents, we shall focus briefly on the variety of situations in which more than one incestuous liaison occurs within the same family. Given the strength of the incest taboo, one might expect that multiple incest would be an extremely rare occurrence, but this prediction ignores some basic facts about the individual and family pathology that produces incest in the first place. In fact, multiple incest cases appear to be quite common, especially when genital intercourse is not stated as the research criterion for incest. In the psychotherapy sample, for instance, nearly 30 percent of the patients had either been sexually involved with more than one family member themselves or knew of other incestuous affairs within their families. Many of these cases have already been mentioned in passing. In this chapter, we shall summarize the various patterns of multiple incest.

The most frequently observed pattern of multiple incest occurs when an older male initiates incestuous relations with more than one female. Large studies of father-daughter incest (for instance, Weinberg, 1955; Gligor, 1966) have consistently found a substantial minority of cases in which the father was involved with more than one daughter, almost always sequentially. In the psychotherapy sample, about 15 percent of the cases of father-daughter incest were multiple in this sense. This figure seems even larger when one considers the fact that in 31 percent of the father-daughter cases there was no possibility of such an occurrence, because the patient was her father's only daughter; in the remaining 54 percent, there were very probably some cases in which the reporting daughter never became aware of incestuous approaches to sisters.

Why does the incestuous father (or grandfather or uncle) "move on" to another incestuous relationship so frequently? A truly complete answer to this question would require an extensive review of the factors that allow incest to occur with the original partner. Suffice it to say that many of the father's incest-favoring characteristics, such as psychopathy or an endogamic orientation, persist over a long time period, whereas the incest affair is almost certain to end when the daughter seeks her independence from the nuclear family. In addition, after the end of his first incest affair, the father has often been participating in incest over a period of several years and has built up a structure of defensive rationalizations that reduce his guilt and may allow him to initiate another incest affair more easily than the first.

When more than one daughter is involved in incest, the older daughter sometimes helps the younger daughter to avoid or terminate the incest affair in lieu of help from an absent or overly passive mother. Clinicians should also be aware of the possibility of "incest envy" arising in this type of multiple incest case. As used by Berry (1975), this term refers to the conflicts experienced by an unchosen daughter when she is aware of father-daughter incest in her family. Another possibility is that the incestuous daughter, even when she is seeking to escape the affair, will become jealous of her father's attention to younger sisters. At least two of the incestuous daughters in the psychotherapy sample, when asked whether their younger sisters had also been approached, became so angry that their therapists suspected that they were not merely being protective of their sisters but also harbored some unconscious feelings of jealousy. If such incest envy exists, it is not necessarily a sexual possessiveness akin to that of husbands and wives. One should remember that parental affection and physical tenderness are rare commodities in many incestuous families, and the prospect of losing these aspects of the incest relationship may be very unpleasant for the daughter even if she dislikes the sexual activity itself. Such feelings of ambivalence about losing the father to another sister are very likely to produce strong guilt feelings in the daughter.

Another variety of multiple incest occurs when the female participant has incestuous relationships with more than one male relative, either simultaneously or sequentially. In some cases in the psychotherapy sample, incest was initiated as a group activity by more than one male. Among the twelve cases of sibling incest, for example, there were three in which two brothers joined forces to engage a sister in sex play; in all these cases, the sister described herself as unwilling and felt that she had been sexually humiliated by brothers who wanted to demonstrate their power over her. Except for the fact that intercourse usually did not occur, this multiple incest situation had much in common with adolescent gang rape. This pattern of simultaneous involvement with two or more males is rare in nonsibling cases, but there was one instance in the psychotherapy sample where a daughter was molested not only by her father but also by her grandfather, two uncles, and various neighbors. The molestation occurred during drunken parties, the male relatives evidently thinking it was humorous.

When a daughter or sister is involved with two or more male relatives sequentially, one tends to suspect that the female participant is somehow creating the incest situation, at least the second time around. There are some published case studies (Rhinehart, 1961; Machotka, Pittman, and Flomenhaft, 1967) in which a daughter who had incestuous relations with her father as a child went on to incest with a stepfather as an adolescent, and it appeared that the daughter had played some active role in initiating the second incest incident. In the psychotherapy sample, there were also two cases in which teen-age daughters complained of incestuous approaches by step-fathers several years after incest with their natural fathers. In one of these cases, the neurotic daughter may have fantasized the approach; in the other, the daughter may have been moti-vated by a desire to get rid of her new stepfather. Other expla-nations for such instances of repeated incest are also possible and should not be overlooked by clinicians dealing with such cases. For instance, the girl's mother may enter a second mar-riage that is merely a "replay" of the first—a domineering hus-band with a taste for alcohol in most cases—and thus set the stage for incest to recur, especially if she abdicates her sexual role in the second marriage.

Weinberg (1955) described five cases of girls who had intercourse with fathers and brothers sequentially, and he con-cluded that these cases of multiple incest occurred in families that were much more disorganized than father-daughter or sib-ling incest families. Father, brother, and daughter all tended to be sexually promiscuous both before and after incest, and some of the daughters had taken an active role in initiating incest, es-pecially with the brother. These daughter-sister participants often became prostitutes after being rejected by their families because of their aggressive sexual behavior. However, Weinberg's impression of extreme promiscuity in association with this par-ticular kind of multiple incest may have been partly condi-tioned by the fact that his cases were all reported to social or legal authorities and thus were especially likely to involve fla-grant sexual behavior. There were no cases of combined father-daughter and brother-sister incest in the psychotherapy sample, but the clinical literature contains at least three case histories (Eist and Mandel, 1968; Magal and Winnick, 1968; Raphling, Carpenter, and Davis, 1967) in which the daughter-sister partici-pant, although psychologically disturbed, was not sexually ag-gressive. In fact, Eist and Mandell described the thirteen-year-old girl whom they saw in psychotherapy as a "typical teen-ager" who was not promiscuous and who was not rejected by her family when it was revealed that she had had intercourse with her father and two older brothers. There are a variety of outcomes observed in this kind of multiple incest.

A third major category of multiple incest situations might be termed *intergenerational*. Instead of one male or female being involved with more than one incest partner in the same family setting, a child may be involved in incest in his or her family of origin and later "carry" incest to the next generation by becoming a parent participant or by fostering incestuous behavior in other family members. Berry (1975) and Raphling, Carpenter, and Davis (1967) have emphasized that incest should be thought of as a transmissible phenomenon—that once a person has been involved in incest or has had knowledge of its occurrence in the family, incest is never again as "unthinkable" as it would be to the noninvolved person. Even if the original incest experience was unpleasant, the firsthand knowledge of incestuous relations can at least suggest the possibility of incest as a form of sexual outlet during a period of personal instability in later life. Gebhard and others (1965, p. 58) observed that men imprisoned for sexually molesting children had often been sexually molested themselves as children, and they speculated that "the early experience may have impressed them with the realization that adult males do sexually approach children." A similar kind of modeling process is suggested for incest, at least in a minority of incest cases.

One form of intergenerational incest occurs when a male has incestuous experience in his family of origin and then becomes an incestuous father. There were no known instances of this pattern in the psychotherapy sample, although one male who had been involved in incest as a child became a pedophile as an adult and might well have engaged in incest were it not for the fact that he had no daughters. Gebhard and others (1965) found that about 4 percent of imprisoned incestuous fathers had had incestuous experience in their families of origin, but this figure includes only males who admitted to having sexual intercourse with females in their nuclear families, so it is possible that many more fathers had sexual contact short of intercourse or knew of incestuous liaisons within their families. Weiner (1962), for example, has described a psychotherapy patient whose family of origin had disintegrated when he was five years old because his father had been accused of incest with his (the patient's) sister; as an adult, he sexually molested his daughter, son, and various schoolchildren in classes that he taught.

Raphling, Carpenter, and Davis (1967) have recounted the most detailed case of intergenerational multiple incest in the literature, and the interested reader is urged to consult their original article for an especially insightful description of this phenomenon. Briefly, their patient was a thirty-nine-year-old male who was referred for psychiatric treatment by his family physician. He had grown up in an isolated rural area of the Midwest and had witnessed intercourse between his father and older sister when he was eleven years old. He then became sexually involved with this sister, and their relationship continued until she ran away from home. When he was fourteen, his mother made sexual overtures to him, but he was repelled by the idea of mother-son incest. At eighteen, he began to have intercourse with two younger sisters who had also been initiated into sexual relations by their father. After his marriage at twenty-one, he had very frequent sexual intercourse with his wife until his eldest daughter was twelve; he then began an incestuous relationship with this daughter that lasted more than five years, and he also attempted to establish sexual relationships with his other daughters and even urged his son to approach his sisters and mother for sexual relations. It seemed that this male, who was quite a conventional person in most ways, had been provided with a model of a patriarchal family in which the father presided over multiple incestuous liaisons, and he had emulated his father, creating a multiple incest situation in the next generation of his family.

Another way in which incest can be transmitted from one generation to the next is through a female participant who either approaches her children sexually or "sets up" her children for incest with their father or some other relative. A few instances of the first possibility have appeared in the literature. Yorukoglu and Kemph (1966) reported that a woman who had sexual relations with both her son and her daughter in their preadolescent years had been traumatized by being raped by a brother-in-law when she was twelve years old. In a case of mother-son incest briefly described by Lukianowicz (1972), a mentally retarded woman conceived a son during an incestuous relationship with her brother and then attempted to have sexual relations with this son when he was eleven years old. A similar case occurred in the psychotherapy sample. A mother who had encouraged sibling incest among her children and seduced her adolescent son into intercourse had a background of incest with a brother during her own adolescent years. In another case, a woman with a background of sibling incest did not actually approach her son for incest but was so overtly seductive toward him that he became extremely uncomfortable in her presence and left home.

Perhaps it is significant that, in all of the incest transmission cases just described, the woman had had incestuous experience with a sibling rather than with a father, uncle, or grandfather. In our discussion of sibling incest in Chapter Seven, we noted that sexual experiences with brothers are more likely to be consensual and to result in sexual pleasure for the sister than are father-daughter relationships. Thus the original sibling incest experience not only provides a model for incest by suggesting the possibility of such relationships but also induces some expectations of pleasure in the second incestuous relationship. When the woman has experienced father-daughter incest, the expectation of pleasure is probably less likely to occur, and to the extent that incest with the father was unpleasant and conflict producing, the daughter might be expected to avoid incestuous involvement in the next generation of her family. However, there is a mode of incest transmission that does not require sexual participation on the part of the "incest carrier."

Weinberg (1955) remarked that some of the daughters who later married became extremely suspicious of their husbands' relationships with their own daughters. In the psychotherapy sample, there was one daughter who had strongly suspected incest between her husband and daughter prior to their divorce; her therapist also thought that the husband and daughter were unusually close and that an incest affair was in the preliminary stages of development if it had not actually occurred. Berry (1975) has also observed a woman with a history of father-daughter incest who appeared to be setting up a classical father-daughter incest situation by dressing her daughter in sexually suggestive clothing, putting her in charge of household duties, and urging her to "Take good care of Daddy!" on the numerous occasions when she left the home in the evening.

It appears, then, that a small minority of women who have been involved in father-daughter incest in their families of origin may somehow transmit incest to the next generation even though they do not become personally involved in the sexual activities. It is possible that the daughter (who is now the mother) sets up her own daughter for incest in the same way that she herself was set up and betrayed by her own mother in the original incest situation. One can also imagine various kinds of unconscious motives that the daughter may have for recreating the incest situation: She may wish to vicariously experience incest again in order to regain her childhood; she may be seeking revenge against her mother, who is symbolized by her daughter; or perhaps she desires to make her husband over in her father's image. However, although such neurotic patterns of motivation may occasionally occur, the simplest explanation is that many daughters become passive, masochistic, and sexually unresponsive women when they grow up. Their adult personality characteristics are such that they endure marriages to abusive, alcoholic, or psychopathic men, marriages that are conducive to the occurrence of father-daughter incest when the wife withdraws from her sexual role. The probability of father-daughter incest in the next generation is therefore increased by virtue of the kind of person that the daughter tends to become, and there is no necessity for invoking explanations involving unconscious motivation unless they seem to be required to fit the facts in an individual case of incest transmission.

11

Treatment Recommendations

Throughout the incest literature, there are repeated references to the intensity of the incest taboo and the horror that its violation inspires in the average person. In an attempt to debunk folk beliefs about incest, some authors (for example, Masters, 1963) have given the impression that the fear of incest is irrationally based and thus outmoded; others (for example, Rascovsky and Rascovsky, 1950) have gone so far as to suggest that incest may be beneficial under certain circumstances. However, the evidence presented in this book suggests that incest is usually a negative life event that is followed by adjustive difficulties that vary widely with social circumstances and preexisting personality characteristics. A hackneyed joke that plays on our incest horror tells us that "Vice is nice, but incest is best!" But, seriously, for the overwhelming majority of persons who have experienced it, incest definitely was not best.

Incest horror is unfortunate, not because it expresses disapproval of incest but because its intensity impairs our ability to think about incestuous behavior in a calm and rational way. I believe that we can greatly improve our social policies in regard to incestuous families and our therapeutic interventions with individuals who have suffered incest trauma. A horrified attitude prevents us from recognizing the true scope of the problem by relegating incest to the realm of events that are so bizarre that they occur only among the scum of society or in the context of extreme psychopathology. We need to adopt the attitude, as professionals, that incest is an unfortunate event that is preventable, detectable, and treatable. The image of Oedipus with his eyes gouged out may be good theater, but the incest horror it expresses can only impede the search for real solutions to the problems presented by incest.

Prevention

In the broadest sense, prevention of incest is tied to improvement in the functioning of society as a whole and to the prevention and early treatment of individual conditions that contribute to a lack of self-control. A long list of social and individual evils that have been associated with incest (and many other forms of undesirable behavior) could be set forth for the reader, but such a listing seems a fruitless exercise in the absence of any new and realistic ideas of how such noble goals as the eradication of alcoholism, for instance, are to be accomplished. Instead, let us focus on some limited prevention goals.

The present rate of divorce in our culture creates numerous family situations in which the risk of incest is somewhat increased because the strong feelings of relatedness that ideally characterize the traditional nuclear family unit have been diluted. Divorced or estranged fathers who infrequently see their natural daughters may lose some of the feeling of relatedness that they originally experienced; stepfathers may never develop real fatherly feelings toward their stepdaughters, especially if they enter the family unit when the stepdaughter is already approaching or past puberty. (The same considerations apply to all of the other dyads within the nuclear family, of course, but the relative frequency of father-daughter incest situations com-

pels an especially close examination of this incest possibility.)
Messer (1969) has written of the potential incestuous attrac-
tions between stepparents and stepchildren, suggesting the term
Phaedra complex to describe these kinds of family romances,
after the Greek myth in which Phaedra, the wife of Theseus,
falls tragically in love with her handsome young stepson. In
addition to suggesting a name for this increasingly common situation, Messer sets forth some ideas for enhancing the feelings
of filial relationship in such newly created families and thus
heightening the effectiveness of the incest taboo. He suggests
formal adoption of children by the stepparent in cases where
this is possible, equal participation of the step- and natural parent
in the administration of discipline, and use of the words *mother*
and *father* by the children as terms of address for stepparents.
All of these measures would have the effect of emphasizing the
parental role of the new stepparent and thus of militating
against the formation of sexual liaisons within the family. En-
hancement of the romantic, sexual nature of the bond between
the parents is also a safeguard against incest temptation, and
Messer therefore urges that the parents periodically renew their
relationship by taking time off from their parental roles to go
on "second honeymoons."

Prevention of incest would be furthered by education of
authorities, such as family physicians, religious advisers, and
marriage and family counselors, who are often consulted by
concerned family members. Simply knowing about the incidence of incest can help these professionals to give more realistic advice. They should not look for incest under every stone,
but neither should they assume that it will not happen in a
"nice family" and thus brush off the concerns of family members with bland reassurance that incest will not occur. Browning
and Boatman (1977) noted that none of their fourteen cases of
incestuous children in psychiatric treatment had been referred
by a family physician despite the fact that concerned family
members had often been in consultation with the physician, and
they recommended that physicians be apprised of the factors
that put a family "at high risk" for the occurrence of incest.
Among these risk factors, they cited an alcoholic or violent

father; a mother who is absent from home, chronically ill, or depressed and passive; and an eldest daughter who has been forced to play the "little-mother" role with regard to household duties and the care of younger siblings. In addition to those given by Browning and Boatman, there are several other fairly well-established risk factors that could be added to the list: failure of the parents to maintain a mutually gratifying sexual relationship; any circumstance that causes a father and daughter to be alone together for long periods of time or to share the same bed; in addition to alcoholism, any other condition that impairs self-control in a parent, such as psychosis, psychopathic personality, or subnormal intelligence; a hostile, paranoid attitude toward outsiders to the family, especially on the part of the father; and the previous occurrence of incest in the family or in the parents' families of origin.

When physicians or other authority figures perceive a number of risk factors in a family situation and thus suspect that incest is a real possibility, professional counseling should be strongly recommended to the family. If a family member has expressed a fear that incest is occurring or will occur in the future, this possibility should be openly discussed as a reason for the referral. However, it is debatable whether the authority figure should specifically mention the perceived risk of incest in cases where no family member has expressed such a fear. Such frankness may make the authority feel totally honest, and it may also increase the family's motivation to follow up on the referral for counseling in a few cases, but there is also the serious risk that the family will feel threatened and refuse to enter counseling after the incest possibility has been raised. The pathological interactions that are already occurring in these families are sufficient justification for a referral for treatment, and this fact should be emphasized whether or not the subject of incest has been broached. Remember that the presence of the risk factors noted earlier raises the probability of incest, but the majority of families at high risk probably never experience overt incest situations.

If, in addition to some or all of the risk factors previously mentioned, the father and daughter (or other family dyad) seem to be developing a special, romantically tinged relationship, if they engage in an unusual amount of physical contact, or if the father seems extremely interested in the daughter's sexual activities with boyfriends, the need for counseling should be seen as especially urgent. While there is never any guarantee that the family will accept a referral or successfully utilize counseling when it is provided, there are several case descriptions in the literature (for instance, Cormier, Kennedy, and Sangowicz, 1962; Berry, 1975) in which one or more family members recognized the impending incest situation and took steps to prevent the actual occurrence of incest. Although these families at risk were diagnosed by professional psychotherapists, there is no reason why the incest risk could not have been detected by some other authority figure, such as a physician, and the family referred for counseling.

Detection and Case Handling

Once incest has occurred, the probability that anyone in authority will gain knowledge of it during or immediately after the incest affair is rather low, judging from the case histories in the psychotherapy sample. The adults in the family have a realistic fear of social shame and legal sanctions, while the involved child often feels too fearful of family dissolution or retaliation by the adults to risk disclosure to outside authorities. For these reasons, most current incest cases will continue to go undetected no matter how well informed and well intentioned authority figures may become. Nevertheless, the rate of incest detection can be improved and, more importantly, the response of society to detected incest cases can be much more humane and effective in preventing future pathology than is currently the case. Getting Support.

Social agencies that encounter disturbed children and adolescents are especially likely to detect current or recent cases of incest. Child guidance clinics and rape crisis centers specializing in sexually traumatized children are obviously agencies where incest victims will be encountered with some frequency. In-patient psychiatric facilities are also involved with incest detection, and recent studies (Molnar and Cameron, 1975; Browning and Boatman, 1977) have disclosed a rate of 4 or 5 percent for detected incest in children and adolescents admitted to these facilities, a rate that certainly justifies special training and sensitivity to incest-related problems for personnel in these settings. Even more frequent is the detection of incest in homes or detention centers for delinquent girls. Halleck (1962) gave a figure of 15 percent from his experience with the residential treatment of girls in Wisconsin; concerning girls in English "remand homes," Cowie, Cowie, and Slater (1968) have emphasized that sexual approaches by adult male relatives or friends of the family were commonly found to have precipitated runaway behavior that often led the girls into acts of more serious delinquency. Personnel in such settings should thus be prepared to evaluate reports of incest and take appropriate action.

When incest is reported to some authority outside the family, the report should generally be believed. Incest should be treated like any other socially undesirable act when evaluating the truth or falsity of a report that it has occurred. That is to say, one recognizes that there is some possibility that the accusation is false due to confusion or malice on the part of the "victim," but there are some very good reasons for believing the report to be true until proven otherwise. Obvious skepticism increases the confusion and hostility of the incest victim, just as it does in cases of rape, and treatment efforts in cases of incest-related psychological disturbance may be stymied until the patient confides the incest occurrence and is able to ventilate the emotional conflicts that it has aroused (Molnar and Cameron, 1975; Peters, 1976). Of course, it is the duty of law enforcement agencies to probe the possibilities of false reports of incest, however small they may be, and in any court proceedings an alleged perpetrator of incest must be assumed innocent until proven guilty. However, the *victim* of an alleged crime surely deserves to be treated with the same policy of innocent until proven guilty when she or he seeks help from authorities *outside* the courtroom.

Believing reports of incest not only facilitates the treatment process but also is in accord with the best evidence currently available on the veracity of such reports. For many years, it was thought that incest reports were especially likely to be false because Freud had come to the conclusion that his belief of patient accounts of early sexual trauma had been naive. The history of this attitude has been discussed in Chapter Three. Suffice it to say that psychoanalytically inspired disbelief of incest reports is going out of vogue even with psychoanalytically oriented therapists (for example, Berry, 1975). The few researchers, such as Kubo (1959), who have carefully investigated a sample of incest reports by interviewing persons other than the victim and alleged perpetrator have concluded that most of the reports were true. Even in the case of reports from delinquent girls, Cowie, Cowie, and Slater (1968) found only a small minority of reports of sexual abuse by adult males to have been fabricated, although they were alert to the possibility that a delinquent girl might use such a report to excuse her own behavior or to escape the supervision of authority figures in her home.

When a current or recent case of incest has been reported, the incest victim should be assured that he or she will be protected against any further incestuous incidents, and the responsible authority should take whatever steps are necessary to guarantee the security of the child. Peters (1976), who has dealt with a large number of cases of sexual assaults on children, has emphasized that this basic assurance of protection is the cornerstone of treatment, which often dictates what kinds of therapeutic interventions will be employed. In father-daughter incest cases where a younger daughter is also present in the home, this principle of protection should also be extended to her, since there is abundant evidence that such daughters are at high risk for incest should the elder daughter be removed from the home. Any therapeutic approach to an incest crisis situation must be judged first and foremost by its ability to meet this most basic requirement in the case at hand.

In many cases of incest, the authority is almost immediately faced with the problem of "collusion" on the part of members of the incestuous family, including the child herself (or himself). Suddenly the person who reported the incest as a crisis situation may become uncooperative, have a thousand excuses why appointments cannot be kept, or insist that the family is "cured" and needs no further assistance. An incestuous daughter may even retract her accusation of incest in public or go through a series of accusations and retractions that tend to bewilder everyone who tries to help her. Such behavior creates the impression that the family is colluding in order to preserve the incestuous status quo. The professional attempting to deal with such a situation needs to understand the source of such uncooperative behavior in order to put it into proper perspective and continue to help the family.

The term *collusion* is somewhat unfortunate, because it is borrowed from criminology and tends to imply that the family members are actively conspiring to frustrate the treatment intervention, which is seldom the case. Thinking of vacillation and uncooperativeness as collusion therefore tends to pit the authority against the family members as if they were adversaries, in a situation where the authority should be striving to convince the family members that their ultimate best interests will be served by whatever kind of therapeutic intervention is underway. If the concerned professionals, instead of immediately applying the *collusion* label, can develop a thoroughgoing understanding of the family's present circumstances and future prospects in light of the incest accusation, they will be in a much more favorable position to ensure that incest is ended and that the trauma to family members is minimized. The tensions within the father-daughter incest family, especially the ambivalence of the mother and daughter, have been discussed in Chapter Five and will not be reiterated here. The key to understanding the family's behavior is to realize that its members perceive themselves as being on the brink of disaster in the form of separation, public shame, loss of financial support, and possibly severe punishment for the perpetrator of incest. With occasional exceptions, the "collusive" family members have not demonstrated that incest is their preferred way of life by their uncooperativeness—they have only demonstrated that they are fearful of the alternatives to the status quo.

The severity of laws against incest and the possible long prison sentences that can be meted out to incest offenders have probably served to increase the ambivalence and fearfulness of incestuous family members and thus made it more difficult for incest victims to seek help outside the family and for the family to fully cooperate with authorities once incest has been disclosed. Harsh penalties are intended to deter people from committing serious crimes or to protect society from a repetition of such crimes, but in practice they often backfire. The existence of a possible death penalty for rape in some states, for instance, may make judges and juries so hesitant to convict the offender that he often is back in the streets in an uncomfortably short period of time. In the case of incest, long prison terms are not always imposed, but the public mortification of undergoing a trial for incest plus the possibility of being victimized by other inmates, who hold the incest offender in very low esteem (Gebhard and others, 1965), are sufficiently repugnant to the alleged incest offender and his family that they may be motivated to frustrate law enforcement authorities.

A more rational mode of public response to incest could surely be devised, and disclosure and cooperation with authorities would then be encouraged. It is beyond the scope of this book to suggest exactly how incest laws should be revised and how social agencies should administer such new laws. However, it is my belief that the laws on incest should be such as to maximize protection of the child and any other children in the home rather than to emphasize punishment of the incest offender for the sake of exacting social revenge. Incest victims and other family members would probably be much more willing to report incest and cooperate with treatment efforts if they could be assured in advance that there would be no trial and no public consequences *unless* the alleged perpetrator refused to cooperate with arrangements that were deemed necessary to ensure the security of the incest victim from further sexual approaches. In addition to reducing the level of realistic fear in the incestuous family, such an understanding would benefit the child victim by alleviating the guilt associated with disclosure of incest, an act that may become equated in the child's mind with betrayal of a parent who is often at least partially loved. Cormier, Kennedy, and Sangowicz (1962) have stressed the fact that the harsh prison sentences given to fathers increased the guilt of the daughters in their clinical sample and therefore exacerbated the incest trauma that they suffered.

It has been suggested (Cormier, Kennedy, and Sangowicz, 1962) that the disclosure of incest to authorities outside the family virtually assures that incest will not recur within that family because the mother then becomes conscious of her duty to protect the daughter and because the disclosure itself erects a psychological barrier between father and daughter. Prison sentences, or the threat of them, therefore may be entirely unnecessary in the majority of incest cases that are disclosed to authorities. However, several studies (for example, Weiss and others, 1955; Weinberg, 1955; Lukianowicz, 1972) have reported case histories in which a father resumed incestuous relations or initiated incest with a younger daughter after full public disclosure and, in some cases, after serving a prison term for incest. We should therefore not be complacent after incest has been disclosed—the family may still need therapy in order to modify the circumstances that led to incest, and the possibility of a prison sentence may have to exist in order to motivate compliance with requirements for therapy or placement of the child.

It is important to be aware of the several different types of incestuous fathers; case-handling recommendations will be quite different for each type. (The reader is referred to Table 5 in Chapter Four for a summary of a proposed typology of incestuous fathers.) As Bagley (1969) has already pointed out, effective case handling will vary considerably, and the responsible authorities should gear their recommendations in each case to the father's personality type and perceived ability to benefit from therapy. If the father is acutely psychotic, for instance, psychotherapeutic measures are definitely in order; if he is psychopathic, there may be no alternative to foster home placement for the child. In other words, since parent-child incest is committed by so many different kinds of parents, it is not possible to adhere religiously to any one prescription for handling disclosed cases.

Masters (1963) suggests that laws against incest per se be

repealed, and this suggestion has some merit. A good argument can be made from a civil libertarian point of view that society has no right to dictate to consenting adults whom they can or cannot enter into sexual relationships with or legally marry. True, there are genetic risks in incestuous unions, but we may ask whether it is the prerogative of the state to forbid individuals to take these risks. There is widespread agreement that laws are needed to protect children from sexual abuse, but Masters asks whether laws against incest are really required, since sexual abuse of minors is already amply proscribed by laws against "child molestation" in general. However, although there might be some benefit in dropping the term *incest* from the legal code in the interest of minimizing the stigma attached to those who are prosecuted, society should somehow formally recognize that sexual abuse by a parent or parent surrogate is more injurious to a child than abuse by a stranger. Perhaps there are ways of legally emphasizing the proscription of parent-child sexual relationships without invoking the irrational horror that the term *incest* carries with it.

Treatment of Immediate Aftereffects

Once incest has been detected, what kinds of therapeutic interventions can be considered? Obviously, a child victim should receive some kind of individual attention in order to assess and alleviate trauma resulting from the incest experience. But what about the family as a whole? How can one ensure that the family relationships will improve to the point where the child can be guaranteed sexual security in the home? Is it possible to avoid shattering the family as a unit?

During the 1960s, family therapy was enthusiastically recommended as the treatment of choice in incest situations (Cormier, Kennedy, and Sangowicz, 1962; Lustig and others, 1966; Eist and Mandel, 1968). Eist and Mandel reported on an incestuous family that remained in therapy for over two years without any coercion from legal authorities, although the incestuous father refused to be involved after several months. Their well-balanced account of the difficulties and rewards inherent in "therapizing" a chaotic family group is highly recommended reading for clinicians who wish to apply family therapy to incest cases. But, although family therapy remains an option in handling incest cases, it has proven to have difficulties that prevent its routine application.

The major difficulty cited by clinicians who have more or less despaired of family therapy (for example, Molnar and Cameron, 1975; Browning and Boatman, 1977) is the lack of cooperation of the incestuous father in the therapeutic efforts. Even when he is required to attend therapy sessions by legal authorities, he may be extremely difficult for a therapist to work with in the family therapy context, perhaps because he experiences it as a mortification process. It may be wiser to work with these men individually if they seem sufficiently anxious to explore their motivation and come to grips with their responsibilities as parents. Since the incestuous father varies widely in personality type and level of psychopathology, as was discussed in Chapter Four, his ability to utilize individual therapy must be carefully assessed in each case.

Even when all members of an incestuous family are cooperative, there are some possible drawbacks in the family therapy approach that should be carefully considered by the clinician. First, in most incestuous families one can expect to uncover serious sexual problems in the husband-wife relationship, so an insistence that all family members be present during therapy sessions will either inhibit discussion of these problems or expose the children to more knowledge of their parents' sexual relationship than they can handle. In a parent-child incest family, the intergenerational boundary against sexual expression has already been violated, and it is difficult to see what therapeutic purpose would be served by further involvement of the children in the sexual concerns of the parents. Therefore, it seems desirable to confine at least part of the therapy efforts to conjoint sessions with the husband and wife.

A second, more subtle problem can occur with the family therapy approach to incest cases—the child's guilt can actually be increased by the therapeutic process. Commonly, a family therapist takes the spoken or unspoken stance that all family members are equally responsible for the family's difficulties and thus all of them are responsible for working toward a healthy family equilibrium. This approach is often very useful because it prevents a destructive family wrangle about who the "bad guy" is by making an assumption of equal responsibility that discourages attempts to pin the blame on individuals. However, unless the therapist handles the issue very carefully, this approach may lead children to believe that they were to blame for incest and thus compound their guilt. If the family therapy approach is used, the therapist should emphasize repeatedly to the children that nothing they may have done justified the parent's incestuous behavior, that many children are innocently "seductive" to parents without being subjected to sexual approaches by them, and that it is possible for them to understand and forgive the parents for breaking the incest taboo. This assurance to the child, of course, places the responsibility for incest squarely on the parents.

The therapeutic approach to an incestuous family usually emerges as a compromise between, on the one hand, the desire to include as many family members as possible in the therapeutic process and, on the other, the difficulties involved in family therapy. Some recent authors (Molnar and Cameron, 1975; Peters, 1976) have emphasized that the major focus should be a crisis intervention approach with the child, which may take the form of individual sessions with her (or him) plus conjoint sessions with the other available family members whenever indicated. Some therapists have elected to concentrate on the mother-daughter dyad, since the father is often out of the picture or uncooperative. Browning and Boatman (1977) have recently reported a notable degree of success in therapy with the mothers in father-daughter incest families, having found that the passivity of these women was often due to a chronic depression that could respond to appropriate treatment interventions. The evidence for continuing destructive interactions between the mother and daughter after the father-daughter incest affair has been terminated certainly justifies a specific effort to involve the mother in the treatment process wherever possible, and Browning and Boatman found that the mother's dependency needs were often so strong that she could be induced to stay in therapy long enough to make real progress. Also, group therapy for incestuous parents has been reported (Kates, 1975) and may be considered in agencies that handle a sufficient number of incest cases.

When a young, preadolescent child has been involved with incest, an appropriate use of crisis intervention techniques can help to minimize effects in later life. Peters (1976), who has dealt with a large number of such cases, has stressed the importance of giving the child the opportunity to ventilate the emotions and concerns that have been evoked by the incestuous experience. In doing so, the therapist should not be deceived by the child's blandness and apparent lack of concern about the incest, for such an external appearance often masks a protective emotional withdrawal, and the skillful therapist can draw the child out with appropriate encouragement and emotional support. Once the child has verbalized concerns about the incest, the therapist can correct any misconceptions that the child may have formed about the incest and its aftermath—that all men are bad, that sex is evil, and so forth. Although the therapist should be concerned and sympathetic, it is important to avoid an anxious overreaction that may communicate to the child that there is something drastically wrong with her (or him) now, and if parents or other adults have given the child this impression, the therapist should strive to correct it. And, again, the child should be given assurance that no further sexual approaches will be made, and the therapist must take all necessary steps to back up this assurance, including placement of the child outside the home, if necessary.

Crisis intervention with an adolescent child should also emphasize ventilation of emotions and the correction of misconceptions about the meaning of the incest experience. Occasionally, in-patient treatment may be required for the postincest depression and suicidal behavior that often characterize the adolescent daughter. The emphasis of therapy often must shift to preparation of the daughter for independence from the incestuous family in the near future and to prevention of runaway behavior and precipitous early marriage; both of the latter may only serve to magnify the effects of incest. While it is certainly desirable to reconcile the adolescent daughter with her parents, Molnar and Cameron (1975) concluded that this ideal solution is seldom possible; in the majority of cases studied by them, placement in a foster home was necessary. Self-help groups for adolescents who have recently left incestuous situations would also be desirable, and Kates (1975) has briefly reported the formation of such a group of postincest daughters by a therapist dealing with a large number of court-referred incest cases. One hopes such self-help groups will be as beneficial to future incest victims as similar groups have been to the victims of rape.

Treatment of Long-Term Aftereffects

Even if social and psychotherapeutic responses to the disclosure of incest were ideal and many children and adolescents were afforded the opportunity to master the incest trauma very soon after it has occurred, therapists would continue to encounter patients for whom incest is still an important personal issue many years after the incest affair has ended. Judging from the psychotherapy sample, the typical patient of this sort is a woman in her twenties or thirties who has a history of incest with her father or stepfather and occasionally with an older brother, uncle, or grandfather. Therapists will continue to treat these patients with whatever methods they have found effective with their other patients, of course, but it is now possible to suggest some general therapeutic policies for such cases based on the accumulated evidence in the incest literature.

The first issue, which has been raised several times in this book, is that of belief or disbelief of the patient's confession of incestuous experience. There is no evidence that reports of incest are more likely to be false or grossly distorted than are reports of other kinds of emotionally charged events in a person's case history, especially when the incest report is given so long after the event that there seems to be no immediate motive for fabricating it. Incest accounts given by psychotics may be more questionable but should not be *automatically* discounted. An overt attitude of skepticism on the therapist's part when the incest report is given can severely disrupt rapport with the patient and serves no valid therapeutic purpose, since the issue of fantasy can always be raised at a later time should the account of incest begin to seem questionable.

Ascribing patient memories of incest to fantasy may severely disrupt the therapeutic process, because the patient is discouraged from ventilating and resolving conflicts directly related to the incest experience. She may also become confused and hostile to the therapist. Peters (1976, pp. 407-408) presents some case history evidence of the unfortunate effects of failure to deal directly with incest trauma and then summarizes this point as follows: "Therapeutically, these cases emphasize the importance of dealing with the actual incident, if it can be established that one did in fact occur. Relegating these traumas to the imagination may divert treatment into a prolonged unraveling of natural developmental processes in which fantasy is a component. . . . Ascribing these events to psychological fantasy may be easier and more interesting for the therapist, but it may also be counterproductive for the most efficient resolution of symptoms. I am not discounting the role of fantasy in psychic development. It is important, however, to distinguish between fantasy and the fact of child molestation."

Once the incest admission is received, many therapists seem uncomfortable with it and may convey to the patient, purposefully or not, the sense that the issue should not be brought up again. A number of therapists seem to believe that a patient who reveals an incest history during an intake interview is very likely to be psychotic because he or she is not displaying adequate ego defenses. This question was discussed in Chapter Six; it appears that any relationship between premature incest disclosure and psychosis is a very weak one and does not justify the therapist's being especially wary of allowing the patient to describe the incest experiences. Another source of concern mentioned frequently by therapists is that patients may use the incest revelation as a diversionary tactic to escape the responsibility of dealing with problems in their present life situations. If so, then the therapist would be justified in deemphasizing the importance of the incest incident and avoiding further discussion of it. In avoiding discussion of incest, however, the therapist takes the risk of leaving patients with the feeling that they have been "cut off" and that an event that still seems very important to them has been minimized. Therapists should therefore carefully explore their motivation for avoiding a discussion of incest before jeopardizing the patient-therapist relationship; in particular, they should ask whether their own discomfort with the topic of incest may not be at the root of their unwillingness to discuss it with a patient.

Simply telling the therapist about incestuous experience provides some sense of cathartic release to the patient, but she is also commonly seeking reassurance about some aspects of the incest experience. She may have heard about the special importance attributed to incest in Freudian psychology and may express the fear that incest has warped her personality in some fundamental way or doomed her to become psychotic. Therapists differ in their willingness to give reassurance, but those who are willing can honestly tell such a patient that incest is an unfortunate life event that often creates serious conflicts for the individuals involved in it but that these conflicts can be resolved. There is no evidence that incest, in and of itself, causes such serious clinical conditions as schizophrenia or psychopathic personality.

The patient may also seek reassurance about her responsibility for the incest as a child. Even though she may describe an incest situation in which she felt that she was the victim, there may still be strong feelings of guilt about many aspects of the affair. Like the rape victim, she may feel that there must have been something she could have done to prevent incest or to terminate the affair earlier than she did. In my opinion, it is a mistake for the therapist to be drawn into an attempt to assess the responsibility for a series of long-past events. It is preferable to emphasize the basic point that *nothing* that a child does justifies sexual approaches from a parent, for parents are adults and are expected to be fully responsible for their actions. A corollary to this statement is that the patient is now an adult who must assume responsibility for her own behavior in the present regardless of her past misfortunes, including the incest experience that she has described.

After the patient has been allowed to discuss her concerns about her incest experience as a child, she may gain the sense that the therapist understands her residual feelings about the incest and is now her ally in the effort to scrutinize her self-defeating behavior patterns as an adult. If the therapist is male, he will sometimes find that the postincest patient begins to act sexually seductive toward him. While it is not known whether these patients are significantly different from other psychologically disturbed females in this regard, it has often been remarked that the postincest patient has a tendency to confuse sex and affection or to "sexualize" all relationships. A skillful male therapist may be able to utilize this relationship to work through conflicts about heterosexual relationships, but in cases where the patient feels extremely threatened by men it may be necessary to consider transfer to a female therapist. For other patients, of course, it may be the female therapist who seems unusually threatening, given the postincest daughter's tendency to be hostile toward her mother as an adult.

The major focus of therapy with the postincest female patient is likely to be her "masochistic" orientation to life in general and to sexual partners in particular. Therapists of different "schools" will have their own conceptions of how to carry out a sustained and thoroughgoing attack on the pervasive set of attitudes that underlie the continued enactment of the victim role in adult life. The goals of therapy, however, are much the same for all schools—competence, assertiveness, personal responsibility, and satisfactory sexual functioning. In working toward the achievement of the first three goals, the therapist may want to consider recommending that the patient join a self-help group for women in order to obtain social support in striving toward meaningful adult relationships.

If a sexual problem exists, specific treatment for it may be necessary. Although the patient may make significant strides in terms of obtaining insight into her problems and restructuring her attitudes in ways that allow healthy adult relationships to develop, sexual functioning will not always improve without specific attention being focused on it. Thus, a referral for sex therapy may be desirable when it is felt that the patient has worked through her incest-related conflicts sufficiently. Until the patient is mature enough to establish an adult love relationship, however, it is doubtful that sex therapy alone can provide the solution for her problems with sexual functioning.

References

Aberle, D. F., and others. "The Incest Taboo and the Mating Patterns of Animals." *American Anthropologist,* 1963, *65,* 253-265.

Abraham, K. "Neurotic Exogamy." *Psychoanalytic Review,* 1921, *8,* 101-102.

Abraham, K. "The Significance of Intermarriage Between Close Relatives in the Psychology of the Neuroses." (H. Abraham, Trans.) In H. Abraham (Ed.), *Clinical Papers and Essays on Psychoanalysis.* Vol. 2: *Selected Papers of Karl Abraham.* New York: Basic Books, 1955. (Originally published 1909.)

Adams, M. S., and Neel, J. V. "Children of Incest." *Pediatrics,* 1967, *40,* 55-62.

Arndt, W. B., and Ladd, B. "Brother-Sister Incest Aversion, Guilt, and Neurosis." Unpublished paper, Department of Psychology, University of Missouri, 1976.

Awad, G. A. "Father-Son Incest: A Case Report." *Journal of Nervous and Mental Disease,* 1976, *162,* 135-139.

Bagley, C. "Incest Behavior and Incest Taboo." *Social Problems,* 1969, *16,* 505-519.

Barry, M. J., Jr. "Incest." In R. Slovenko (Ed.), *Sexual Behavior and the Law.* Springfield, Ill.: Thomas, 1965.

Barry, M. J., Jr., and Johnson, A. M. "The Incest Barrier." *Psychoanalytic Quarterly*, 1958, *27*, 485-500.

Bender, L., and Blau, A. "The Reaction of Children to Sexual Relations with Adults." *American Journal of Orthopsychiatry*, 1937, *7*, 500-518.

Bender, L., and Grugett, A. E., Jr. "A Follow-Up Report on Children Who Had Atypical Sexual Experience." *American Journal of Orthopsychiatry*, 1952, *22*, 825-837.

Berry, G. W. "Incest: Some Clinical Variations on a Classical Theme." *Journal of the American Academy of Psychoanalysis*, 1975, *3*, 151-161.

Bieber, I., and others. *Homosexuality: A Psychoanalytical Study*. New York: Vintage, 1962.

Bigras, J., and others. "En Decu et au Dela de l'Inceste chez l'Adolescente" ["On Disappointment and the Consequences of Incest in the Adolescent Girl"]. *Canadian Psychiatric Association Journal*, 1966, *11*, 189-204.

Brown, W. "Murder Rooted in Incest." In R. E. L. Masters (Ed.), *Patterns of Incest*. New York: Julian Press, 1963.

Browning, D. H., and Boatman, B. "Incest: Children at Risk." *American Journal of Psychiatry*, 1977, *134*, 69-72.

Cavallin, H. "Incestuous Fathers: A Clinical Report." *American Journal of Psychiatry*, 1966, *122*, 1132-1138.

Cormier, B. M., Kennedy, M., and Sangowicz, J. "Psychodynamics of Father-Daughter Incest." *Canadian Psychiatric Association Journal*, 1962, *7*, 203-217.

Cory, D. W. "Homosexual Incest." In R. E. L. Masters (Ed.), *Patterns of Incest*. New York: Julian Press, 1963.

Cowie, J., Cowie, V., and Slater, E. *Delinquency in Girls*. Atlantic Highlands, N.J.: Humanities Press, 1968.

Eist, H. I., and Mandel, A. U. "Family Treatment of Ongoing Incest Behavior." *Family Process*, 1968, *7*, 216-232.

Ellis, A. *Reason and Emotion in Psychotherapy*. New York: Stuart, 1962.

Fleck, S., and others. "The Intrafamilial Environment of the Schizophrenic Patient." In J. Masserman (Ed.), *Science and Psychoanalysis*. Vol. 2: *Individual and Familial Dynamics*. New York: Grune & Stratton, 1959.

Ford, C. S., and Beach, F. A. *Patterns of Sexual Behavior.* New York: Harper & Row, 1951.

Fox, J. R. "Sibling Incest." *British Journal of Sociology,* 1962, *13,* 128-150.

Frances, V., and Frances, A. "The Incest Taboo and Family Structure." *Family Process,* 1976, *15,* 235-244.

Freud, S. *Totem and Taboo.* (A. A. Brill, Trans.) New York: Vintage, 1946. (Originally published 1913.)

Freud, S. "The Etiology of Hysteria." (J. Strachey, Trans.) In J. Strachey (Ed.), *The Standard Edition of the Complete Psychological Works of Sigmund Freud.* Vol. 3. London: Hogarth Press, 1962a. (Originally published 1896.)

Freud, S. "Further Remarks on the Neuropsychoses of Defence." (J. Strachey, Trans.) In J. Strachey (Ed.), *The Standard Edition of the Complete Psychological Works of Sigmund Freud.* Vol. 3. London: Hogarth Press, 1962b. (Originally published 1896.)

Gebhard, P. H., and others. *Sex Offenders: An Analysis of Types.* New York: Harper & Row, 1965.

Gligor, A. M. "Incest and Sexual Delinquency: A Comparative Analysis of Two Forms of Sexual Behavior in Minor Females." Unpublished doctoral dissertation, Case Western Reserve University, 1966.

Gordon, L. "Incest as Revenge Against the Preoedipal Mother." *Psychoanalytic Review,* 1955, *42,* 284-292.

Greenland, C. "Incest." *British Journal of Delinquency,* 1958, *9,* 62-65.

Greenwald, H. *The Call Girl: A Social and Psychoanalytic Study.* New York: Ballantine, 1958.

Gundlach, R. H., and Riess, B. F. "Birth Order and Sex of Siblings in a Sample of Lesbians and Nonlesbians." *Psychological Reports,* 1967, *20,* 61-62.

Halleck, S. L. "The Physician's Role in Management of Victims of Sex Offenders." *Journal of the American Medical Association,* 1962, *180,* 273-278.

Heims, L. W., and Kaufman, I. "Variations on a Theme of Incest." *American Journal of Orthopsychiatry,* 1963, *33,* 311-312.

Henderson, D. J. "Incest: A Synthesis of Data." *Canadian Psychiatric Association Journal*, 1972, *17*, 299-313.

Henderson, D. J. "Incest." In A. M. Freedman, H. I. Kaplan, and B. J. Sadock (Eds.), *Comprehensive Textbook of Psychiatry*. Vol. 2. (2nd ed.) Baltimore, Md.: Williams & Wilkins, 1975.

Herman, J., and Hirschman, L. "Incest Between Fathers and Daughters." *The Sciences*, October 1977, pp. 4-7.

Hersko, M., and others. "Incest: A Three-Way Process." *Journal of Social Therapy*, 1961, *7*, 22-31.

Howard, H. S. "Incest—The Revenge Motive." *Delaware State Medical Journal*, 1959, *31*, 223-225.

Karpman, B. *The Sexual Offender and His Offenses*. New York: Julian Press, 1954.

Karpman, B. "Citizen William K." In R. E. L. Masters (Ed.), *Patterns of Incest*. New York: Julian Press, 1963.

Kates, M. "Incest: The Taboo Next Door." *San Francisco*, February 1975, pp. 24, 36-38.

Kaufman, I., Peck, A. L., and Tagiuri, C. K. "The Family Constellation and Overt Incestuous Relations Between Father and Daughter." *American Journal of Orthopsychiatry*, 1954, *24*, 266-277.

Kinsey, A. C., Pomeroy, W. B., and Martin, C. E. *Sexual Behavior in the Human Male*. Philadelphia: Saunders, 1948.

Kinsey, A. C., and others. *Sexual Behavior in the Human Female*. Philadelphia: Saunders, 1953.

Krafft-Ebing, R. von. *Psychopathia Sexualis: A Medico-Forensic Study*. (H. E. Wedeck, Trans.) New York: Putnam's, 1965. (Originally published 1886.)

Kubo, S. "Researches and Studies on Incest in Japan." *Hiroshima Journal of Medical Sciences*, 1959, *8*, 99-159.

Landis, J. T. "Experiences of 500 Children with Adult Sexual Deviation." *Psychiatric Quarterly* (supplement), 1956, *30*, 91-109.

Langsley, D. G., Schwartz, M. N., and Fairbairn, R. H. "Father-Son Incest." *Comprehensive Psychiatry*, 1968, *9*, 218-226.

Lester, D. "Incest." *Journal of Sex Research*, 1972, *8*, 268-285.

Lindzey, G. "Some Remarks Concerning Incest, the Incest Taboo, and Psychoanalytic Theory." *American Psychologist,* 1967, *22,* 1051-1059.

Lombroso, C. *Criminal Man.* (G. Lombroso-Ferrero, Trans.) New York: Putnam's, 1911. (Originally published 1876.)

Lukianowicz, N. "Incest." *British Journal of Psychiatry,* 1972, *120,* 301-313.

Lustig, N., and others. "Incest: A Family Group Survival Pattern." *Archives of General Psychiatry,* 1966, *14,* 31-40.

McDougall, W. *Introduction to Social Psychology.* London: Methuen, 1908.

Machotka, P., Pittman, F. S., and Flomenhaft, K. "Incest as a Family Affair." *Family Process,* 1967, *6,* 98-116.

Maddox, B. *The Half-Parent: Living with Other People's Children.* New York: Evans, 1975.

Magal, V., and Winnick, H. Z. "Role of Incest in Family Structure." *Israel Annals of Psychiatry and Related Disciplines,* 1968, *6,* 173-189.

Maisch, H. *Incest.* (C. Bearne, Trans.) New York: Stein & Day, 1972.

Malinowski, B. *Sex and Repression in Savage Society.* London: Routledge & Kegan Paul, 1927.

Malmquist, C. P., Kiresuk, T. J., and Spano, R. M. "Personality Characteristics of Women with Repeated Illegitimacies: Descriptive Aspects." *American Journal of Orthopsychiatry,* 1966, *36,* 476-484.

Marcuse, M. "Incest." *American Journal of Urology and Sexology,* 1923, *16,* 273-281.

Martin, J. O. "A Psychological Investigation of Convicted Incest Offenders by Means of Two Projective Techniques." Unpublished doctoral dissertation, Michigan State University, 1958.

Masters, R. E. L. (Ed.). *Patterns of Incest.* New York: Julian Press, 1963.

Masters, W. H., and Johnson, V. E. *Human Sexual Response.* Boston: Little, Brown, 1966.

Masters, W. H., and Johnson, V. E. *Human Sexual Inadequacy.* Boston: Little, Brown, 1970.

Medlicott, R. W. "Parent-Child Incest." *Australia and New Zealand Journal of Psychiatry,* 1967, *1,* 180-187.

Merland, A., Fiorentini, H., and Orsini, J. "A Propos de 34 Expertises Psychiatriques se Rapportant a des Actes d'Inceste Père-Fille" ["Concerning 34 Psychiatric Cases in Which Acts of Father-Daughter Incest Were Reported"]. *Annales de Médecine Legale,* 1962, *42,* 353-359.

Messer, A. A. "The 'Phaedra Complex.' " *Archives of General Psychiatry,* 1969, *21,* 213-218.

Middleton, R. "Brother-Sister and Father-Daughter Marriage in Ancient Egypt." *American Sociological Review,* 1962, *27,* 603-611.

Molnar, G., and Cameron, P. "Incest Syndromes: Observations in a General Hospital Psychiatric Unit." *Canadian Psychiatric Association Journal,* 1975, *20,* 373-377.

Morgan, L. H. *Ancient Society.* Chicago: Kerr, 1877.

Murdock, G. P. *Social Structure.* New York: Macmillan, 1949.

Parsons, T. "The Incest Taboo in Relation to Social Structure and the Socialization of the Child." *British Journal of Sociology,* 1954, *5,* 101-117.

Peters, J. J. "Children Who Are Victims of Sexual Assault and the Psychology of Offenders." *American Journal of Psychotherapy,* 1976, *30,* 398-421.

Raphling, D. L., Carpenter, B. L., and Davis, A. "Incest: A Genealogical Study." *Archives of General Psychiatry,* 1967, *16,* 505-511.

Rascovsky, M. W., and Rascovsky, A. "On Consummated Incest." *International Journal of Psychoanalysis,* 1950, *31,* 42-47.

Rasmussen, A. "Die Bedeutung Sexueller Attentate auf Kinder Unter 14 Jahren fur die Entwickelung von Geisteskrankheiten und Charakteranomalien" ["The Role of Sex Crimes Against Children Under 14 in the Development of Mental Illnesses and Character Disorders"]. *Acta Psychiatrica et Neurologica,* 1934, *9,* 351-434.

Raybin, J. B. "Homosexual Incest." *Journal of Nervous and Mental Disease,* 1969, *148,* 105-110.

Rhinehart, J. W. "Genesis of Overt Incest." *Comprehensive Psychiatry,* 1961, *2,* 338-349.

Riemer, S. "A Research Note on Incest." *American Journal of Sociology,* 1940, *45,* 566-575.

Rohleder, H. "Incest in Modern Civilization." *American Journal of Urology and Sexology,* 1917, *13,* 406-411.

Rosen, D. H. *Lesbianism: A Study of Female Homosexuality.* Springfield, Ill.: Thomas, 1974.

Santiago, L. P. *The Children of Oedipus: Brother-Sister Incest in Psychiatry, Literature, History and Mythology.* Roslyn Heights, N.Y.: Libra, 1973.

Schachter, M., and Cotte, S. "Etude Médico-Psychologique et Social de l'Inceste, dans la Perspective Pédo-Psychiatrique" ["A Medical-Psychological and Social Study of Incest from the Perspective of Child Psychiatry"]. *Acta Paedopsychiatry,* 1960, *27,* 139-146.

Schull, W. J., and Neel, J. V. *The Effects of Inbreeding on Japanese Children.* New York: Harper & Row, 1965.

Schwartzman, J. "The Individual, Incest, and Exogamy." *Psychiatry,* 1974, *37,* 171-180.

Seemanova, E. "A Study of Children of Incestuous Matings." *Human Heredity,* 1971, *21,* 108-128.

Segner, L., and Collins, A. "Cross-Cultural Study of Incest Myths." Unpublished manuscript, University of Texas, 1967.

Shelton, W. R. "A Study of Incest." *International Journal of Offender Therapy and Comparative Criminology,* 1975, *19,* 139-153.

Slater, M. K. "Ecological Factors in the Origin of Incest." *American Anthropologist,* 1959, *61,* 1042-1059.

Sloane, P., and Karpinski, E. "Effects of Incest on the Participants." *American Journal of Orthopsychiatry,* 1942, *12,* 666-673.

Szabo, D. "Problemes de Socialisation et d'Integration Socioculturelles: Contribution à l'Etiologie de l'Inceste" ["Problems of Socialization and Sociocultural Integration: A Contribution to the Etiology of Incest"]. *Canadian Psychiatric Association Journal,* 1962, *7,* 235-252.

Tessman, L. H., and Kaufman, I. "Variations on a Theme of Incest." In O. Pollak and A. Freedman (Eds.), *Family Dynamics and Female Sexual Delinquency.* Palo Alto, Calif.: Science & Behavior Books, 1969.

Tompkins, J. B. "Penis Envy and Incest: A Case Report." *Psychoanalytic Review,* 1940, *27,* 319-325.

Vestergaard, E. "Fader-Datter Incest" ["Father-Daughter Incest"]. *Nordisk Tidshift for Kriminalvid,* 1960, *48,* 159-188.

Wahl, C. W. "The Psychodynamics of Consummated Maternal Incest: A Report of Two Cases." *Archives of General Psychiatry,* 1960, *3,* 188-193.

Weinberg, S. K. *Incest Behavior.* New York: Citadel, 1955.

Weiner, I. B. "Father-Daughter Incest: A Clinical Report." *Psychiatric Quarterly,* 1962, *36,* 607-632.

Weiner, I. B. "On Incest: A Survey." *Excerpta Criminology,* 1964, *4,* 137-155.

Weiss, J., and others. "A Study of Girl Sex Victims." *Psychiatric Quarterly,* 1955, *29,* 1-27.

Westermarck, E. *The History of Human Marriage.* (5th ed.) New York: Allerton, 1922.

White, L. A. "The Definition and Prohibition of Incest." *American Anthropologist,* 1948, *50,* 416-435.

Woodbury, J., and Schwartz, E. *The Silent Sin: A Case History of Incest.* New York: Signet, 1971.

Yorukoglu, A., and Kemph, J. P. "Children Not Severely Damaged by Incest with a Parent." *Journal of the American Academy of Child Psychiatry,* 1966, *5,* 111-124.

Index

Masters, W. H., 75, 224, 237, 240, 242-244, 302-303, 355
Medlicott, R. W., 40, 47, 54, 70-73, 100, 197, 224, 230, 258, 300, 303, 314, 321, 355
Merland, A., 46, 93, 100, 176, 356
Messer, A. A., 74, 333, 356
Middleton, R., 2, 75, 356
Molnar, G., 48, 170, 188-191, 197, 224, 258, 336, 342-343, 345, 356
Morgan, L. H., 5, 356
Mother-son incest: aftereffects of, 309-311; analysis of, 298-311; and personality development, 298-299; sexual activity in, 302-305
Mothers: absence or incapacitation of, 116-118; aversion of, to sexuality, 123-126; characteristics of, 111-130, 302-303, 305; dominance by, 92; emotional background of, 113-116; passivity, dependency, and masochism of, 118-121; promiscuity of, 121-123; reaction of, to father-daughter incest, 168-176, 183-184; role of, in brother-sister incest, 265-266; role of, in father-daughter incest, 343-344; role reversal of, 126-130
Murdock, G. P., 4, 9, 11-12, 19, 23, 26, 356

N

Nadine, 62, 218, 236, 251-253, 254, 256
Nancy, 65, 275-276, 278-279
Neel, J. V., 19-21, 76, 351, 357
Neurotic exogamy, after father-daughter incest, 210-211
New Zealand, 47, 54, 224
Norway, 45, 197

O

Obesity, and incest, 198-200, 275
Olivia, 62, 199
Orgasmic dysfunction: and brother-sister incest, 281; after father-

daughter incest, 231-232, 234-245
Orsini, J., 46, 93, 100, 176, 356

P

Pamela, 63, 171
Paranoid personality disorder, of fathers, 102-105
Parsons, T., 10, 12, 25, 299, 356
Passivity, dependency, and masochism, of mothers, 118-121
Pauline, 65, 92-93, 120, 174, 250
Peck, A. L., 45, 50, 53, 76, 85, 89-90, 93, 114, 119-121, 127-128, 133-134, 168, 175, 188, 191-192, 221, 230, 258, 354
Pedophilia, of father, 105-106, 111
Peters, J. J., 37-39, 49, 54, 73, 165, 186-187, 203-204, 233, 288, 336-337, 343-344, 346, 356
Phaedra complex, 333
Pittman, F. S., 47, 127-128, 137, 146, 168-169, 172-173, 320, 325, 355
Pomeroy, W. B., 30, 72, 77, 81, 354
Pregnancy: and brother-sister incest, 273-274; and father-daughter incest, 176-177
Promiscuity: adolescent, defined, 134-135; of daughters, 134-136, 191-192, 227-232, 240-241; of mothers, 121-123; of sisters, 268, 281-282, 284-285
Prostitution, by daughters, 232-234
Psychopathy, of father, 95-97, 111, 156, 179
Psychosis: of daughters, 202-204; of fathers, 100-102, 111; incest related to, 40-41
Psychotherapy, as setting for incest research, 34-36, 51-82

R

Rachel, 63, 88, 123
Raphling, D. L., 47, 87, 91, 98, 103, 115, 267, 303, 326-328, 356
Rascovsky, A., 45, 160, 207-209, 211, 224, 230, 240, 331, 356